IFIP Advances in Information and Communication Technology 395

IFIP – The International Federation for Information Processing

IFIP was founded in 1960 under the auspices of UNESCO, following the First World Computer Congress held in Paris the previous year. An umbrella organization for societies working in information processing, IFIP's aim is two-fold: to support information processing within its member countries and to encourage technology transfer to developing nations. As its mission statement clearly states,

> *IFIP's mission is to be the leading, truly international, apolitical organization which encourages and assists in the development, exploitation and application of information technology for the benefit of all people.*

IFIP is a non-profitmaking organization, run almost solely by 2500 volunteers. It operates through a number of technical committees, which organize events and publications. IFIP's events range from an international congress to local seminars, but the most important are:

- The IFIP World Computer Congress, held every second year;
- Open conferences;
- Working conferences.

The flagship event is the IFIP World Computer Congress, at which both invited and contributed papers are presented. Contributed papers are rigorously refereed and the rejection rate is high.

As with the Congress, participation in the open conferences is open to all and papers may be invited or submitted. Again, submitted papers are stringently refereed.

The working conferences are structured differently. They are usually run by a working group and attendance is small and by invitation only. Their purpose is to create an atmosphere conducive to innovation and development. Refereeing is also rigorous and papers are subjected to extensive group discussion.

Publications arising from IFIP events vary. The papers presented at the IFIP World Computer Congress and at open conferences are published as conference proceedings, while the results of the working conferences are often published as collections of selected and edited papers.

Any national society whose primary activity is about information processing may apply to become a full member of IFIP, although full membership is restricted to one society per country. Full members are entitled to vote at the annual General Assembly, National societies preferring a less committed involvement may apply for associate or corresponding membership. Associate members enjoy the same benefits as full members, but without voting rights. Corresponding members are not represented in IFIP bodies. Affiliated membership is open to non-national societies, and individual and honorary membership schemes are also offered.

Tobias Ley Mikko Ruohonen
Mart Laanpere Arthur Tatnall (Eds.)

Open and Social Technologies for Networked Learning

IFIP WG 3.4 International Conference, OST 2012
Tallinn, Estonia, July 30 – August 3, 2012
Revised Selected Papers

Springer

Volume Editors

Tobias Ley
Mart Laanpere
Tallinn University
Narva mnt 25, 10120 Tallinn, Estonia
E-mail: {tobias.ley, mart.laanpere}@tlu.ee

Mikko Ruohonen
University of Tampere
Kalevantie 4, 33100 Tampere, Finland
E-mail: mikko.j.ruohonen@uta.fi

Arthur Tatnall
Victoria University
City Flinders Campus
PO Box 14428, Melbourne, VIC 8001, Australia
E-mail: arthur.tatnall@vu.edu.au

ISSN 1868-4238 e-ISSN 1868-422X
ISBN 978-3-642-37284-1 e-ISBN 978-3-642-37285-8
DOI 10.1007/978-3-642-37285-8
Springer Heidelberg Dordrecht London New York

Library of Congress Control Number: 2013934553

CR Subject Classification (1998): K.3, K.4.3, H.3, H.4, H.5, C.5.3

Typesetting: Camera-ready by author, data conversion by Scientific Publishing Services, Chennai, India

Printed on acid-free paper

Springer is part of Springer Science+Business Media (www.springer.com)

Preface

Sometimes shifts in technology prove to be a game-changer in certain application fields. The shift to open and social technologies plays an increasingly important role in many educational settings. Social technologies are naturally entering primary, secondary, and higher education where they blur the boundaries between formal and informal learning. Social technologies also enter the workplace where they connect learners and bridge the boundaries between individual learning and organizational knowledge processes. Not only do these technologies connect learners independent of place and time, they have also been found to exert emergent properties. For example, wikis or social tagging environments are increasingly used for collaborative knowledge construction where new knowledge emerges from a large-scale interaction of individuals. These properties and their impact on individual, group, and organizational learning have only started to be researched.

Open source software (OSS) and technologies have received extensive research attention owing to some favorable properties contrasting with a traditional understanding of software development and the use of those systems. Many OSS issues are motivations for OSS developers and licensing bodies. However, important research areas in OSS are product and implementation success and the use of OSS in different educational and enterprise settings. OSS can also serve as a platform for providing services to user communities. Especially in developing countries, OSS provides an attractive opportunity.

To address these topics, the IFIP-sponsored open conference on Open and Social Technologies for Networked Learning took place in Tallinn, Estonia, from July 30 to August 3, 2012. The conference brought together participants from five continents, and engaged them in a broad and diverse programme. All submitted papers were peer reviewed and we accepted 16 full research papers for presentation at the conference with an acceptance rate of roughly two thirds of all submissions. These were complemented by presentation of three short papers and five doctoral student papers that presented emerging topics of young researchers in this area. These research papers comprise the main body of this volume, covering topics of "Mobile Learning," "Social Networks, Analytics and Recommendation," "Workplace Learning," "Learning Analytics in Higher Education," "Collaborative Learning in Higher Education," and "Managing Open and Social Education." The authors of the accepted papers were then given the opportunity to make improvements to their papers following suggestions and feedback from other conference participants. We thank the reviewers for their dedication that helped to ensure the high quality of the final papers.

In addition to these presentations and following the tradition of earlier IFIP conferences, three discussion groups offered the opportunity for in-depth discussion of more focused topics. Kati Tikkamäki and Nicholas Mavengere from the

University of Tampere convened a group on "Organizational learning, agility and social technologies in contemporary workplaces". Jane Andersen from the IT University of Copenhagen, Denmark, convened a group on "Social technologies for improving quality and efficiency in the area between teaching/learning and administrative student support," and Mart Laanpere and Peeter Normak from Tallinn University lead a group on "Digital learning ecosystems: rethinking virtual learning environments in the age of social media." This volume includes a paper that synthesizes the discussions of the Tikkamäki and Mavengere discussion group and points toward further research.

Last but not least, the program included presentations of three invited speakers. Stefanie Lindstaedt, from Graz University of Technology, Austria, talked about a research program in which she examined the important role of reflection at the workplace. Different technological means included work-integrated learning technologies, knowledge maturing services, and different types of context-detection mechanisms from desktop and mobile applications.

Alberto Cañas from the Institute for Human and Machine Cognition, in Florida/USA presented concept mapping as a way to support knowledge construction. Several tools that his group has been developing for this purpose were also demonstrated. It is increasingly important to formulate concepts for the mass of social media phenomena, otherwise it is difficult to observe the changing arena of discussion.

Lastly, Jari Multisilta from CICERO Learning at the University of Helsinki, Finland, talked about mobile social technologies and their use in schools and beyond. His message was to pinpoint the value of a richer social media environment with massive use of digital images and, increasingly, videos. The next generation will learn by socializing their video inputs.

With the tag #ifipost12, the conference was also represented in several social media services, such as Twitter, Flickr, and Slideshare.

The conference was co-sponsored by IFIP Technical Committee 3 Education with the organizing working group WG 3.4 Professional and Vocational Education in Information Technology. This working group has focused its activities in the last few years on many of the emerging movements in the field of ICT and education, one of the editors of this book, Arthur Tatnall, is the Chair of the WG.

Whether the increased use of social and open technologies proves to be a game-changer in education has not been decided. The contributions in this volume, however, show that significant progress has been made in the application of open and social technologies in all areas of education, and a number of exciting research questions still remain to be tackled.

Tobias Ley
Mikko Ruohonen
Arthur Tatnall
Mart Laanpere

Organization

Organizing Committee

Conference Co-chairs

Tobias Ley	Tallinn University, Estonia
Mikko Ruohonen	University of Tampere, Finland

Organisation Chair

Mart Laanpere	Tallinn University, Estonia

Social Media Chair

Hans Põldoja	Tallinn University, Estonia

Doctoral Consortium

Pertti Järvinen	University of Tampere, Finland
Terje Väljataga	Tallinn University, Estonia

Posters and Demos

Karin Schöfegger	Tallinn University, Estonia
Kaido Kikkas	Tallinn University, Estonia

Program Committee

Graham Attwell	Pontydysgu, UK
Dirk Börner	Open University of The Netherlands
Linda Castañeda	University of Murcia, Spain
John Cook	London Metropolitan University, UK
Raquel M. Crespo García	Universidad Carlos III de Madrid, Spain
Bill Davey	Royal Melbourne Institute of Technology, Australia
Valentina Dagiene	Vilnius University, Lithuania
Michael Derntl	RWTH Aachen, Germany
Hannes Ebner	KTH Stockholm, Sweden
Helen Edwards	University of Sunderland, UK
Alev Elci	Eastern Mediterranean University, Magusa, North Cyprus
Dragan Gasevic	Computing and Information Systems, Athabasca University, Canada
Israel Gutiérrez Rojas	Universidad Carlos III de Madrid, Spain

Anneke Hacquebard	CEN ICT/SKILLS Workshop, The Netherlands
Raimo Hälinen	University of Applied Sciences, Hämeenlinna, Finland
Marek Hatala	Simon Fraser University, Canada
Teresa Holocher-Ertl	Zentrum für Soziale Innovation, Vienna, Austria
Malinka Ivanova	Technical University of Sofia, Bulgaria
Pertti Järvinen	University of Tampere, Finland
Jelena Jovanovic	University of Belgrade, Serbia
Kaido Kikkas	Tallinn University, Estonia
Ralf Klamma	RWTH Aachen, Germany
Tomaž Klobucar	Jožef Stefan Institute, Ljubljana, Slovenia
Milos Kravcik	RWTH Aachen, Germany
Timo Lainema	University of Turku, School of Economics, Finland
Effie Law	ETH Zürich, Switzerland
Teemu Leinonen	Aalto University, Helsinki, Finland
Stefanie Lindstaedt	Graz University of Technology & Know Center, Austria
Allison Littlejohn	Glasgow Caledonian University, UK
Johannes Magenheim	University of Paderborn, Germany
Claudia Müller-Birn	Free University of Berlin, Germany
Paul Nleya	University of Botswana, Botswana
Jan M. Pawlowski	University of Jyväskylä, Finland
Sandra Schön	Salzburg Research, Salzburg, Austria
Melody Siadaty	Simon Fraser University and Athabasca University, Canada
Rory Sie	Open University of The Netherlands
Lampros Stergioulas	Brunel University
Antti Syvänen	University of Tampere, Finland
Arthur Tatnall	Victoria University, Melbourne, Australia
Stefan Thalmann	University of Innsbruck, Austria
Stefaan Ternier	Open University of The Netherlands
Riina Vuorikari	European Schoolnet, Belgium
Martin Wolpers	Fraunhofer FIT, Germany

Table of Contents

Learning Analytics in Higher Education

Collaborative Learning in Higher Education

Managing Open and Social Education

Doctoral Student Papers

Discussion Groups

Mobile Learning

Mobile Phones and Voice-Based Educational Services in Rural India: Project RuralVoice

Mikko Ruohonen[1], Markku Turunen[1], Gururaj Mahajan[1], Juhani Linna[1], Vivek Kumar[1], and Himadri Das[2]

[1] School of Information Sciences, University of Tampere, Finland
{mikko.j.ruohonen,markku.turunen,gururaj.mahajan, juhani.linna,vivek.kumar}@uta.fi
[2] Great Lakes Institute of Management, Gurgaon, India
himadri.das@greatlakes.edu.in

Abstract. Voice-based services offer major business opportunities in developing areas such as India and Africa. In these areas mobile phones have become very popular, and their usage is increasing all the time. In this project, we study the deployment of voice-based mobile educational services for developing countries. Our study is based on a Spoken Web technology developed by IBM Research Labs, and our focus is on India's Bottom of the Pyramid (BoP). It is being built as a service that runs on the telecom infrastructure similar to World Wide Web that runs as a service on the Internet infrastructure. Spoken Web proposes to build an alternate web for the underprivileged population that is yet untouched by the enormous benefits of Internet and World Wide Web. In this research project RuralVoice we also investigate how Finnish service and technology companies can co-create novel services for this challenging target population in three educational areas i.e. agriculture, healthcare and entrepreneurship education.

Keywords: Bottom of the Pyramid, Mobile Education, Professional Education, India, Illiteracy.

1 Introduction: Indian BoP Market for Mobile Services

A large market opportunity exists for businesses to tap at the bottom of the pyramid (BoP) in India [11]. This market segment is mostly in rural India, which is difficult to reach compared to urban India. The total population of India is 1.21 billion with a break up of 833 million from rural India and 377 million from urban India. This indicates a huge 69% to 31% rural to urban skew. Accessibility to this large rural BoP market is a huge challenge especially for services. The distribution channels for products have been established with large investments by some of the large consumer product companies but services have been a hitherto more or less unexplored category for this market.

The poor are vulnerable by virtue of lack of education, lack of information, and economic, cultural, and social deprivations [5]. Accessibility to this large rural bottom of the pyramid market is a huge challenge especially for services. The distribution

T. Ley et al. (Eds.): OST 2012, IFIP AICT 395, pp. 3–11, 2013.

channels for products have been established with large investments by some of the large consumer product companies but services have been a hitherto more or less unexplored category for this market. A notable exception to this service drought in rural India has been telecommunication services.

Mobile phone penetration in India, in general, and rural India, in particular, has been growing at a breakneck pace. According to TRAI's (Telecom Regulatory Authority of India) latest Telecom Subscription Data as 3rd May 2012, the total number of mobile phone connections in India is 919.17 million with 595.90 million connections in urban India and 323.27 million connections in rural India. This higher share of urban subscribers at 64.83% as compared to the lower share of rural subscribers at 35.17% is because mobile connectivity was originally rolled out exclusively in urban centers as that was where the purchasing power existed for the then expensive service. As the service prices have dropped drastically the market in rural India has now opened up and that is where the growth is much higher than that in urban India. Every month 8 million new mobile connections are added across India at a monthly growth rate of 0.88%.

This is made up of 1.79 million new connections in urban India at a monthly growth rate of 0.30% and 6.02 million new connections in rural India at a monthly growth rate of 1.96%. It is expected that by 2013, the number of mobile phone subscribers will be 1 billion. The national mobile connection teledensity is 76.00 with an urban teledensity of 162.82 and a rural teledensity of 38.33. It is should be noted that more subscribers are coming from rural areas. What appears to be a comparatively low rural teledensity for mobile connections is very misleading in terms of a measure of the power of the mobile phone for accessing the rural market. This is because in rural India the mobile phone is not a personal device like in urban India but a shared device across the entire family. This makes the addressable market size using mobile phones larger than that suggested by the teledensity figures.

2 Voice-Based Services for BoP Markets

Typically value added services through mobile phones have been delivered through text and web platforms. Both of these require the service consumer to be literate. Whereas literacy is a given in developed markers for mobile value added services, it is not the necessarily the case in the rural India bottom of the pyramid market segment. The illiteracy rate in India is 26%, with 31% illiteracy in rural India and 15% illiteracy in urban India. This problem is likely to persist, since elementary education is not targeted to adults, and children's drop-out rates are high. Illiteracy makes text based and web based service delivery platforms unusable. This creates a need for services that can be delivered on a voice platform instead of text or web. Currently, spoken services are used successfully in many areas in many countries. Typical examples of speech applications include transport information services, such as automated train and bus timetable services. The current trend is that DTMF (touch-tone) inputs are replaced by speech inputs. This may promote both greater user satisfaction and cost savings in some application areas. In addition to IVR applications, many other forms of telephony applications have dominated the field. To address these challenges, IBM Research Labs have developed the Spoken Web to deliver data and information to illiterate people. In a nutshell, Spoken Web content is stored in the form of voice-sites instead of text based web-sites. The content is in local dialects, making it much easier for illiterate people to access this information. It has been observed that IT systems with a voice-based feedback have much more appeal for the illiterate and semiliterate population of these regions [8][9] as compared to GUI-based systems such as Internet Kiosks. Voice-links allow for navigation between voice-sites using voice commands from a limited permissible vocabulary set. The interconnection of voice-sites leads to a WWTF or World Wide Telecom Web on the lines of the traditional World Wide Web. The lack of internet access limits access to the World Wide Web. Voice-sites can be accessed by dialing a phone number. The much higher access to mobile phone connections, therefore, makes access to voice sites much easier. In addition to fulfilling service needs for these BoP markets it also provides a platform to create and develop first in developing countries context and then "reverse" the innovation to developed countries [3] and probably building an institutional innovation system through creation nets [4].

3 Target Service Domains

According to Prahalad and Hart [11] the commercial infrastructure and ecosystem for BoP markets is driven by the following four drivers: creating buying power, shaping aspirations, improving access and tailoring local solutions (see Figure 1). The other drivers after this phase are reverting innovation back to developed countries [3] and building an institutional innovation system through creation nets [4].

Based on our preliminary studies and strategic documents, we have identified the people at India's BoP markets require professional educational services and knowledge sharing in the following three urgent areas:

1. Agriculture education and knowledge sharing (local production)
2. Healthcare education and access to primary care (well-being)
3. Education for entrepreneurship and employment (economic growth)

Our work focuses initially on agriculture education provision. The existing work done in the area allows us a rapid start, and in particular concrete field studies can be conducted already in the initial phases of the project. Furthermore, the potential of other domains will be studied so that the results from studies on agriculture knowledge sharing can be applied to these fields as well.

In the area of agriculture, the problem is that of information asymmetry where people at the BoP do not have access to information on agri-commodity prices, weather, seeds, pesticides, fertilizers, and agricultural equipment. They need real time information access as and when required. Examples of information needed include agri-commodity prices, weather, seeds, pesticide, fertilizer, and agricultural equipment. There are three phases in agriculture i.e., production, processing and

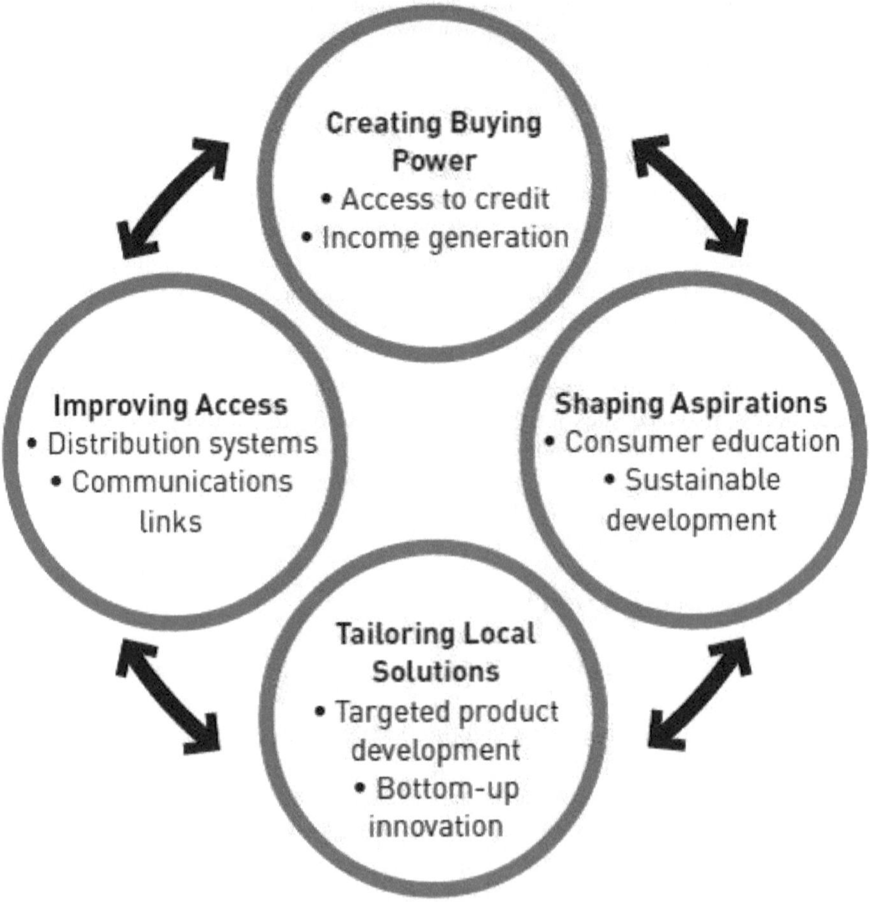

Fig. 1. The commercial infrastructure at the Bottom of the Pyramid [11]

marketing of the crops. Farmers are in need of education and consultation for their problems during all these phases. So, this need based information is very vital for the farmers.

For primary healthcare education, the condition of health care in the BoP is very poor. Doctors are not present and access to any kind of modern health care is virtually non-existent. People in many villages have no option but to go to village quack and often face life threatening consequences. General knowledge on dealing with potential disease symptoms is limited. These people need genuine medical advice and access to consultation facilities.

In the area of professional education, a key contributor to India's growth story in a globalized economy has been the English speaking skills of the educated population. The illiterate population, who also do not know spoken English, have missed out on the opportunities that knowledge of the English language provides. Even without having requisite literacy levels for other jobs, knowledge of spoken English opens up several employment avenues that currently do not exist for the rural BoP. The focus on inbound tourism opens up possibilities in the hospitality industry where spoken English becomes a boon. This includes jobs for drivers, hotel housekeeping staff, tour guides, etc. In addition, knowledge of spoken English also opens up doors for employment for these people in urban centers for cleaning staff and errand runner jobs in MNC offices as well as expatriate managers' residences. These people in the rural BoP would like access to spoken English courses that do not need basic literacy as a prerequisite. In addition to English language education, there is a need for entrepreneurial education to grow their microenterprises and increase employability which supports the opportunities of poor people and growth of small businesses in rural India.

4 Farmer's Voice Case Study

The baseline Spoken Web technology is currently ready to be deployed commercially. Next, we present case studies carried out by its developers and the project team. Farmer's Voice [1][2] is Kannada language voice site created for the purpose of field study. Kannada is one of the official and classical languages in India. This is field study was carried out in close collaboration with University of Agricultural Sciences (UAS) Dharwad, IBM Research Lab, India and University of Tampere (UTA).

The Department of Extension, UAS works to transform the best agricultural practices, research work and agricultural technologies created by its staff to the farming community. In order to accomplish this goal, they have adopted several modern communication media such as Television, Krishi (Farming) Community Radio Station. Even though adopting all new mediums for communication, they are still not reaching entire farming community. In recent times most of the farmers in Rural India owns mobile phones. Thus now the University is willing to propagate services through mobile phone medium. Their objective is to find ways to propagate agricultural information services through mobile phones using spoken web as a platform. This was prime research question of our field study.

In order to attain user experience and feedback about Raitarinda Raitara Dhwani – voice site application, we decided to interview participants from different age group i.e., from age group 20-30, 30-40 and above 40. We carried out two field studies, in the first we interviewed 16 participants and second field study we interviewed 35 participants. There were total 51 participants in the field studies, out of them 16 are female participants and remaining 35 were male participants. Most of the participants are illiterate or having very little formal school education. The content of this voice site is provided by the Krishi (Farming) Community Radio Station. The content is in local Kannada language, spoken throughout Karnataka state. There were total five sections in the voice site, like Krishi Chintana (Farming Information), Pakshika Salahegalu – (Tips to the farmers), Weather forecast, Market Forecast and Varada Basanna(Talk by veterinary doctor in colloquial Kannada language).

There were two prototypes of this voicesite, one is with background music and another one without background music. We went to total 5 villages near by University of Agricultural Sciences. The prototype was installed on mobile phone (Nokia C6 touch screen phone). The field study process included following steps

1. Voice site introduction
2. Demographics information – Noted participants demographics
3. Requested participants to use the prototype
4. Took participant's feedback

Findings:

- All the participants liked this initiative and service.
- Most of the farmers liked service with music, upon asking why they liked service with music, they replied "The background music helps them to concentrate and understand content clearly".
- Some of the Illiterate participants did not notice the background music.
- All the participants understood the content in the service very clearly. They said "As this information is in our local Dharwad rural accent, so we understood clearly".
- Most of the participants had their own mobile phones, thus they were very familiar with using mobile phones.
- For those who did not have mobile phones, they have used the mobile phones owned by their family members. These participants were also comfortable while using our prototype.
- For the illiterate users, initial guidance was needed, as some of them didn't knew few symbols like '#' and' *'. But after initial guidance and introduction, these participants were comfortable in using this prototype.
- Most of the participants said they would be happy to use this service without any subscription charges. Some of the participant said they are willing to pay small subscription charges if the service is very helpful for them.

Suggestions:

- Spoken medium is very powerful in rural India. From our field study, it is clear that, even though the some of the participants did not have formal schooling, they are very comfortable and very quickly able to use this service.
- However it is very important to keep the content in local dialect, when you are designing information services for the rural India.
- When developing business models it is very important to know that most of the rural users are from economically poor background. Most of them are unable to pay large subscription charges.

5 Previous Other Case Studies on Using Speech-Based Technology

In addition to the mentioned research collaborative study, IBM has carried out a number of successful cases in using the Spoken Web technology:

Avaaj Otalo. Avaaj Otalo [7] is a VoiceSite in Gujarati language providing an application for farmers to access agri-information over the phone. It allows farmers to access latest information regarding farming practices; it enables them to interact with agriculture experts by posting their questions on the VoiceSite. These questions may also be answered by other farmers, encouraging more peer interaction and community building.

VoiAvatar. VoiAvatar [7] system enables individuals to create their own personal/business oriented VoiceSites. Each of these VoiceSites acts as an online avatar or proxy of those individuals. A VoiAvatar VoiceSite for a small business owner (such as plumbers, electricians, carpenters or craftsmen) could include information such as area of operation, service charges and work hours.

Folksomaps. Sparsely populated semi-urban and vast rural areas of developing countries such as India do not have detailed map systems built for most locations. The semi-literate, low income, non-IT savvy population residing in these areas cannot use such services even if they were offered online over the internet. Secondly, lack of structured addressing conventions and poor road signs makes it difficult to follow the maps. So, even people comfortable with maps, often need to ask people on the streets to find their way. Folksomaps [6] is a community driven map system offered as a VoiceSite and a website that leverages Semantic Web technologies to create and manage a community generated knowledge base and makes use of web and voice applications to provide access to its services.

Applications for Visually Impaired. Websites in the Web are primarily meant for visual consumption. Accessibility tools such as screen readers that render the visual content in audio format enable the visually impaired to access information on the websites but they have their own limitations. Since the access to VoiceSites is a simple phone call, it can become a pervasive and low cost IT access mechanism for the blind [12]. Surveys were conducted at two institutions for the institutions of blind in New Delhi which indicate that the learning curve for using applications on the Spoken Web is relatively low and does not require extensive training.

University of Tampere (UTA) has worked with spoken and multimodal mobile services for more than ten years[13] [14]. Its existing research prototypes include numerous applications which have been piloted in large-scale pilots with real users in Finland. For example, the publicly available TravelMate application offers spoken and multimodal public transport guidance for mobile users, and the MobiDic application was developed for mobile dictation and notetaking needs. Currently, UTA is developing spoken mobile applications for medicine and healthcare. Another recent work includes speech and symbol based tablet applications for illiterate people. In these applications (and many others), UTA has applied the technology for special user groups, such as visually-impaired people, who share many issues with illiterate people. Most importantly, the work done with these systems completes the work of IBM Spoken Web in many ways. First UTA is the one the key players in world in the area of spoken mobile applications, and is thus in an excellent position for helping to deploy the Spoken Web technology with IBM and Finnish SMEs. Second, UTA has developed multimodal technologies which can be applied for future applications of Spoken Web and tablets. In particular, UTA and IBM have planned to apply novel auditory, haptic, gestural and symbol based technologies for Spoken Web.

6 Conclusion

In the preliminary studies, we have identified that India's BoP people require educational and knowledge sharing services in the following three large areas: agriculture, primary healthcare, and entrepreneurial education. The baseline Spoken Web technology is currently ready to be deployed commercially. In this paper we presented case studies carried out by its developers and the project team. We also show how the spoken technology development carried out can make advanced multimodal Spoken Web services possible. Proposed results of the research and development project are i) viable business models to deploy voice based services for the Indian BoP market, ii) improved multimodal Spoken Web technology, iii) several deployed Spoken Web services and iv) several documented field studies conducted in India. We will work in close collaboration of the network partners to apply the results into real world services. In this way, the results of this project make also commercial products possible in the company driven actions which run after and in parallel with the proposed base project. In addition to the Indian BoP market, the results of the project can be applied for similar market areas, such as African countries, with similar processes.

Acknowledgements. This research and publication has been funded by National Funding Agency for Technology and Innovation (TEKES) and supported by grants of Economic Education Foundation, Jenny and Antti Wihuri Foundation and Finnish Association of Information Processing. We are grateful for this financial support.

References

1. Agarwal, S.K., Jain, A., Kumar, A., Nanavati, A.A., Rajput, N.: The Spoken Web: A Web for the Underprivileged. SIGWEB Newsletter Summer (2010), http://doi.acm.org/10.1145/1796390.1796391, doi:10.1145/1796390.1796391
2. Das, H., Ruohonen, M.J., Mahajan, G.: Delivering Interactive Voice based Services through Mobile Phones to Rural India's Bottom of the Pyramid. In: Ström, P., Dolles, H., Alvstam, C., Middel, R. (eds.) 28th Euro-Asia Management Studies Association Conference 2011. Palgrave-McMillan (2013) (to be published)
3. Govindarajan, V., Trimble, C.: The Other Side of Innovation: Solving the Execution Challenge. Harvard Business School Press (2010)

4. Hagel, J., Seely Brown, J.: Creation nets: Harnessing the Potential of Open Innovation (2006), https://www.johnhagel.com/creationnets.pdf (checked October 17, 2012)
5. Karnani, A.: The Mirage of Marketing to the Bottom of the Pyramid: How The Private Sector Can Help Alleviate Poverty. California Management Review 49(4), 90–111 (2007)
6. Kumar, A., Chakraborty, D., Chauhan, H., Agarwal, S.K., Rajput, N.: Content Creation and Dissemination by-and-for Users in Rural Areas. In: IEEE/ACM International Conference on Information and Communication Technologies and Development (ICTD), Doha, Qatar (2009)
7. Kumar, A., Rajput, N., Agarwal, S.K., Chakraborty, D., Nanavati, A.A.: Organizing the Unorganized - Employing IT to Empower the Under-privileged. In: WWW 2008: Proceedings of the 17th International World Wide Web Conference, Beijing, China (2008)
8. Newell, A.F.: Speech technology: Cross fertilization between research for the disabled and the non-disabled. In: Proceedings of the First ISAAC Research Symposium in Augmentative and Alternative Communication, Stockholm (1990)
9. Parikh, T.S., Lazowska, E.D.: Designing an Architecture for Delivering Mobile Information Services to the Rural Developing World. In: Proc. Intl. Conf. on World Wide Web, WWW (2006)
10. Patel, N., Chittamuru, D., Jain, A., Dave, P., Parikh, T.S.: Avaaj Otalo – A Field Study of an Interactive Voice Forum for Small Farmers in Rural India. In: ACM Conference on Human Factors in Computing Systems (CHI 2010), USA (2010)
11. Prahalad, C.K., Hart, S.L.: The Fortune at the Bottom of the Pyramid. Strategy+Business (January 2002), http://www.strategy-business.com/article/11518?gko=9a4ba (checked October 17, 2012)
12. Rajput, N., Agarwal, S., Kumar, A., Nanavati, A.A: An Alternative Information Web for Visually Impaired Users in Developing Countries. In: ASSETS 2008 (poster) (2008)
13. Turunen, M., Hakulinen, J.: Spoken and Multimodal Communication Systems in Mobile Settings. In: Esposito, A., Faundez-Zanuy, M., Keller, E., Marinaro, M. (eds.) COST Action 2102. LNCS (LNAI), vol. 4775, pp. 227–241. Springer, Heidelberg (2007)
14. Turunen, M., Hakulinen, J., Räihä, K.-J., Salonen, E.-P., Kainulainen, A., Prusi, P.: An architecture and applications for speech-based accessibility systems. IBM Systems Journal 44(3), 485–504 (2005)

Challenges in Mobile Teaching and Safety – A Case Study

Birgy Lorenz[1] and Kaido Kikkas[1,2]

[1] Institute of Informatics, Tallinn University, Narva Road 25, 10120 Tallinn, Estonia
[2] Estonian Information Technology College, Raja St 4C, 12616 Tallinn, Estonia
{Birgy.Lorenz,Kaido.Kikkas}@tlu.ee

Abstract. This paper is based on two studies about mobile learning in one secondary school in Estonia. The main question for this research was how should schools harness the increasing use of mobile phones, tablets at home in order to make it also beneficial for the schools? What are the emerging trends in mobile devices security that schools are facing when introducing m-learning to students? According to our findings, Estonian schools face various problems which must be addressed before any serious attempt at m-learning is made.

Keywords: mobile safety, didactics, mobile learning, integrated innovation, teacher attitudes.

1 Background

1.1 School and Home Today

The ITU Statistics from 2009 shows that 8% of the global population is using fixed-line broadband and 14% mobile broadband [9]. The Pisa 2009 results in Estonia reports higher usage of ICT tools at home (96%) than at school (53%). Students who use ICT and mobile phones just for leisure tend to get lower results than those who use ICT also for home- or classwork [14].

Despite the increasing use of mobile gadgets, availability to exploit these technologies and opportunities in real classrooms usually remains low because K12 education still focuses on laptops instead of mobile devices [6]. There is ongoing debate about whether schools should allow mobile phones, tablets to the classroom or not. Teachers say they need new methods and didactics before opening learning to mobile technologies, what students already experience every day [23]. There are several studies about edutainment using ICT and portable solutions in education [19]; however, the use of mobile phones and tablets is still emerging in education in the area of implementations [16].

Since the beginning of 2000, the European Commission has funded m-learning projects in three categories: Authoring and publishing, Delivery and Tracking, Content Development. The main goal of R&D was aimed at young adults aged 16-24 [15]. Over the dozen years, E-learning has changed from sharing documents to

T. Ley et al. (Eds.): OST 2012, IFIP AICT 395, pp. 12–21, 2013.

co-working at creating the document from the start, from a closed system to an open one – the m-tools will further allow to experience that anyplace and anytime [1]. There are studies about pedagogical aspects of m-learning [12], engaging and measuring [7] as well work-based learning environments [2].

While the trends for the next decade have been promising, including the fusion of e-learning, m-learning and social networking, personal learning experience, tablets and cloud computing, some of them also raise caution - with the cloud-based data and high-speed mobile broadband to connect to it, security will become a much bigger issue [8].

M-learning is not yet implemented on the K-12 level in Estonia, but there are several good initiatives from Tallinn University Centre for Educational Technology for training teachers [11] and Estonian Information Technology College opened a software development laboratory for mobile devices [20] in 2011. Still, the training in these areas is lacking continuity. As Tiger Leap Foundation (foundation whose main purpose is to implement new technologies into schools in Estonia) has pointed out that mobile software should be in Estonian language rather than English to get better implementations for secondary schools. The cost of hardware and broadband has also been mentioned as a reason why m-learning is not implemented at schools yet [24].

There have been some studies about implementing m-learning or promoting it to children, e.g. Baker et al. [3] [5]. They list various practices used worldwide, but also outline new challenges, e.g. children becoming more of a researchers and publishers than consumers or information [10].

1.2 Area of m-safety

As tablets and mobile devices become ubiquitous, the safety risks also evolve. These could be divided into three categories: a) technical risks, related to how the mobile phone works (data protection, PINs/fingerprints, avoiding malware etc.), [4] [26] b) behavioral risks, related to users' habits and awareness (what to download, what to do when the phone is lost etc.) [25] [17] [22] c) policy risks, related to either too lax or too restrictive regulations (e.g. forbidding the use of phone or WiFi completely even when it is needed to teach or study) [21].

Some of the key differences in m-and e-safety are noted by Andero Sepp, an Estonian e-police official: first ignorance can be costly. Paid services, downloading virtual non-free gadgets, accidental roaming can result in a large bill. Secondly it is crucial to understand that not everything is meant to be shared and it is necessary to ask permission before taking e.g. a picture. On the other hand, crimes made with m-devices are easier to detect as mobile operators gather information about the phone (location etc.). At the moment, mobile devices do have fewer viruses than ordinary computers. This also means that people are less aware of security.

We note that the studies about m-learning at school tend to focus on positive aspects like inclusiveness, flexibility and variability [18] [13]. The potential threats to e-safety are studied remarkably less.

2 Methods

Our study focused on fifth- to ninth-grade students. We used survey, interview and observation methods. Most of the quantitative data was collected by means of closed questions or Likert scale options. The questionnaire and interview also included some open questions that concerned mainly about specific addressed questions. The study was carried out twice (2009 and 2012) at the same school.

Stage I In 2009, the participants were 153 students, 47% girls and 54% boys (46 from grades 5-6 and 107 from grades 7-9). 51% of all students from grades 5-9 took part in the survey. In the follow-up in 2012 the number of participants was 156 - 80 girls (19 from grades 5-6 and 61 from grades 7-9 – referred to as G1 and G2 respectively) and 76 boys (22 from grades 5-6 and 54 from grades 7-9 - referred to as B1 and B2 respectively). This time, the participants formed 36% of the student population.

Stage II – learning exercises and observation. We used 3 exercises in 2009 and 5 in 2012 to test how students were able to use mobile devices in school environment as a tool for working with curricular assignments in two months' time.

Stage III – an interview with a diverse choice of respondents from older age groups (18 students from grades 10-11, 6 teachers and in 2012 also 32 Master students from Tallinn University).

Stage IV – a group interview with 14 teachers conducted during an introductory course on m-learning in spring 2012.

3 Results

The results from the assignments reveal that in 2009 there were only 1-3 phones in every class that were useful as a learning device - by 2012 a half or more of the students have that opportunity. It is interesting that even when students use mobile every day still feel that mobile phone is not a learning device. The same idea was also expressed by teachers.

In 2009 students preferred to use photo camera to take pictures or videos. They were proud to appear in the video and share it to the world. 2012 students were more active using smartphones, but they were not interested to appear on the video anymore, the agreed solution was that they filmed hands and dolls or other props.

In 2009, finding software was more difficult due to different operating systems and abundance of software errors. By 2012 there are three major providers of apps. The numbers of available Estonian language apps as well as the applications that can be used in educational setting have increased a lot.

Results from the survey reveal that 2012 13% of respondents use calling cards. The biggest difference between the card users in different factions was between B1 (17%) and others (10-12%). New gadgets are mostly given to younger children, the difference between older is 5-8% depending of the gender. The main reason to have a phone is said to be reachable for parents (70%) and others (86%), phone is a status indicator to only 7% of students, it has raised 4%.

Girls have more numbers recorded on the phone than boys. Older students have more of them (the difference with the younger age group is 27%). The numbers recorded belong mostly to the family (87%), friends (76%), classmates (88%), but also teachers (31%), casual acquaintances (30%), companies or other (6%) and strangers (20%). In particular, B1 (27%) and G2 (23%) keep more strangers' numbers than others (15-16%). Compared to 2009, having strangers' numbers in one's phone is risen by 8% while the parental interest and control over the content has stayed the same –3/4 of parents have never asked to check their children's phones.

Older students spend more time in social networking (13%) and direct communication (10%) than younger. Girls tend to listen to music (17%) and send SMS more than boys, especially notable is the difference between G1 (23%) and others. Compared to 2009, the regularity of using the phone as an internet device has risen from 9% to 64% and smartphone-related skills (e.g. watching videos, listening to music, using online social network, sending e-mail or using direct communication) have risen from 24% to 52%.

50% of students have used phone as a learning device, G2 leads in this sense. The phone skills analysis reveals that 54% of students play games coming with the phone. Gaming is more important to B1 - 77% play games that come with the phone and 27% play also Internet games, older boys (B2) would download most of the new games. 31% of G2 and 32% of B1 think about their selves as routine gamers.

Mobile services are of more interest to girls (23%), but 23% of B1 having tried it out, just like calling to TV or radio programs. Calling to adult phone lines and services is more interest to the B group – 18% have already tried it. It is more of interest to B1. Other fee-based services like wallpapers, music, videos, games, other services or buying things over mobile phone are more common among younger students.

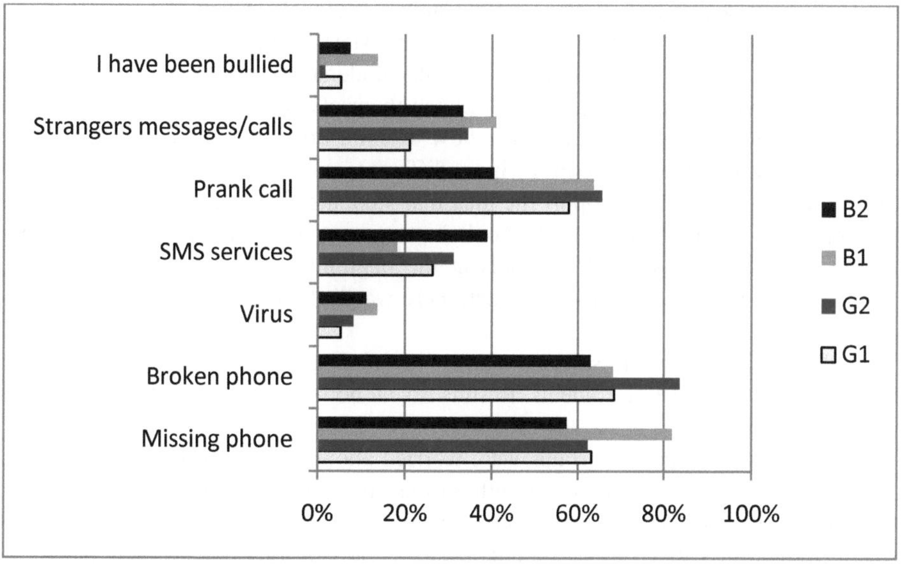

Fig. 1. What problems have risen of using phone 2012?

Regarding other unpleasant cases all the numbers have raised from 2009 compared to 2012. 15% more phones get lost, there are 31% more broken phones, 4% more viruses, 43% more prank calls (see more results and diagrams go to goo.gl/C4nD1). To see 2012 results look at the Fig 1.

The M-training for students revealed strong interest in hands-on participation - they wanted to be active participants in the process, not just passive listeners.

The students were given the following tasks:

- using QR codes to enhance and promote literature reading and knowledge building and a "treasure hunting" game to find solutions to the e-safety problems;
- making videos and worksheets in math using real life situations;
- finding hidden pupils using only mobile phones (and only up to 12 yes/no answers were allowed);
- learning about 10th anniversary of the Euro using the Euro Coins application on Android;
- finding and identifying animal tracks in snow using an Estonian mobile application "Kes käis?" (Who Walked Here?);
- tagging problematic places near the school, e.g. trash, dangerous traffic locations like big piles of snow in the pedestrian area etc.

Students were also tasked to find and analyze mobile applications for education to use in teaching different subjects. The top three subjects were math and science, arts and music. The students emphasized that the programs should be in Estonian, but actually managed well with English apps as well.

The M-learning discussion group of teachers displayed sincere interest in these tools, even if only two participants did already own the smartphone. The interest increased after seeing and feeling that the mobile phone is in fact very intuitive and there were a lot of programs to discover in the Market application. Discussing the challenging part they pointed out that to really understand the m-world they should have the option to own a tablet or smartphone themselves. They also wanted to have examples of worksheets and guidelines how to build up lessons in a situation where every student or student group is in a different stage in his/her learning. Also the participants tended to support the idea that students should use their own gadget (as opposed to school-owned) at school. In this case, the teacher would have less responsibilities (e.g. to distribute tools at the beginning of a lesson, maintenance, accountability in case of misuse). In fact, there was little difference between teachers and students.

In the three areas of m-safety we interviewed 3 groups of people: gymnasium students, teachers and ICT students. Results reveal both differences and similarities in opinions and fears.

In the technical sense all groups were worried about accidental roaming expenses. The ICT students were divided in whether to use passcode or finger lock (to use it or not), as the gymnasium students and teachers were in the favor of it. Some ICT students suggested that people should install a tracking program to their phone so when a thief would use the phone they may get their phone back.

In the behavioral sector they listed a lot of problems: activating paid services, stolen or missing phone, bullying, when and where and how long to use the phone, but usually all the problems were stated as moderate – reportedly it either usually don't happen to them or it is somebody else's problem.

In school policy sector, the restriction of school resources mirrored different understandings – the teachers pointed out problems with school policy to use mobile devices, while students thought it was their constitutional right to have access to the networks. Using their own mobile broadband connection (as opposed to the schools) was not considered a problem by anybody. Concerning awareness training and introducing m-learning to students, the students suggested that teachers should implement new technologies in educational way; teachers said that they did not have proper tools and training to do it, and it rather should be a responsibility for parents.

4 Discussion

Over the last three years, the challenges have increased as the use of smartphones, tablets has skyrocketed due to the increasing competition between service providers and phone manufacturers, as there is a lack of training in this field and supervision of students by their parents has stayed the same (i.e. very low). Students know how to make use of the new features offered by new gadgets - download, upload, share etc. At the same time, neither teachers nor parents are able to keep pace with them.

Schools should regulate how the m-tools are used in the class. When the teacher is not prepared to use these tools then he/she will not be pleased and the quality of teaching will be low. The teacher may view mobile phones, tablets as a threat to their existence because the students can go online and look for answers and undermine their position. Younger teachers using smartphones themselves are more willing to try it out in order to learn more about their phones.

The findings of the study confirmed that there is interest in using mobile learning in math, science and art classes. Students and teachers do not usually see m-learning as a part of their curriculum, but after practical experiences their fears start to vanish and they were more active and in control of their learning process.

The students' positive confidence using mobile phones has improved the results, raised interest in participating in math and science classes and also their willingness to do their mobile project related homework (the more exact impact is being tested yet). These findings lead to the conclusion that implementing mobile learning into school life gives better results than restricting it. We noticed that the participants still feel somewhat uneasy due to the urge to succeed at once. So our recommendation is to give a lot of feedback to students and teachers - discuss what went wrong and how the problems could be overcome next time.

From the study we see also that there are too many strangers in children's phonebook (20%). Sometimes the strangers will appear after synchronizing phones with Facebook, but that also indicates that those children accept everybody as their friend on the Net. Also we found out that 18% of the boys have tried calling to adult services. It seems too easy to do that. Service providers can offer parents solutions which can block children's access to several services. It is possible in UK and US, but in Estonia providers are not interested in implementing such features as 'no parent has ever asked that'. A visible problem is also the rise of prank calls and bullying. Even if children say it is hardly more than a joke then after discussing these issues more deeply they admit that both bullying and cyber-bullying are an everyday problem.

A major problem with mobile phones, tablets in Pelgulinna Gymnasium is the possible accidental activation of paid services, because of the direct loss of money involved - school wanting to implement m-learning should seriously address the issue as well what are listed here:

Problem 1: in the purely technical sense, students are better equipped than schools. At the same time, they are unable to use the technology in a reasonable manner, as neither parents nor schools are unable to guide them. As the educational features are not shown to them, their activities tend to be limited to entertainment.

Problem 2: students are also left on their own in terms of e-safety and networking. As schools do not promote e-safety, the whole mobile technology has become a sort of „Wild West“ - to make it worse, neither students nor their parents consider schools as reliable partners in this matter.

Problem 3: as a rule, the school and teachers deny any responsibility in these matters – most teachers claim it to be the responsibility of the parent who bought the gadget. When a training program is offered (e.g. by some international project), teachers are happy to accommodate them and when the training is complete, all problems are considered to be either solved or disappeared.

Problem 4: the digital divide will prevail until teachers acquire the necessary knowledge and skills – and also gain practical experience of the services used by students (e.g. Facebook). Teachers, being seriously overworked, typically do only as much as prescribed by the national curriculum – as e-safety is considered a pervasive topic not strictly related to any specific topic, it can be overlooked as 'irrelevant'.

Problem 5: the students are considered 'too smart' to need any additional training. According to the 2009 PISA study in Estonia [2], 2/3 of the school principals claimed to have no additional needs for ICT. Due to the national curriculum dropping the experimental ICT test in Grade 9, ICT seems to be not so important any more. Children are considered to 'be born with a mobile in their hands', but in reality, they lack a lot of crucial skills which result in education rather than technology.

Problem 6: for a while, the digital divide between smartphone users and those who cannot afford one may pose an issue. However, in a longer perspective this problem is likely to lose its urgency as smartphones are rapidly losing the luxury item status and becoming common tools (as both the prices of devices and related services are coming down). In the past, the same divide existed in computer use - right now, 98% of students in Pelgulinna Gymnasium are able to use computer at home. The comparison with an earlier study (2 years ago) shows that mobile phone ownership rates have increased a lot.

We note that while this particular study focused on just one school, the results can mostly be applied to other urban schools (which involve a large majority of students) in Estonia as well. A larger survey is underway, but the preliminary results show strongly similar findings at large rural schools as well.

This study is still valuable to the Safer Internet in Estonia program that deals with e-safety issues and training in schools and kindergartens. The program so far has not yet focused on mobile technology and this is a big gap to be filled during the next stages of the program.

5 Conclusion

In analyzing problems with mobile phone use, we found the majority of the most crucial ones to be related to plain, everyday human behavioral issues: how to avoid large bills stemming from exceeding Internet quota, how to safely lend a phone to somebody, how to deal with paid services etc. Likewise, cyber bullying with phones, prank calls or strangers calling/texting can pose problems for children. As explained above, the parents and teachers are usually in a weak position to supervise students; they are usually left alone with these problems and have to develop their own strategies to deal with these matters.

The schools who have understood the circle of problems (having had awareness training or set up some regulations regarding the issue) are also in a better position to discover problems in advance, training parents and teachers. Those schools who forbid m- and e-learning as well as using laptops and phones at school premises just postpone the problem and banish it outside, while it keeps evolving in social networks and off the school time - and may finally outburst in a different way (in the worst case, a school shooting or any other comparably grave incident).

The students will only learn educational applications when these are taught them. The opportunity and resources of m-learning are seriously underexploited. There is a need for teaching materials and handbooks in Estonian language. Smartphones are new in the whole world, not only in Estonia – but there are several good examples and pilots to learn from. With half of the children already having these devices at home, we don't have the time to wait for the results of some multi-year academic studies. Teachers should have access to new technologies now rather than later. Schools should be open but at the same time also prepared for safety incidents.

Schools do have an option to open their classrooms to students' gadgets. Local authorities should provide broadband connection in the school area (WiFi). E-safety training should be mandatory for all teachers graduating from universities, be available via Tiger Leap training programs and also have an option to ask trainers or volunteers to visit the school. School leaders and government must provide teachers with modern technologies. Service providers could also provide more help to parents – both in well-designed services and better support in incident handling.

References

1. 2009 Horizon Report (ID: CSD5612): In Educause (2009), http://www.educause.edu/ELI/2009HorizonReport/163616
2. Attwell, G.: Work based mobile learning environments: contributing to a socio-cultural ecology of mobile learning. In: Pachler, N. (ed.) Mobile Learning in the Context of Transformation (2010); In Special Issue of International Journal of Mobile and Blended Learning
3. Baker, A., Krull, G., Mallinson, B.: Proposed Theoretical Model for M-Learning Adoption in Developing Countries. In: Proceedings mLearn Education, pp. 17–22 (2005)
4. Cheng, J., Wong, S.H.Y., Yang, H., Lu, S.: SmartSiren: Virus Detection and Alert for Smartphones. In: MobiSys 2007, San Juan, Puerto Rico, USA, June 11-14 (2007)
5. Ching, D., Shuler, C., Lewis, A., Levine, M.H.: Harnessing the Potential of Mobile Technologies for Children and Learning Mobile Technology for Children, pp. 23–42. Morgan Kaufmann (2009)
6. Dias, A., Carvalho, J., Keegan, D., Kismihok, G., Mileva, N., Nix, J., Rekkedal, T.: An Introduction to mobile learning. In: GISMA, Socrates Project "The Role of Mobile Learning in European Education" (2008)
7. Diaz, V.: Mobile Teaching and Learning: Engaging Students and Measuring Impact. Presentation at the 2010 EDUCAUSE Center for Applied Research Symposium, Carlsbad, CA, December 7 (2010), http://www.educause.edu/ecar
8. Gadd, R.: My mLearning Predictions for 2010. In: Mlearning Trends (2010), http://mlearningtrends.blogspot.com/2010/01/my-mlearning-predictions-for-2010.html
9. ITU Statistics: ICT Data and Statistics (IDS) (2009), http://www.itu.int/ict/statistics
10. Koszalka, T., Ntloedibe-Kuswani, G.S.: Literature on the safe and disruptive learning potential of mobile technologies Distance Education. Routledge Journals 31(2), 139–157 (2010)
11. Laanpere, M.: E-õppest m-õppeni. In: M-õuesõpe Lemill.net (2011), http://lemill.net/content/webpages/e-oppest-m-oppeni
12. Laurillard, D.: Pedagogical forms for mobile learning. In: Pachler, N. (ed.) Mobile Learning: Towards a Research Agenda. WLE Centre, IoE, London (2007)
13. Lam, P.H.-C.: Students' Voices: Enriching Learning Experiences through M-learning. In: IEEE International Conference on Wireless Mobile and Ubiquitous Technology in Education, pp. 171–176 (2010)
14. Lorenz, B.: Eesti õpilaste PISA 2009 IKT-alased küsimuste vastused vihjavad kasutamata ressurssidele koolides. In: National Exam and Qualificaton Centre Pisa Research results page (2011), http://uuringud.ekk.edu.ee/fileadmin/user_upload/documents/PISA2009_IKT_analyys.PDF
15. M-learning project background. In: M-Learning Ultralab and Stac (2005), http://www.m-learning.org/archive/background.shtml
16. Mobile learning for expanding educational opportunities. Workshop Report. In: International Workshop on Mobile Learning for Expanding Educational Opportunities, Tokyo, Japan (2005)
17. Mobile phone safety. In: Physicians and Scientists for Responsible Application of Science and Technology (2011), http://www.psrast.org/mobileng/mobilstarteng.htm
18. Prensky, M.: Digital Game-Based Learning. McGraw-Hill, New York (2011)

19. Pozzi, F.: The impact of m-learning in school contexts: An "Inclusive" perspective. In: Stephanidis, C. (ed.) HCI 2007. LNCS, vol. 4556, pp. 748–755. Springer, Heidelberg (2007)
20. Puusaar, M.: IT Kolledžis avatakse mobiilseadmete tarkvaraarenduse labor. ITK Press Release (2011)
21. Sheperd, I.J., Reeves, B.: iPad or iFad - The reality of a paperless classroom. In: Mobility Conference, Abilene Christian University (2011)
22. Speak up 2010 report, National Findings. In: K-12 Students and Parents Project Tomorrow (2011)
23. Stockwell, G.: Investigating learner preparedness for and usage patterns for mobile learning. ReCALL 20/3, 253–270 (2008)
24. Zova, K.: Kohtumine teemal "e-õppevarast mobiilsete seadmetele". In: Tiigrihüppe Sihtasutus Protokoll (2012), http://goo.gl/41QjT
25. Tippett, N., Thompson, F., Smith, P.K.: Research on Cyberbullying: Key findings and practical suggestions. In: Bullying Special Edition Contributor (2011)
26. Westervelt, R.: Smartphone theft, loss outweighs malware risk, McAfee report finds. In: SearchSecurity (2011)

Social Networks, Analytics and Recommendations

Social Learning Analytics to Study Teachers' Large-Scale Professional Networks

Riina Vuorikari and Santi Scimeca

European Schoolnet, Brussels, Belgium
{Riina.Vuorikari,Santi.Scimeca}@eun.org

Abstract. A growing interest in research focuses on teachers' large-scale socio-technical networks. Social learning approaches such as social constructivist theory is well established, however, the current challenges lie in creating reliable methods to gather evidence of how and under which conditions social learning takes place in such socio-technical networks and how does it support teachers' lifelong learning goals. The field of Learning Analytics (LA) addresses the issue of individual learners, whereas Social Learning Analytics (SLA) addresses that of groups' processes in knowledge construction.

The eTwinning action is used as a case study for applying the concepts of Social Learning Analytics. Our interest is on teachers' co-operation behaviour and patterns within a socio-technical network and how that can support teachers' continuous professional development. The eTwinning platform currently hosts more than 160000 European teachers. We first introduce the underlying pedagogical and lifelong learning related assumptions regarding teachers' co-operation. To better understand the type of activities that teachers undertake in eTwinning, they are classified according to the OECD's indices for teachers' co-operation. This creates the core of the eTwinning Analytics framework, which operationalises activities and allows them to be better measured and monitored. A snapshot of data from the platform is used as a proof of concept.

Keywords: Socio-technical networks, teachers' professional development, social learning analytics, eTwinning, Tellnet.

1 Introduction

Learning networks are technology-supported communities through which participants share knowledge with one another and jointly develop new knowledge [1]. They potentially enrich the experiences and form a viable setting for professional development and lifelong learning. They can also be called socio-technical networks as they enable knowledge and expertise to be shared indirectly as well, for example, when a message is read by someone other than the person to whom it was originally addressed [2]. Examples of such networks for teachers' professional development are communities who want to improve their work through exchange of experiences and collaboration, e.g. Tapped-in [3], Teachernet [4], eTwinning [5].

The underlying assumption is that teachers' networks, like other learning networks, can offer participants informal ways to support *competence building* and *personal and*

T. Ley et al. (Eds.): OST 2012, IFIP AICT 395, pp. 25–34, 2013.

professional development. Such competences include 21st century key competences, e.g. teachers gaining new digital competences, learning new methods to use ICT to support teaching and learning, learning to communicate in foreign languages, as well as gaining in other areas of personal development such as intercultural dialogue and social competence.

The second important assumption is that teachers' activities in collaboration networks can also have a relation to their teaching and instructional practices in the classroom. The OECD's TALIS study indicates to the direction that teachers' professional development may be effective in instructing and inspiring teachers to use modern and multifaceted practices, especially *student-oriented practices* (e.g. students work in small groups to come up with a joint solution to a problem or task; different work is given to the students that have difficulties learning and/or to those who can advance faster) and *enhanced activities* (e.g. students work on projects that require at least one week to complete; students make a product that will be used by someone else) [6]. Especially activities that take place at regular intervals and involve teachers in a rather stable social and collaborative context (i.e. networks or mentoring) have a significantly stronger association with teaching practices than regular workshops and courses [6, p. 101]. Thirdly, according to the same study, *co-operation* among teachers can also create opportunities for social and emotional support, exchange of ideas and practical advice that can thus enhance professionalism, feelings of self-efficacy and prevent stress and "burnout".

With the above-listed benefits, teachers' networks also offer challenges. How can evidence be gathered of how and under which conditions teachers gain new competences in such socio-technical network? Do certain activities support better teachers' lifelong learning goals and professional development? How do the activities undertaken in such networks eventually translate into actions in classroom (e.g. student-oriented and enhanced activities)? The first step towards this challenge is to create and test a framework that allows defining, operationalising, measuring and monitoring activities teachers undertake in socio-technical networks.

In this paper, we present a case study on the teachers' professional network in eTwinning. In section 2, a general description of eTwinning is offered focusing on the motivations behind this research. Section 3 offers a concept of a framework to define and operationalise teachers' activities in networks so that they eventually can be measured and better monitored. In section 4, a proof of concept is offered elaborating on a small number of research questions. The following section reflects on results and methods, and offers direction for future work.

2 eTwinning

eTwinning is defined as "The community for schools in Europe" [5]. It promotes school collaboration through the use of Information and Communication Technologies (ICT). In August 2012, 32 countries in Europe participate in eTwinning and the platform hosts more than 170000 registered members. Since 2005, eTwinning has been one of the most successful actions of the school education programme (Comenius) under the European Union's Lifelong Learning programme.

The main actors of the platform are eTw*inners*, i.e. teachers from 32 different European countries that currently participate in the initiative. The platform is also used by the National Support Services (*NSS*) that function in each participating country and support local users in eTwinning. The platform is managed by the Central Support Service (*CSS*), who is responsible for the implementation and considered as a *service provider*. The Central Support Service, run by European Schoolnet [7], is in the position to collect and process data according to the data protection rules defined in the eTwinning privacy statement[1]. It also observes all communications and interactions between eTwinners (*data processor*). The platform is run under a service contract for the European Commission, whereas the ultimate *data controller* is the Education, Audiovisual & Culture Executive Agency.

eTwinning offers teachers three main streams of activities:

1. Teachers can find schools from other countries to run *school collaboration projects* using Information and Communication Technologies (ICT) provided by the platform[2].
2. Various *formal and informal professional development* (PD) activities are offered. These include online Learning Events[3], a distance course for teachers, and more informal PD activities such as online interest Groups[4] and Teachers Rooms on topics of interest.
3. Additionally, the participating teachers have a set of *social networking tools* available, these include a profile page with personal and professional information[5], a display of connections to other members (i.e. contacts) and posting on a personal journal (e.g. status updates), but also on contacts' journals.

The development of eTwinning and its community building aspects are described in [8] and [9]. We call these micro-level studies focusing on the actions of individual teachers and students. These studies focus on active members and interesting cases that may not represent the larger community. As argued by [2] "such accounts serve to show the field what is attainable under particular conditions, interventions, or context, but we are still unable to rigorously measure their value, much less predict, guide, or replicate results reliably or at scale".

On the other hand, there are studies on eTwinning on the macro-scale: the growth of the network and its spread within each country is presented in [10] using measurements such as *eTwinning Reach*. Synergies between eTwinning and national teachers' professional development schemes are elaborated in [11]. These macro-scale studies also include the use of Social Network Analysis (SNA) and information

---

[1] `http://www.etwinning.net/en/pub/misc/privacy_statement.htm`

[2] `http://www.etwinning.net/en/pub/tools/twinspace_tools.htm`

[3] `http://www.etwinning.net/en/pub/professional_development/learning_events.htm`

[4] `http://www.etwinning.net/en/pub/professional_development/etwinning_groups.htm`

[5] `http://www.etwinning.net/en/pub/tools/desktop_tools.htm`

visualisation to study eTwinning (e.g. [12], [13], [14]). In addition to the two approaches explained above, the CSS also has a need to understand eTwinning at the meso-level. This middle-layer allows zooming on social structures that emerge from activities such as interactions among members and their interactions with content and tools. But instead of focusing on individuals, the meso-level is interested in the emerging behavioural patterns as a unit of study.

3 The eTwinning Analytics Framework

eTwinning Analytics *focus on the measurement, collection, analysis and reporting of data about eTwinners and their contexts, for purposes of understanding and optimising their co-operation and the environment in which it occurs. The goal of eTwinning Analytics, therefore, is to offer eTwinning stakeholders better tools to monitor the action through emerging trends and patterns upon which they can better base their decisions.*

Table 1. Mapping between TALIS activities to eTwinning activities

Category	TALIS: examples of activities	eTwinning: examples of activities
Index of **Exchange and co-ordination for teaching**	o Discuss and decide on the selection of instructional media (e.g. textbooks, exercise books). o Exchange teaching materials with colleagues. o Attend team conferences for the age group taught. o Ensure common standards in evaluations for assessing student progress. o Engage in discussion about the learning development of specific students.	o Participate in a Group to discuss and exchange on o a topic of interest o pedagogical practices o ICT tools and practices o teaching materials o Comments and ratings on Kits o Posts and comments on Project Cards o Applications for Quality Labels
Index of **Professional collaboration**	o Teach jointly as a team in the same class. o Take part in professional learning activities (e.g. team supervision). o Observe other teachers' classes and provide feedback. o Engage in joint activities across different classes and age groups (e.g. projects). o Discuss and co-ordinate homework practice across subjects.	o Take part in Learning Lab (A short intensive online event offered on a number of themes. They are led by an expert and include active work and discussion among teachers across Europe.) o Engage in a cross-country project using ICT. These projects can be either within or across disciplines or age groups.

The definition follows that of Learning Analytics in general [15], more particular, eTwinning Analytics are part of Social Learning Analytics focusing on building knowledge together in cultural, social and technological settings [16].

As explained previously, teachers' co-operation carries many promises for lifelong learning opportunities. The aim of the eTwinning Analytics is therefore to operationalise the *construct* of teachers' co-operation in eTwinning to allow it to be monitored and measured. Teachers' co-operation implies *teachers working together in groups or teams to improve educational processes and outcomes,* Table 1 shows TALIS examples of such activities across the two indices: "teachers' exchange and co-ordination activities" and "professional collaboration" [6]. Similar to this division, a mapping between TALIS' activities and their counterpart in eTwinning is presented.

Table 2 gives brief details of eTwinning Analytics framework version 1. Two additional categories have been added to the core of eTwinning Analytics Framework, namely "social networking activities" which includes the use of personal profile, social networking tools such as writing status updates, collection of contacts and receiving their status updates. A category for general statistic is created to allow monitoring trends in engagement with the activity.

Table 2. Elements of the eTwinning Analytics framework (v1)

eTwinning Analytics Framework	
General	o Logging on to the Desktop o Sending messages
Social networking activities	o Journal posts, comments, "I like it!" o Adding Contacts o Participation in Teachers' rooms
Teachers' coordination and exchange activities	o Participation in Groups o Commenting: on Kits, other people's Project Diary, Project Card, Quality Label applications
Teachers' professional collaboration	o Participation in Learning Events o Project collaboration and Twinspace o Writing Project Diary

Various requirements have been gathered from eTwinning stakeholders for the framework; they wish to monitor the action by the country from which the eTwinner originates, the year of registration and whether the eTwinner has engaged in any collaborative cross-border school projects within eTwinning. Although school collaboration projects are not a mandatory part of the action, in terms of professional development gains they offer great advantages (i.e. construct "teachers' professional collaboration"). Additionally, understanding how various tools under the three main streams of activities are used is an asset (as explained in section 2: project collaboration, formal and informal PD, social networking).

Interest in these emerging trends and behavioural patterns can be turned into simple research questions (RQ) which we will answer in the following section. These questions are as following: RQ1: Is there evidence of eTwinners remaining engaged with the action over a long period of time (i.e. 6 years)? RQ2: There are eTwinners who run school collaboration projects and the ones who do not: do these two groups use the Social networking tools in the same way? RQ3: Over a long period of time (i.e. 6 years), are there any trends that emerge in teachers' co-operation activities?

To answer to our research questions, authentic data from the eTwinning platform is used. The *SteerCom*-Desktop tool, which offers a set of pre-determined queries on the data within a certain period (e.g. from 2005 to 2011), was used. Additionally, some custom queries were made where the data was extracted on Nov 2011. In the following section we provide results to our research questions, discussion of which is offered in the last section with future work.

4 Demonstrating the Use of eTwinning Analytics

RQ1: eTwinning retention rate. *Is there evidence of eTwinners remaining engaged with the action over a long period of time (i.e. since its start in 2005)?*
"Retention rate" is a term used in Web Analytics to indicate to the percentage of users who sign up for the service and come back within a period of time.

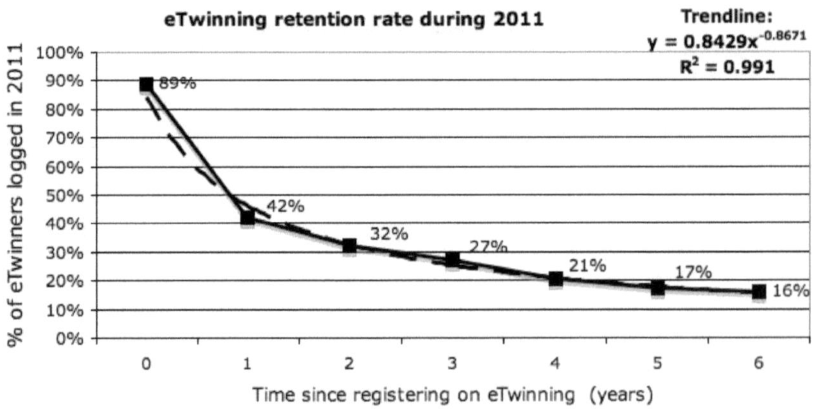

Fig. 1. eTwinning retention rate in 2011. Data on returning eTwinners by the year of their registration: "0 year" refers to eTwinners who registered in 2011; "1 year" = in 2010, etc.

Retention rate for eTwinning refers to the percentage of eTwinners who have registered on eTwinning since its beginning in 2005, and who still return to log-in to the eTwinning platform in 2011. Figure 1 shows the eTwinning retention, the x-axis represents the number of years since registration on eTwinning and the vertical one represents the percentage of eTwinners.

We can observe that in year 0, the retention rate is 89%. This means that 89% of users who registered on eTwinning in 2011 returned to login onto eTwinning at least once during that year. In year 1, the retention rate is 42%, indicating that 42% of those who signed up in 2010 returned to eTwinning at least once in 2011. The retention curve is closely fitted with the power law curve (dashed line).

Finally, the retention curve shows evidence that among early eTwinners (i.e. registered in '05 and '06), about 1 in 6 still remains engaged in 2011. We were not able to find similar retention rates available for other professional learning networks or social networking sites, but the annual version of eTwinning Analytics will keep track of the trend in the future.

RQ2: Use of social networking tools. *There are eTwinners who engage in "professional collaboration" (i.e. run school collaboration projects) and the ones who do not: do these two groups use Social networking tools in the same way?*
Figure 2 shows the usage of four different Social networking tools available for eTwinners (Contact, Profile picture, Journal Wall posts and Teachers' rooms) divided by the two groups. As a general trend, eTwinners using social networking tools are more involved in projects (average 64%) than the ones not engaged in projects (36%). This indicates that between these two groups, there are different ways in which they engage using the available Social networking tools. It is noteworthy to mention that the data does not give any indication of the amount of activities in which these two groups engage, nor of the causality of the usages (e.g. does social networking precede project collaboration).

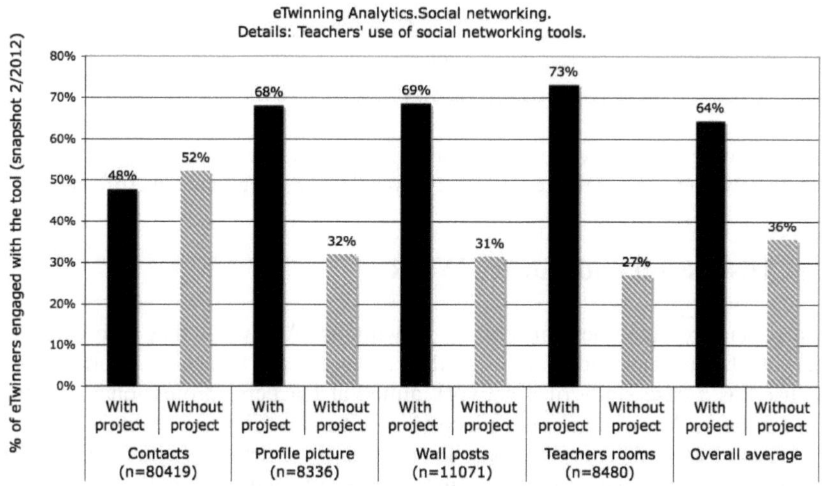

Fig. 2. eTwinners' use of social networking tools, divided by eTwinners with projects and without. Snapshot of data extracted from *SteerCom*-Desktop tool (Feb 2012).

RQ3: Teachers' co-operation activities. ***Over a long period of time (i.e. 6 years), are there any trends that emerge in teachers' co-operation activities?***
Figure 3 shows the percentage in which eTwinners have engaged in various co-operation activities, namely in *professional collaboration activities*, e.g. participation in cross-border school collaboration and in *Social networking activities,* e.g. adding Contacts and participating in Teachers' rooms. The x-axis represents the year since registered on the portal. Two patterns can be observed:

1. Professional collaboration: eTwinners in their early years (registered in year 0 and 1) seem to be less engaged in project collaboration (line: triangular) than those who have been on the platform for 3 years or more (average 18% vs. 30%).
2. Social networking: eTwinners in their early years (registered in year 0 and 1) seem slightly more involved in Teachers Rooms than others. On the other hand, even in the early years, Contacts feature seems to be well used by almost half of the eTwinners (45%), and the use seems to intensify after that.

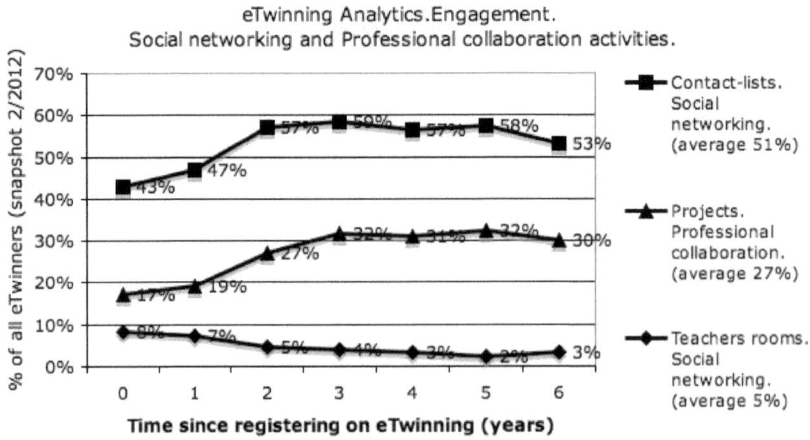

Fig. 3. eTwinners engagement on the portal disaggregated by the year of registration. "0 year" refers to eTwinners who registered in 2011; "1 year" to those registered in 2010, etc.

5 Discussion and Future Work

This paper presents the concept of eTwinning Analytics that allows observing emerging behaviours and patterns within a large-scale teacher network. eTwinning was used as a case study of a network aimed at teachers' professional development where building knowledge takes place in a cultural, social and technological setting. The focus of analysis is on the meso-level using the emerging behavioural patterns as the unit of analysis. Three research questions were used to demonstrate the usage of such analytics. In the following, we offer some discussion on the results and the method, as well as new directions for this work.

From the RQ1 it becomes clear that eTwinning has a potential to engage its users over a long period of time (e.g. over 5 years). Evidence was found that *one eTwinner in six who registered on the platform between 2005 and 2006 still returns to it.* More studies are needed to understand whether eTwinning serves the evolution of teachers' competences; how well it can serve their lifelong learning goals over such a long period of time; and how to make sure that more "mature" eTwinners can contribute back to the community, for example, by mentoring newcomers.

The RQ2 looked at the use of Social networking tools on the platform by two groups: eTwinners engaged in project collaboration and the ones not. About 2/3 of the users of Social networking tools were active in project collaboration, showing that this group of active users use a large variety of tools and engage in many activities. However, *one third of the users of Social networking tools are eTwinners with no project experience engaging in a positive activity for building weak ties in the network.* Weak ties are important for connecting people and bringing new ideas so that information can travel through a network [17]. More studies are needed to understand whether there is a sequence in using the different tools, e.g. social networking precedes project collaboration or whether they are complementary and overlapping activities. Such sequential interaction models would allow better insights into supporting teachers' competence building over time, as well as to offer better support for new comers.

The RQ3 shows that to experience a full range of professional development activities in eTwinning (i.e. teachers' co-operation as defined by TALIS), and therefore to gain full advantage of it, *a substantial time investment is needed.* However, it is not clear whether we can infer that there is "an eTwinning life-cycle" with an assumption that it takes around two full school years for most eTwinners to "mature" and get involved in school collaboration - a topic needing a further investigation.

In this paper we have demonstrated the concept of eTwinning Analytics highlighting new insights into teachers' activities within a socio-technical network aimed at professional development. Even if some limitations with the available data were shown, the results are encouraging. They allow new hypothesis being created for further investigation on how teachers' co-operation takes place within a large-scale socio-technical network, and eventually take steps towards understanding when such networks better support teachers' personal and professional continuous development.

The future research proposes to investigate how the Uptake Analysis framework by [18] could offer a suitable methodological framework to further develop eTwinning Analytics and advance the study on teachers' large-scale socio-technical networks. More specifically, we are interested in investigating sequential interaction models and artefact-mediated collaborative activities within the eTwinning network that potentially lead us to gather better evidence of how, when and why socio-technical networks support lifelong learning. Evidence from the previous research [18] indicates towards the direction that the Uptake model offers an interesting methodological framework, especially thanks to its ability to achieve media independence, which has been deemed problematic for the studies in the past (e.g. [19]).

Acknowledgements. The paper has been made possible thanks to collaboration and funding through the LLP project called Teachers' Lifelong Learning Network [20] and eTwinning [5].

References

1. Sloep, P., Berlanga, A.: Learning Networks, Networked Learning. Comunicar. 9(37), 55–64 (2011)
2. Schlager, M.S., Farooq, U., Fusco, J., Schank, P., Dwyer, N.: Analyzing Online Teacher Networks: Cyber Networks Require Cyber Research Tools. Journal of Teacher Education 60(1), 86–100 (2009)

3. Tapped-in, http://tappedin.org
4. Teachernet: webarchive.nationalarchives.gov.uk/*/http:/www.teachernet.gov.uk/
5. eTwinning, http://www.etwinning.net
6. Creating Effective Teaching and Learning Environments: First results from TALIS. OECD (2009)
7. European Schoolnet (EUN), http://www.europeanschoolnet.eun.org
8. Crawley, C., Gerhard, P., Gilleran, A., Joyce, A. (eds.): eTwinning 2.0 Building the community for schools in Europe. European Schoolnet (2010)
9. Crawley, C., Gilleran, A., Scimeca, S., Vuorikari, R., Wastiau, P.: Beyond School Projects, A report on eTwinning 2008-2009. In: Central Support Service for eTwinning (CSS), European Schoolnet (2009)
10. Vuorikari, R., Berlanga, A., Cachia, R., Cao, Y., Fetter, S., Gilleran, A., Klamma, R., Punie, Y., Scimeca, S., Sloep, P., Petrushyna, Z.: ICT-Based School Collaboration, Teachers' Networks and their Opportunities for Teachers' Professional Development - A Case Study on eTwinning. In: Leung, H., Popescu, E., Cao, Y., Lau, R.W.H., Nejdl, W., et al. (eds.) ICWL 2011. LNCS, vol. 7048, pp. 112–121. Springer, Heidelberg (2011a)
11. Vuorikari, R., Gilleran, A., Scimeca, S.: Growing beyond Innovators – ICT-Based School Collaboration in eTwinning. In: Kloos, C.D., Gillet, D., Crespo García, R.M., Wild, F., Wolpers, M., et al. (eds.) EC-TEL 2011. LNCS, vol. 6964, pp. 537–542. Springer, Heidelberg (2011b)
12. Breuer, R., Klamma, R., Cao, Y., Vuorikari, R.: Social network analysis of 45,000 schools: A case study of technology enhanced learning in europe. In: Cress, U., Dimitrova, V., Specht, M. (eds.) EC-TEL 2009. LNCS, vol. 5794, pp. 166–180. Springer, Heidelberg (2009)
13. Song, E., Petrushyna, Z., Cao, Y., Klamma, R.: Learning Analytics at Large: The Lifelong Learning Network of 160,000 European Teachers. In: Kloos, C.D., Gillet, D., Crespo García, R.M., Wild, F., Wolpers, M., et al. (eds.) EC-TEL 2011. LNCS, vol. 6964, pp. 398–411. Springer, Heidelberg (2011)
14. Berlanga, A.J., Vuorikari, R. (eds.): Symposium - Learning Networks for Professional Development: Current Research Approaches and Future Trends. In: Proceedings of the 8th International Conference on Networked Learning 2012, The Netherlands (2012)
15. Siemens, G. (2011), http://www.learninganalytics.net/?p=126
16. Ferguson, R., Buckingham Shum, S.: Social Learning Analytics: Five Approaches. In: 2nd International Conference on Learning Analytics & Knowledge, ACM Press, New York (2012)
17. Haythornthwaite, C.: The strength and the impact of new media. In: Proceedings of the 34th Annual Hawaii International Conference on System Sciences (2001)
18. Suthers, D.D., Dwyer, N., Medina, R., Vatrapu, R.: A framework for conceptualizing, representing, and analyzing distributed interaction. International Journal of Computer-Supported Collaborative Learning 5(1), 5–42 (2010)
19. Ley, T., Schweiger, S., Seitlinger, P.: Implicit and Explicit Memory in Learning from Social Software: A Dual-Process Account. In: Kloos, C.D., Gillet, D., Crespo García, R.M., Wild, F., Wolpers, M., et al. (eds.) EC-TEL 2011. LNCS, vol. 6964, pp. 449–454. Springer, Heidelberg (2011)
20. Teachers' Lifelong Learning Network, http://www.tellnet.eun.org

Knowing My Peers: Edentity – To Invite Peer Interaction and Social Learning

Hanna M. Olsson and Thomas Persson Slumpi

Computer and Systems Science,
Mid Sweden University, Östersund, Sweden
{hanna.olsson,thomas.persson}@miun.se

Abstract. Digital spaces designated for learning need to invite to social learning. Oftentimes, however, students express feelings of loneliness in their learning in online courses. Making the students more visible to each other is hence crucial. In this article we present a study of students' self-presentations. We find that they are rather unelaborated, and we propose an alternative solution to making students identities visible within the learning space. Our proposed solution is a separate system that can be plugged into any digital learning system: the edentity.

Keywords: Edentity, social learning, digital identity, awareness.

1 Introduction

Digital learning spaces (DLS) have become increasingly important in contemporary higher education and in some cases they present the sole environment in which education takes place. A challenge that has emerged related to DLSs is that the students to a greater extent are feeling alone and isolated [1]. Learning is as such a social activity, which takes place in-between people [2], thus loneliness and isolation do not promote learning. A solution is to support the students' effort in establishing a social learning setting and encourage them to interact. But interaction requires knowledge of whom one is interacting with [3]. We argue that a first step towards creating a social learning setting in which interaction is central is that the students reveal cues about their identity to others. Identity is in this article, inspired by Callero [4], viewed as a subjective self-representation; it is a dynamic, context-dependent, hierarchically organized complex. Hence, different types of self-presentations in DLSs should reveal important identity cues.

In this article we present empirical data on how learners present themselves in a DLS related two different courses in the Swedish higher education, and what influence the teacher might have on these self-presentations. Based on this data, we propose an alternative way to make learners identities explicit in DLSs, with the purpose to invite peer interaction and social learning. We hypothesize that this would lead to increased motivation, learner experience and learning outcome.

T. Ley et al. (Eds.): OST 2012, IFIP AICT 395, pp. 35–40, 2013.

2 Method

This research departs from the most fundamental principle in hermeneutics, the hermeneutic circle which illustrates the relationship between the whole and the parts, and the continuous movement between the two [5]. The identity communicated through the self-presentation is viewed as the whole while the different cues revealed are viewed as the parts. Our approach to hermeneutics can be argued to be sender-oriented and has its base in the work of Schleiermacher [6]. The sender-orientation implies that we as researchers try to reconstruct the meaning (the identity) the writer of the self-presentation intended to communicate (through the cues in the self-presentation). In this article the identification of identity cues, hence the parts, are in focus of our attention. In order to identify the cues we have applied what Bergsröm and Boréus [6] label content analysis. The basic principle of content analysis is to count different occurrences in a text [6]. We have read through the students' self-presentation repeatedly and counted different identity cues. The count of cues will contribute with 1) indication what students seem to find important to communicate and 2) indication if there is a difference what is communicated if the self-presentation is an assignment or not, e.g. what role the teacher plays.

In this article we have analyzed the self-presentation in two different courses in Informatics at Mid Sweden University. Course A concerns searching and critically evaluating information on the web. Course B concerns the design and construction of usable websites. Additional information concerning the courses is summarized in Table 1:

Table 1. Information related to the studied courses

	Course A	Course B
Duration	5 weeks	5 weeks
Number of students enrolled	36	48
Age span	21-67	20-55
Median age	31	35
Self-presentation assignment on course	Yes	No
DLS	WebCT	WebCT

What should be added to the above is that WebCT offers a function where the students can create a profile. This profile is however very static in nature and rarely used by the students. Also, related to the assignment in course A, there was a short instruction of what the presentation could include such as background, interests, why are you taking this course, expectations on the course and experiences of problems regarding searching the Internet for information (subject of the course). For course B there was a discussion forum with the heading of "Presentations", and a message from the teacher to "make a short presentation of your-self".

3 Theoretical Bpackground and Related Research

Theoretically this article draws on two different theoretical approaches to identity creation: identity theory and social identity theory. These approaches over lap to some extent and complement one another on others according to Hogg et al. [7]. Three distinct categories related to the creation of an identity can be identified: master statuses, role identities, and group memberships. Master statuses include for example race, ethnicity or sex, and overrides other statuses and sometime they override each other depending on the context [8]. In identity theory, identity is viewed as a structural unit consisting of hierarchically organized roles [4]. Those roles can be more or less salient, and the more salient a role is, the more relevance it is given [4]. It is also the case that relationships with others influence the salience of a role [4]. Thus, salient roles should get greater focus in self-presentations. Finally, in social identity theory the membership in different groups are emphasized as important in the construction of an identity [7]. Identity is the meeting point of the individual and the group/society [9]. Thus, it is influenced by both the individual and the social context. Learning in itself also contributes to the development of one´s identity [9]. Hence, identities are very much intertwined in any (social) learning situation.

When it comes to communicating identity cues in online environments, the most basic identity cues communicated in online environments (a baseline) can be synthesised from the work of Rusman et al. [10] and Berlanga et al. [11] and is summarized in Table 2 below. Rusman et al. [10] also provide a more elaborate set of cues comprising in total of 157 different cues. Due to space limitations we cannot include the complete list.

Table 2. Baseline of identity cues (synthesis of Rusman et al. [10] and Belanga et al. [11])

Identity cues	
Name (first and surname)	Pseudonym (alias/display name)
Personal description	Age/Date of birth
Reference to personal URL (blog, website, etc.)	Social network sites or communities participating in
Contact method	Location data (business/ private)
Occupation/ function/ position/role	Company/ organization/ employer
Education	Interests (private/ professional)
Languages (level, preferred language for communication)	Testimonials (references, info from others about person)
Number of contacts	Contact data (business/private)
Expertise	Intentions for participation

Besides research on identity cues, research on the relation between identities and online environments often concerns identification and often refers to management of digital identities. For example, Milikic et al. [12] indicate the importance of benefitting from and merging available identity cues from diverse sources through diverse systems and propose a technical solution for this. It is however not only a technical issue. The users need to be in control of their digital identity(-ies) in order to feel secure and confident to provide personal information as well. A way to achieve this is for example by embedding it in mobile devices [13]. Since the user always carries the device with them, it is seen as a natural extension of themselves [13].

Student profiles are discussed by for example Kear [1] as a mean to enhance the sense of presence (i.e. the extent to which the users perceive each other as real [14]). Also E-portfolios have been proposed as a way to mediate student identity both with administrative [15] and didactic/promotion [16] motives. However, e-portfolios have been criticized by Olsson [17] for not being a suitable way of representing one's identity since it is traditionally used for showcasing only one's abilities. However, identity expression is about much more than abilities, as shown in Table 2.

4 Results

The result of the conducted studies of the courses is as is summarized in Table 3.

Table 3. Cues identified in student self-presentations

	Course A		Course B	
	Actual numbers	Percent	Actual numbers	Percent
Total number of registered students	36	100%	48	100%
Number of presentations	34	94%	26	54%
Number of pres. receiving reply	0	0%	3	12%
Name	23	68%	22	85%
Place of birth	4	12%	3	12%
Age	20	59%	18	69%
Occupation	15	44%	20	77%
City of residence	17	50%	24	92%
Family/Status	10	29%	17	65%
Parallel studies	14	41%	13	50%
Pre-knowledge	19	56%	11	42%
Interests	15	44%	11	42%
Expectations/Attitude in rel. to class	26	76%	17	65%
Future aims	4	12%	4	15%

The key findings are that the identified 11 identity cues to a large extent overlap with the baseline cues in Table 2, with a few exceptions like "Place of birth" and "Future aims". However, the cues identified in the students' self-presentations also did not include several identity cues found in the baseline like for example "Reference to personal URL (blog, website, etc.)" or a "Photo" (some, but far from a majority of the students, in fact had included a photo in the profile function provided in WebCT).

5 Discussion and Conclusions

The identity cues communicated in the self-presentations that we have studied are rather limited and unelaborated. But a person's identity is a dynamic, context-dependent, hierarchically organized complex. Hence, an identity cannot be communicated by only a few cues. A minimum could be argued to be the cues in the baseline, but even these are perhaps too few. It might be the case that the baseline needs to be complemented with cues found in the extended set of cues identified by Rusman et al. [10]. The lack of several of the baseline identity cues might indicate that the students' self-presentations were not sufficiently elaborated to establish interaction based on them. An indication that making the self-presentation an assignment actually prevented the students to initiate any social interaction was that the students sparsely commented on someone else's presentation. The few times this happened were in course B. That it only occurred when the presentation was not mandatory could indicate a more casual attitude towards the presentation and that they then become more usable. When students do comment, it is regarding something they can relate to, and the impression is that they seem to grasp onto anything that gives a familiar feeling.

When it comes to the teacher's influence on the self-presentation, it did not seem to influence the content of the presentations whether the self-presentation was an assignment with instructions or not. The same cues where roughly included in both cases. The only influence the teacher seems to have had, was that the number of students making a self-presentation became higher (94%) if it was an assignment compared to (54%) if it was not. Hence, the teachers seem to rather easily be able to influence the quantity of presentations within a course by making an initial assignment but not the content or the quality of it.

Self-presentations in DLSs seem not to be an efficient way to communicate identity cues. There is a need for a tool that can help mediate the identity with all its complexity and thereby enhances learning, motivation and user experience. The identity cues along with the tool are what we label the edentity. We picture the edentity as a separate system, platform independent, completely student-owned and student-controlled. This private system can then be plugged into any digital learning space at choice. At the time of the initial plugging in (or later through settings) to another system, the student chooses what information to share in this specific other system. This could be facilitated through predefined sets.

Our work towards the edentity has only just started. Further research is first to establish what needs to be part of an edentity. This is crucial in order to make it easier for students to communicate their identity in digital learning spaces and establish social relations with other students. Secondly it is about how the edentity should be associated with the student so it can be carried around at all times, become accessible for other students, but also be controlled by the student so he or she can increase or decrease the number of cues revealed to others.

References

1. Kear, K.: Social presence in online learning communities. In: The 7th International Conference on Networked Learning, Aalborg, Denmark (2010)
2. Vygotsky, L.S., Cole, M.: Mind in society: the development of higher psychological processes, p. 159 s. Harvard University Press, Cambridge (1978)

3. Ke, F., Chávez, A., Causarano, P.-N.L., Causarano, A.: Identity presence and knowledge building: Joint emergence in online learning environments? International Journal of Computer-Supported Collaborative Learning 63, 349–370 (2011)
4. Callero, P.L.: Role-Identity Salience. Social Psychology Quarterly 483, 203–215 (1985)
5. Klein, H.K., Myers, M.D.: A Set of Principles for Conducting and Evaluating Interpretive Field Studies in Information Systems. MIS Quarterly 231, 67–93 (1999)
6. Bergström, G., Boréus, K.: Textens mening och makt: metodbok i samhällsvetenskaplig text- och diskursanalys, 2nd edn., p. 461 s. Studentlitteratur, Lund (2005)
7. Hogg, M.A., Terry, D.J., White, K.M.: A Tale of Two Theories: A Critical Comparison of Identity Theory with Social Identity Theory. Social Psychology Quarterly 584, 255–269 (1995)
8. Becker, H.S.: Outsiders: studies in the sociology of deviance, p. 179. Free press of Glencoe, London (1963)
9. Lave, J., Wenger, E.: Situated learning: legitimate peripheral participation. In: Learning in Doing, p. 138 s. Cambridge University Press, Cambridge (1991)
10. Rusman, E., Van Bruggen, J., Sloep, P., Valcke, M., Koper, R.: Can I trust you? – Personal profiling for a first impression of trustworthiness in virtual project teams (2010)
11. Berlanga, A.J., Bitter-Rijpkema, M., Brouns, F., Sloep, P.B., Fetter, S.: Personal profiles: enhancing social interaction in learning networks. International Journal of Web Based Communities 71, 66–82 (2011)
12. Milikić, N., Radulović, F., Devedžić, V.: Infrastructure for Exchanging Online Presence Data in Learning Applications. In: ERK Portorož (2011)
13. Satchell, C., Shanks, G., Howard, S., Murphy, J.: Identity crisis: user perspectives on multiplicity and control in federated identity management. Behaviour & Information Technology 301, 51–62 (2011)
14. Gunawardena, C.N., Zittle, F.J.: Social presence as a predictor of satisfaction within a computer-mediated conferencing environment. American Journal of Distance Education 113, 8–26 (1997)
15. Ravet, S.: E-portfolio Interoperability Revised: Position Paper. In: Baumgartner, S.P., Bauer, Z.R. (eds.) The Potential of E-Portfolios in Higher Education, pp. 187–204. Studienverlag GmbH, Wien (2009)
16. Bauer, R.: Construction of One's Identity. A Student's View on the Potential of EPortfolios. In: Baumgartner, S.P., Bauer, Z.R. (eds.) The Potential of E-Portfolios in Higher Education, pp. 173–183. Studienverlag GmbH, Wien (2009)
17. Olsson, H.: Proposing Learner E-dentity to social presence in digital spaces for learning. In: Asproth, V. (ed.) Challenges for the future in an ICT Context ...for Stig, pp. 177–186. Mid Sweden University, Östersund (2011)

An Implicit-Semantic Tag Recommendation Mechanism for Socio-Semantic Learning Systems

Paul Seitlinger[1], Tobias Ley[2], and Dietrich Albert[1]

[1] Knowledge Management Institute, Graz University of Technology, Austria
{paul.seitlinger,dietrich.albert}@tugraz.at
[2] Center for Educational Technology, Tallinn University, Estonia
tley@tlu.ee

Abstract. In recent years Social Tagging (ST) has become a popular functionality in social learning environments, not least because tags support the exchange of users' knowledge representations, a process called social sensemaking. An important design feature of ST-Systems (STS) is the tag recommendation service. Several principles for tag recommendation mechanisms (TRM) have been proposed, which are built upon a technical and statistical perspective on STS and based on aggregated user data on a word level. Up to now, a cognitive perspective also taking into account memory processes has been neglected. In this paper we therefore introduce a TRM that applies a formal theory of human memory to model a user's prototypical tag configurations. The algorithm underlying the TRM is supposed to recommend psychologically plausible tag combinations and to mediate social sensemaking.

Keywords: Tagging, Categorization, Cognitive Modelling, MINERVA2, Tag-Recommendation-Algorithm.

1 Introduction

In recent years, Social Tagging (ST) has become a popular functionality in the Web allowing people to freely associate textual labels (called tags) to resources. Prominent ST-Systems (STS) are http://del.icio.us (social bookmarking platform) or http://flickr.com (photo sharing platform), which we regard as socio-semantic learning environments. Dynamic interactions between representations on an external level (tags and resources) and semantic memory processes on an internal level (categorization) expedite social sensemaking [1], i.e. cooperative categorization and indexing of Web resources. To mediate these social learning processes we need services that analyze statistical structures on the word level and are embedded into a cognitive-psychologically plausible framework.

With respect to its usefulness for educational activities, empirical studies of Kuhn et al. (e.g. [5]) give evidence that ST supports an important aspect of science education in schools and university courses, namely reflecting on the utility of data and annotating this reflection for later recall. A design recommendation of [5] is that teachers or lectors deploying ST for social learning processes should provide a schema for the tagging activity and should categorize tags in a relevant way.

T. Ley et al. (Eds.): OST 2012, IFIP AICT 395, pp. 41–46, 2013.

In this paper we introduce the principles of a tag-recommendation mechanism (TRM), which is motivated by empirical studies [6,6] and built upon MINERVA 2 [3], a formal theory of human memory. This TRM is designed to extract prototypical tag combinations (so called gist traces) from a user's tagging behavior and to suggest tags in a categorized and psychologically meaningful way. The suggestion of gist-traces is supposed to give a supportive schema during the tagging activity. Beyond that, it is conceived to identify and recommend users with similar gist traces, thereby mediating social sensemaking.

The structure of this article is as follows. First, we provide a brief overview of previous TRMs (section 2.1). Second, we briefly summarize some cognitive-psychological work on STS to motivate the principles of our TRM and briefly describe MINERVA2 (section 2.2). Third, we provide simple equations to derive appropriate tag recommendations (sections 2.3 and 2.4).

2 An Implicit-Semantic Tag Recommendation Mechanism

2.1 Previous Tag Recommendation Mechanisms

Referring to [2] there are currently four different approaches to design TRMs. One approach is the analysis of tag quality, e.g. its popularity and semantic distinctiveness to other tags. A second approach is the computation of tag co-occurrence to gather similarities between pairs of tags for the recommendation of appropriate tag combinations. The third approach relies on mutual information between words, documents and tags. One example is collaborative filtering for recommending tags in folksonomies [4]. For a given user a neighborhood is formed consisting of users with similar tag or resource collections. Tags frequently occurring within the neighborhood are then recommended. The fourth approach takes into account the content of a resource and ranks tags according to their relevance to the resource's content. [4] applied an adapted PageRank algorithm, which ranks the importance of vertices (tags, users, resources) as a function of their edge degrees. The most dominant approach simply counts the number of tag occurrences and suggests the most popular ones.

All these approaches are based on aggregated user data and – to some extent – on the "wisdom of the crowd". However, they abstract from users' preferences and neglect their typically verbal categorization behavior. Cognitive-psychological studies (e.g. [1,6,6]), briefly described in the next sub-section, show that these approaches would benefit from mechanisms applying formal theories of human semantic memory. Such an extension would help to realize the suggestion of [5] to provide a categorical schema for the tagging activity during educational tasks.

2.2 Theoretical and Empirical Background

[1] provided a formal model of human categorization in STS. They put emphasis on implicit (automatic) categorization processes of a user during a tag-based inference of a resource's gist (topic) as well as during gist-based tag-assignments. By means of a multinomial model of ST [6] and [6] empirically showed that implicit categorization

processes (gist-based reconstructions) are indeed in play during the generation of tags. More precisely, users retrieve an implicit gist-trace from their semantic memory to reconstruct the meaning of previously perceived tags. Afterwards, tags are chosen to index the implicit gist-trace. Here, we introduce an implicit-semantic tag-recommendation mechanism (isTRM) that mimics the gist-based reconstruction process investigated by [6].

As described above, the isTRM is built upon MINERVA2 [3] that formally describes implicit, reconstructive processes triggered by stimuli (e.g. words or tags). The general assumption is that a stimulus (e.g. the word "bird") strongly activates traces (internal representations) in semantic memory, which share many features with the stimulus (e.g. sparrow, raven, falcon, etc.); all other traces stay relatively dormant (e.g. different dog exemplars). All the features common across the activated traces (e.g. feathers, wings, etc.) constitute the concept that comes into mind. The outcome of this activation process is a prototype or gist: an abstract representation of all single traces activated by the stimulus (e.g. a prototypical bird). MINERVA2 provides a formalization of this reconstructive process. Memory traces as well as stimuli are formalized as vectors where feature values (-1, 1) encode the existence/nonexistence of features. Thus, the semantic memory is represented as a matrix (a set of row vectors). A particular algorithm (see 2.4), which multiplies the matrix by a stimulus-vector, yields a content-vector displaying the prototype.

We draw on the MINERVA2 notations to represent a user's tag assignments (TAS for short) in form of vectors, whose feature values encode the assignment/non-assignment of a tag to a particular resource, and on the MINERVA2 algorithm to extract the user's prototypical tag combinations.

2.3 Notation of a User's Personomy

The basis of the isTRM is the formalization of a user's semantic traces left in the STS, which are verbalized in form of her or his tag assignments (TAS). To define a TAS we refer to [4] and represent an STS as a triple of the finite sets U, T and R, whose elements are the users, tags and resources, respectively. There exists a ternary relation Y between the three sets, i.e. $Y \in U \times T \times R$., and the TAS (u, t, r) are the elements of Y. The collection of all TAS of user u_i is called personomy [4]; the collection of all personomies constitutes the folksonomy.

For m resources and n tags of the whole folksonomy, we notate the personomy of a user u_i in a resource-tag matrix $\mathbf{X} \in \{-1,1\}^{m \times n}$ that can be divided into row vectors: $\mathbf{X} := [\vec{x}_1,...,\vec{x}_m]$ with $\vec{x}_r := [x_{r1},..x_{rn}]$, for $r := 1,\ldots,m$. We call x_{rt} a tag-feature indicating that a user assigned tag t to the resource r, and $x_{rt} \in \{-1,1\}$. Thus, each row vector represents a particular TAS of a user u_i that we call semantic trace. The middle part of Fig.1 schematically presents this resource-tag matrix $\mathbf{X}$. For instance, the first tag-feature of the semantic trace $\vec{x}_1$ indicates that the user assigned the tag "memory" to the resource r_1; the second tag-feature represents the non-assignment of the tag "Java".

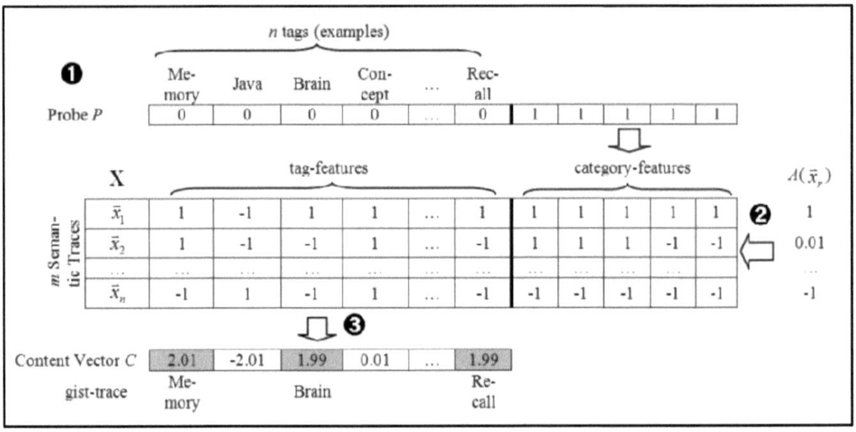

Fig. 1. Schematic presentation of the isTRM mechanics

One prerequisite to apply MINERVA2 is to group the semantic traces of a user into categories. In several social platforms, such as *MENDELEY* (www.mendeley.com), *SemanticScuttle* (www.semanticscuttle.sourceforge.net) or *soboleo* (www.soboleo.com), self-created folders or taxonomies complement the tagging functionality. In such environments, each folder or node of the taxonomy can be interpreted as a category *cat.* In more popular STS, such as *Del.icio.us* (www.delicious.com), some additional computational costs have to be invested to identify categories. The following paragraph provides a suggestion on how to group resources into categories.

Similar to the technique of collaborative filtering, the similarities between pairs of semantic traces, e.g. $(\check{x}_1, \check{x}_2)$, can be computed by the cosine similarity measure (e.g. [4]). This measure can be applied to all pairs of semantic traces and a subsequent multidimensional scaling can represent these vectors as points in a multidimensional space. All pairs of traces whose Euclidean distance d does not exceed a critical threshold τ can be assigned to the same category cat_i. Each vector $\vec{x}_r$ needs a "label" indicating its category membership. Therefore, we extend each semantic trace by o (so called) category-features $t = n+1 \ldots n+o$, representing the category to which resource r belongs. For simplicity, in the example of Fig.1 there are only five category-features (i.e. o=5), which would allow for 2^5 differentiations. For instance, the semantic trace $\vec{x}_1$ is labeled by the sequence [1,1,1,1,1].

2.4 Extracting the Gist of a User's Tag-Assignments

After a new resource r_{new}, has been assigned to a category, e.g. cat_1, the isTRM starts by generating a probe P (circled "1" in Fig. 5). The purpose of P is to activate those semantic traces in the matrix **X**, which belong to the same or similar category as the resource r_{new}. P is also a vector with tag-features [p_t=1 … n] and category-features [p_t=n+1 … n+o] and bears the same label (category-features) as the resource r_{new} (1,1,1,1,1 in the example of Fig.1); its tag-features are set at 0. A particular

MINERVA2 equation yields the similarity $S(\vec{x}_r)$ between P and a semantic trace $\vec{x}_r$ by:

$$S(\vec{x}_r) = (1/N_R)\sum_{t=1}^{n} p_t x_{rt}. \tag{1}$$

N_R is the number of features for which either p_t or x_{rt} is nonzero. Since $S(\vec{x}_r)$ acts in a similar way as the Pearson correlation coefficient, the value of $S(\vec{x}_r)$ will be positive and high (approaching +1) for all traces bearing the same or a similar label as P ($\vec{x}_1$ in the example of Fig.1). The extent to which P activates the trace $\vec{x}_r$ depends on a non-linear function of $S(\vec{x}_r)$ given by $A(\vec{x}_r) = S(\vec{x}_r)^3$. Raising $S(\vec{x}_r)$ to the power 3 has proved to increase the activation differences between similar and less similar traces (see [3]).

To derive tag-recommendations from the matrix a content Vector C with content-features c_t is computed summarizing the activation pattern across the matrix (circled "3" in Fig.1). The activation of each trace $A(\vec{x}_r)$ is multiplied by each of the trace's feature x_{rt} (circled "2" in Fig.1). Then, these products are summed over traces:

$$c_t = \sum_{r=1}^{m} A(\vec{x}_r) x_{rt}. \tag{2}$$

The c_t –values indicate, "which features [in our case tags] are shared by the strongly activated traces" [3] and therefore, which tags belong to a prototypical tag combination of a user. In the example of Fig.1 the tags "memory", "brain" and "recall" constitute such a prototypical tag combination. Finally, we need a simple rule selecting an appropriate subset of tags for the gist-trace, i.e. the final tag recommendations. If the parameter l specifies the number of tags to be selected, an appropriate subset is given by $\textit{gist-trace} := \{c_t \in C \mid rank(c_t) \leq l\}$.

The isTRM is also conceived to mediate social sensemaking by identifying neighborhoods of users with similar categorization behavior. That could be realized by combining collaborative filtering with the content vector C. Referring to [4] the k most similar users to user u can be computed by:

$$N_u^k := \operatorname*{arg\,max}_{v \in U \setminus \{u\}}^{k} sim(C_u, C_v), \tag{3}$$

where $sim(C_u,C_v)$ is the cosine similarity between two vectors, in our case content vectors of the users u and v. We assume that the neighborhood of user u based on content vectors is a valid measure for user recommendations from a semantic memory perspective.

3 Summary and Conclusion

In this paper we introduced the isTRM, an implicit tag recommendation mechanism for the suggestion of psychologically plausible tag combinations and the identification of users with similar categorization behavior. It is based on empirical research on ST, built upon the memory theory MINERVA2 and treats users' TAS as verbalized semantic traces. The outcome of the isTRM is a gist-trace representing a tag combination that is assumed to resonate with the user's implicit semantic memory and thus, to give an appropriate categorical schema during the tagging activity, as suggested by [5]. By incorporating collaborative filtering, the isTRM appears to be a psychologically valid service to mediate social sensemaking within social learning environments.

In the near future, we aim at evaluating the isTRM. We will conduct an empirical study where different groups of participants will be supported by conventional TRMs as well as by the isTRM. On the one hand we will measure group differences with respect to the acceptance ratio, operationalized by the variables recall and precision (see [4]). On the other hand we will investigate the impact of the isTRM) on social sensemaking, operationalized by tag-quality (e.g. semantic distinctiveness) and resource-quality (e.g. coverage of different categories of the knowledge domain).

References

1. Fu, W.-T., Kannampallil, T.G., Kang, R.: A semantic imitation model of social tag choices. In: Proceedings of CSE 2009, pp. 66–73. ACM Press, New York (2009)
2. Gupta, M., Li, R., Yin, Z., Han, J.: Survey on social tagging techniques. In: 17th ACM SIGKDD, pp. 58–72. ACM Press, New York (2010)
3. Hintzman, D.L.: MINERVA 2: a simulation model of human memory. Behav. Res. Meth. Ins. C. 16, 96–101 (1984)
4. Jäschke, R., Marinho, L., Hotho, A., Schmidt-Thieme, L., Stumme, G.: Tag recommendations in social bookmarking systems. AI Commun. 21, 231–247 (2008)
5. Kuhn, A., Cahill, C., Quintana, C., Schmoll, S.: Using tags to encourage reflection and annotation on data during nomadic inquiry. In: Proceedings of CHI 2011, pp. 667–670. ACM Press, New York (2011)
6. Seitlinger, P., Ley, T.: Implicit imitation in social tagging: familiarity and semantic reconstruction. In: Proceedings of CHI 2012, pp. 1631–1640. ACM Press, New York (2012)
7. Seitlinger, P., Ley, T.: Implicit and explicit memory in social tagging: evidence from a process dissociation procedure. In: Proceedings of ECCE 2011, pp. 97–104. ACM Press, New York (2011)

Workplace Learning

Learner Experiences and Perceptions of Using Social Media Tools in Formal Workplace Learning

Juha Leino, Erika Tanhua-Piiroinen, and Johanna Sommers-Piiroinen

The University of Tampere, School of Information Sciences/TRIM, Tampere, Finland
{Juha.Leino,Erika.Tanhua-Piiroinen,
Johanna.Sommers-Piiroinen}@uta.fi

Abstract. As social media tools are increasingly used in e-learning in the workplace, there is also a growing need for case studies to allow us to understand the underlying dynamics in order to develop best practices and to avoid potential pitfalls. Using qualitative approach, we studied a pilot training tailored for a large insurance organization that was conducted largely with chats, blogs, voice conferencing, and discussion forums. Our results show that despite challenges, social media use can produce value to e-learners and thus lend credence to many, so far weakly substantiated claims about their potential. In particular, synchronous tools enabled peer support, experience sharing, and networking. Still, the results also show that interactive learning process does not emerge automatically from adding social tools but needs to be designed and maintained. Based on learner views, we discuss how to improve the overall learning experience and make learning more efficient. Also, we discuss how to improve social media tools to better meet learner needs in e-learning in contrast to their recreational use.

Keywords: E-learning, continuing professional development, user studies.

1 Introduction

Social software is increasingly hailed as a way of integrating social learning—any "learning occurring within a group, an organization, or any social cluster" [14]—into e-learning [4], [12], as peer interaction in social context is thought to lead to effective construction of meaning and to better learning [3], [12]. Social media features are seen as offering educational affordances [2], [10], e.g. support for conversational interaction, social feedback, and social networking [10]. Such "sociability aspects" are seen as having "the most potential for enhancing education" [10]. Consequently, social media features are increasingly used in the education sector [2-4], [9].

At the same time, however, using social media features in the education sector is a new and still rather under-explored field [1], and so many papers today "uncritically ... rejoice in the possibilities of ... knowledge construction, critical reflective thinking and collaboration between learners, often without substantiating the enthusiasm" [2]. Without in-depth case studies [9], there is a clear and present danger of "misunderstandings, disappointments and irrelevant pedagogical practices" [13].

T. Ley et al. (Eds.): OST 2012, IFIP AICT 395, pp. 49–58, 2013.

Such features are also making inroads into continuous professional development trainings and courses in the workplace [2], [4]. However, various ramifications of adding social media features to workplace trainings have been researched even to a smaller degree [1], [9]. Moreover, different perspectives in educational and workplace e-learning mean that we cannot necessarily apply results from one to another directly [1]. This results in a dire need for case studies—in particular, for "qualitative, student-centered work" [6]—to uncover evidence-based best practices and potential pitfalls in designing and running workplace trainings enhanced with social media [1], [3], [9].

In this paper, we look at the perceptions and experiences of learners who took part in a pilot training that was tailored for one of the biggest insurance organizations in Finland. The tools used in the training were chat, voice conferencing, blog, and discussion forum. We used interviewing, questionnaires, and artifacts (e.g. blog texts) in addition to real-time observation of interactions (e.g. chats) and use logs to collect data. The data provides us with an in-depth look at the dynamics of what happens when social media features are used as the main approach in a workplace training. We found that despite many challenges, social e-learning can deliver on its promises, as learner interactions resulted in peer support, tip and experience sharing, and networking. Most value came out of social interactions facilitated with synchronous features.

In addition to describing social media tool use and related learner experiences and perceptions, we also discuss how to approach tackling some of the challenges that emerged in the training. We also discuss how to improve social media tools to better facilitate e-learning use, as goal-directed e-learning process (where people who may not know each other interact) needs different support than recreational use does.

2 Background

Social media is an umbrella term for mobile and web-based technologies that "create highly interactive platforms via which individuals and communities share, co-create, discuss, and modify ... content" [5]. Consequently, social media tools, e.g. wikis, blogs, and discussion forums, offer various educational affordances by e.g. facilitating and enabling sharing, communicating, and discovering information [10].

Using social media features in e-learning is part of the larger paradigm shift from teacher-oriented instruction to more student-centered learning. Learners are seen as active participants and co-produces—*prosumers*—instead of passive consumers and learning as a social process [10]. Consequently, what is learning and how it becomes visible needs to be re-evaluated [8]: Non-engaged learner may still be learning [7] and contributing does not automatically imply learning [8]. Learners may also fail to see social learning as real learning if it does not fit their pre-conception of learning [6].

Moreover, having social media features as part of the training does not guarantee that they are used properly—or at all—or that using them leads to learning [3], [10]. Without both learners and educators internalizing the new approach and its practices and attitudes that first need to be invented and designed, all-important mindset change and resulting behavioral change may fail to materialize [8], [10].

While reflective practices, e.g. writing blogs that others can see and comment instead of learning journals for instructor(s), are still part of social learning, social media in particular provide a community of peers [7] and thus enable getting "feedback, constructive criticism and validation" from interactions with peers [14].

This can function as a source of learning even if none of the learners knows the answer by enabling them to "contextualize current knowledge" and to develop "skills to deal with situations in the future" [7].

In social e-learning, increased social presence—"the degree to which a medium is perceived as conveying the presence" of the communicator [12]—is considered to increase learner satisfaction and both perceived and actual learning [1], [12]. Social presence is seen as having two dimensions, intimacy (interpersonal vs. mediated) and immediacy (synchronous vs. asynchronous) [12]. Social presence theory predicts that different media result in different levels of perceived intimacy and immediacy: Face to-face communication has the highest while asynchronous, technology-mediated communication forms have significantly lower levels of social presence [12].

Social media tools can be characterized by their immediacy as synchronous (e.g. chat and voice conference) or asynchronous (e.g. blog and discussion forum). Asynchronous tools (low feedback but high parallelism) suit information conveyance and reflective work while synchronous tools (high feedback but low parallelism) suit information convergence [12].

Using social media tools in e-learning requires new skills and this can create barriers to learning [1]. Learners with prior experience perceive using social media in learning as more satisfying and rewarding than those with little experience [12]. Importantly, social media skills acquired in other contexts, e.g. recreational use, may not translate directly into e-learning skills, as different contexts have their own use cultures [2].

3 Method

Using social media tools in workplace e-learning is a new field the studying of which necessitates qualitative case study approach that allows investigating complex social phenomena with a rich data set [9], [14]. Consequently, we used a qualitative approach to study adding social media tools to a formal workplace training, i.e. a training having "a structured program of instruction" leading to "a formal qualification or award," e.g. diploma or certificate, as opposed to informal learning, i.e. learning "acquired through everyday work and life" [11].

The two-month pilot training was provided by a professional training organization, Financial and Insurance Institute FINVA, and was tailored for internal trainers in one of the biggest finance and insurance organizations in Finland. The training had previously been taught through contact day lectures, and the role of electronic systems had basically been to allow returning assignments and downloading materials. Consequently, the training allowed us to explore the actual dynamics of adding social media features to a workplace training in real world, and our research goal was to uncover and describe the emerging dynamics and draw conclusions based on actual learner views and behavior rather than test any pre-described hypothesis.

Besides starting and ending days, the training was conducted entirely with social media tools: chat (three sessions), discussion forum (two assignments), blog (three blogs from ten given topics), and voice conferencing (two sessions). The forty employees taking the training were divided into seven small groups (5–6 learners per group) for chats and voice conferences but not for forums or blogs. As the organization has offices in about fifty cities, many learners logged in from different cities.

As data of learner perceptions and experiences, we used chat contents (one chat topic was discussing the tools), blog contents (one of the given topics was to write about one's perceptions of learning with social tools), end survey data, and in-depth interviews of five learners. The semi-structured interviews were conducted at the end of the training by phone and were preceded by the end survey (where we solicited learners for interviews). The interviews were meant to and did provide further insight into survey answers. Table 1 summarizes the data we had on each small group. Apart from only four learners, we had at least one type of input from every learner.

Furthermore, we observed online interactions and learner behavior during interactions (e.g. chats) and through artifacts (e.g. forum postings) and log data (e.g. when postings were made). Consequently, we have a fairly comprehensive set of data of the training. However, at the same time, we have to exercise care in generalizing the results, as any case study inherently represents a specific set of circumstances. Consequently, our results represent more a starting point for further work than be-all-end-all truths.

Table 1. Small groups by data: Numbers represent the number of learners in the small group of whom we had the particular type of material available (*Blog* and *Chat* refer to the tool-related topics mentioned above; *No material* refers to the number of small-group members from whom we had no survey, interview, blog (tool-related topic), or chat (tool-related topic) material available, i.e. the number of learners in the small group on whose views we have no material.)

	n	*End survey*	*Interview*	*Blog*	*Chat*	*No material*
Small group 1	6	1	0	2	6	0
Small group 2	6	3	1	2	4	1
Small group 3	6	4	2	1	6	0
Small group 4	6	4	0	2	3	1
Small group 5	6	5	1	2	6	0
Small group 6	5	2	1	3	5	0
Small group 7	5	2	0	1	3	2
Altogether	**40**	**21**	**5**	**13**	**33**	**4**

The analysis approach was standard qualitative data coding approach. The materials in non-text format were first transcribed and then all material was coded into themes used in the in-depth interviews. Each theme was further divided into subcategories arising from the material, and some of the larger subcategories were further divided into sub-subcategories. While the end survey data provided us with some quantitative data, most of our data was qualitative.

4 Synchronous Tools: Chat and Voice Conferencing Experiences

The two synchronous features, chat and voice conferencing, were widely liked. They were seen as being close to face-to-face conversation and as providing a good amount of social presence: "*...when it was real-time, it felt really nice. Even if the other person is in another city, it feels as if we're in the same room.*" Immediacy led to social presence also in chats: "*...[we] got close. Like we were a chat family.*" Some learners said that synchronous tools enabled better "*corridor conversations*" than contact days by bringing more people and more focus into the exchange. Learning with synchronous tools was seen as more participatory and active than lecture-based learning.

While blog and forum texts were seen as something one produces "*alone*" and then submits, interactivity was seen as inherent in the synchronous features, as learners constantly reacted to each other: "*...you compared your experiences to what others wrote or said...*" This interactive process resulted in instantaneous and abundant feedback that gave learners "*plenty of useful ideas.*"

Synchronous conversations were seen as flowing from "*intuitive thinking,*" in part as the constant flow of interaction required quick responses, and as showing "*how people see things,*" thus supporting experience sharing and peer support: "*...the comments from others, feelings and experiences, they were the best...*"

However, neither tool was without problems. Many learners felt that chats were too fast-paced: "*...while you were writing something longer, others had moved to another topic.*" This led to overlapping of threads: "*...many conversations [were] going on at the same time and it's hard to follow them all.*" As a result, following chats was challenging for many: "*...everybody wrote at super-fast speed, commenting on different things. I was trying to keep up with it, scrolling up and down the message window...*"

Voice conferencing in turn was plagued by turn-taking challenges. Learners found it difficult to know when they could talk: "*...the problem was to know whose turn it was to talk—is the speaker still about to continue or is it proper to say something between...*" and this could lead to some learners dominating the conversation: "*...two people talk to each other and the four others listen in the background and maybe they would have good ideas to contribute but they end up forgetting them or the topic has moved on and the comment would now be out of place.*" Learners felt that moderation should be enhanced to handle such problems in chats and voice conferences.

Also, some learners felt that chats and voice conferences were light on substance—"*just chitchatting*"—and suggested that there should be reading materials on which to base the conversations. In fact, while many felt that sharing experiences was one of the best things in the training, many others did not perceive it as learning: "*...it should have been more professional. ...we were just sharing our own experiences. ... Although it's fun and all, there should have been some concrete teaching, too.*"

Some learners felt that the current group size (5-6 learners) was good while some felt that the groups were too big. Large groups made the pace too frantic for slower, "*more deliberative*" learners; smaller groups could help all learners be able to contribute more equally. Keeping groups small was also necessary to help everybody dare to participate: "*...small enough to make learning efficient, because if the group is too large, people feel too shy or don't dare to participate or don't have time to talk...*"

Finally, using chat and voice conferencing at workplace brought its own challenges. Voice conferencing meant that learners had to watch what they said because other employees could hear them, thus impeding free flowing of conversation. Chats, on the other hand, were prone to interruptions, as the organization culture was to go to others to ask for help at any time; others simply did not realize that learners were busy. Still, chat as silent was seen as perhaps better suiting open office environments.

5 Asynchronous Tools: Discussion Forum and Blog Experiences

The two asynchronous tools used, blog and discussion forum, received a lukewarm reception. At best, they were found useful in that they forced one to slow down and reflect, but otherwise they were seen more as a chore. Postings in the asynchronous, non-real-time features were seen as something done "*alone*" and based on source materials as opposed to emerging from interactive process.

Learners consistently referred to blog and discussion forum texts as "*assignments*" and saw them also otherwise in terms of school assignments. Learners, perhaps consequently, felt that they had to submit "*a well thought-out whole,*" "*a finished article.*" Instead of "*free association,*" blogs and forums produced "*written articles.*"

Learners were not divided into small groups for blog and forum assignments. As most postings were made close to the deadline, learners faced a "*gray mass*" of text that discouraged them from reading and from commenting (not compulsory) them: "*...I couldn't sacrifice so much working time ... people's postings were so long that you simply don't have time for it.*" For example, 70 blog postings (54%) came in on the deadline day (March 18) and the three preceding days. The average length of a blog posting was about 1.3 pages (A4). Thus, within four days, learners received about 93 pages of material to read and to comment in one week—with more material flowing in after the deadline.

The situation was much the same for the forum assignments. Postings "*flooded*" in close to deadlines, resulting in them getting practically no comments and desultory readings at best: "*...just too many messages, it numbs you and then you don't comment anything...*" Neither did it help that all were writing on the same few topics: "*...when there are you know a hundred postings about the same topic, nobody has the patience to read them all [laughed shortly].*"

In fact, not using small groups in blog and forum assignments killed whatever chance there was for interactivity: "*...[you can't] expect us to read ... 40 people's postings and comment them all... You should be able to concentrate on communicating between only a few people and exchange views that way.*" With smaller groups, interactive culture of sharing might have emerged: "*...there might've been more discussion... It would have been more interactive.*"

Many learners experienced the resulting lack of feedback as discouraging: "*...the assignments were rather massive ... but then you got no feedback at all on them. ... I started to wonder if it actually interested anybody at all.*" The situation was aggravated by some learners feeling that some others did the bare minimum but still got the same certificate. This, combined with the lack of feedback, made the more diligent learners question why they worked so hard, thus undermining their motivation. Consequently, one learner mentioned seeing no difference between posting answers to a blog and returning them by email while another one said that "*Putting assignments in blogs felt a bit dumb, since I don't think anybody went there to read or comment them.*"

Many learners expressed hope that this solitary work would have been made more interactive. For example, one learner suggested that the long writings should have been submitted in smaller pieces so that others could have commented them (in small groups) and then the author could have continued based on the feedback.

Also, despite all the work that learners put into them, some learners felt that blog and forum posting contents were "*superficial.*" Many saw them as a good source of ideas and knowledge that could be refined into something useful but not ready as such. Some learners suggested they should have tackled the postings as small groups: "*...we never went through them properly. ...we would have refined them and turned the material into something that would have stayed as ... instructional material. Now it all stayed hanging in the air.*" Not only would this have resulted in more reusable materials, it would also have served to turn individual work into collective work. At the very least, learners would have read more texts with more focus.

6 Discussion on the Implications of the Learner Experiences

6.1 Explicate Learning Goals and Benefits to Learners

While many learners greatly appreciated sharing experiences and peer support, many others did not see this as real learning and missed a more theoretical approach. Some learners also expressed uncertainty about how to approach this kind of learning: "*...we might have gotten a tad off the given topic [in chats] but I don't know if that's a good thing or a bad thing.*" Clearly, there is a need explicate to learners what learning with social media means, how learning takes place, and what is expected of them. Otherwise, some learners will feel confused: "*...I was thematically lost ...the training was very different from what I expected and in that way I didn't get the benefit that I was expecting.*"

Naturally, explicating entails pointing out the benefits of the new approach. One benefit many learners appreciated was **networking** with other learners, including both making new acquaintances and improving ties with old ones: "*Absolute the most fabulous thing about this training has been networking with other trainers. It gives you a certain peace of mind to know who to contact when you need help on something unfamiliar.*" The training also lowered the threshold in contacting: "*It is also easier to contact these people in future when we already kind of know each other.*"

A related benefit is **peer support**: "*It has been very gratifying to discuss various matters with my own small group and share one's sentiments.*" Training led people to emphasize each other: "*You get a feeling that you are not alone with this thing but others are also in the same situation.*" Also, peers were seen to be in a good position to provide **experience-based feedback**, and hearing of "*various experiences, thoughts, and practices*" was felt to be a "*significant*" part of the training.

6.2 Level Differences in Technical Abilities with Tool Training

It is very dangerous to have expectations about the know-how level and technical skills of learners; e.g. even though Live Meeting was installed in everybody's computer as per company policy, not everybody knew how to use it. However, the training offered little tool training. Learners felt that this affected learning: "*…it was a challenge to study the tool itself before you got to the actual matter.*"

Many learners felt that there should be a contact day focused on learning the tools to build confidence and to enable everybody to participate and contribute at equal footing. Learners felt that with proper tool training, they would, in fact, have saved precious time: "*...what we would absolutely have needed was to go through the tools immediately at the beginning… but now we went in cold, and we have constant rush at work. …it took way too much time to start figuring out how to use [the tools] during the working day.*" Also, learners needed training not just in technical use of tools but also in use culture related factors; e.g. not all learners knew how to approach generating content: "*…blog was for me perhaps like, well, what I should write here, what I would talk about…*"

Learners also emphasized tool-training because they saw social media tools as being part of the "*modern*" world and thus essential to know: "*It's important to get to try different ways to study so that we could someday possibly utilize similar methods in our own trainings.*" Besides training purposes, learners were interested in social media tools because they saw in them a potential to support distance working and for getting just-in-time information from colleagues, for instance using chat to ask something while on the phone with a client. Now, however, some learners felt that training failed in teaching them tools: "*It's still a mystery to me how it [Live Meeting] works.*" Some learners also expressed uncertainty about what they had learned: "*I've learned to use social media in studying but do I know how to use it correctly? Maybe not.*"

Finally, some learners felt that using so many tools in the training had a fragmenting effect, especially since they were not familiar with the tools: "*I'd have preferred concentrating on a fewer tools…*" If learning tools is not in the locus of training, using fewer tools than here may be advisable.

6.3 Learner Views on Interface Related Matters

There were clear indications that learner needs for social media tool interfaces and features somewhat differ from the needs in recreational use. The reasons for differences appear related to various aspects of the use situation. In e-learning, the process is goal-oriented (the interaction has an agenda to fulfill), learners may not be familiar with each other but nevertheless need to interact at person-to-person level, and there is a cost-related pressure to have as big groups as possible.

In **chats**, some learners wanted to have texts color-coded by the person. In e-learning, learners deal with people they may not be familiar with and learner-groups tend to be bigger. Consequently, identity awareness should be supported in the interface. If learners do not easily recognize each other and cannot get to know each other through the interface, no closeness develops and interaction stays at superficial level. The fragmentation of discussion into various threads in chats was also a problem for many learners. While recreational chatting can flow freely, e-learning process is goal oriented, and all information concerning an issue needs to stay connected. Thus, being able to tie different pieces of an issue thread together and being able to refer to earlier postings that may have disappeared from the current view need to be supported. Finally, many learners had difficulties writing fast enough and some worried about making typos. Predictive inputting and spell-checking could facilitate these problems. While there is a certain tolerance to typos in social media, e-learners in the workplace are nevertheless professional people who wish to make a professional impression on others.

In **voice conferencing**, learners had the same need as in chat to recognize the speaker with whom they may not be familiar and to get to know other learners. The interface should therefore support identity awareness. Also, there was a clear need to support turn-taking. Interfaces could support gesturing, turn-reserving and such e.g. through icons or other indicators. Moreover, being able to indicate agreement or disagreement in the interface—e.g. thumbs up or down—would allow learners to contribute to interaction without requiring a speaking turn.

In **blogs** and **discussion forums**, especially since the number of posting was high, there was a clear need to support learners to find postings that interested them. Many wished to read a particular person's postings or postings by their own small group. In social media, it is natural to allow sorting postings based on social aspects, such as authors and social connections between learners. Learners also wished to be able to have a summary, abstract or some other preview of a posting content to decide if they wanted to read it. While learners can be asked to write abstract to postings, there are also many automatic approaches that could be used, e.g. keyword clouds, that could also be used to help learners locate salient items.

7 Conclusion

Despite many problems evident in this pilot training, the learner perceptions and experiences lend credence to many claims about the potential of social e-learning. The interactive process, where it took place, resulted in experience sharing, abundant feedback, and peer support in addition to facilitating networking. That so much value materialized despite challenges further underlines the potential of social e-learning once the wrinkles have been smoothed out and best practices have been outlined.

However, the study also shows that benefits are not automatic. The social e-learning process has to be designed and maintained to make sure e.g. that group sizes suit the tools, the interactive process takes place, and learners have enough technical skills to focus on learning rather than on learning the tools.

Neither is social e-learning necessarily a be-all-end-all of workplace trainings. Now some learners found the learner-generated content somewhat lacking in substance. Consequently, it is necessary for future work to establish how best to use social e-learning for various types of learning goals. The implication from this study is that social e-learning works well when the knowledge exists within the learner community. However, when new, more theoretical matters are studied, it may be better utilized as supporting rather than as the sole approach to learning; e.g. contact days still appear to have their place, as some things, such as social media tools themselves, are best learned hands-on and face-to-face.

While more case studies are needed to understand how best to use social e-learning in workplace trainings, our results substantiate many promises and encourage further research.

References

1. Daneshgar, F., Van Toorn, C., Chan, S.C.E.: E-learning in Workplaces. In: ITI 6th Int. Conference on Information & Communications Technology, pp. 65–70. IEEE (2008)
2. Dohn, N.B.: Teaching with Wikis and Blogs: Potentials and Pitfalls. In: 7th Int. Conference on Networked Learning, pp. 142–150 (2010)
3. Judd, T., Kennedy, G., Cropper, S.: Using Wikis for Collaborative Learning: Assessing Collaboration through Contribution. AJET 26(3), 341–354 (2010)
4. Kane, K., Robinson-Combre, J., Berge, Z.L.: Tapping into Social Networking: Collaborating Enhances both Knowledge Management and e-Learning. VINE 40(1), 62–70 (2010)
5. Kietzmann, J.H., Hermkens, K., McCarthy, I.P., Silvestre, B.S.: Social media? Get serious! Understanding the functional building blocks of social media. Business Horizons 54, 241–251 (2011)
6. Kirkpatrick, G.: Online 'Chat' Facilities as Pedagogic Tools: A Case Study. Active Learning in Higher Education 6, 145–159 (2005)
7. Ladyshewsky, R.K., Gardner, P.: Peer Assisted Learning and Blogging: A Strategy to Promote Reflective Practice during Clinical Fieldwork. AJET 24(3), 241–257 (2008)
8. Leino, J., Tanhua-Piiroinen, E., Sommers-Piiroinen, J.: Adding Social Media Features to Work-related Adult Learning: Educator Views, Expectations and Experiences. In: BIR 2011: Assoc. Workshops and Doctoral Consortium (Local Proc.), pp. 226–233. RTU (2011)
9. Lockyer, L., Patterson, J.: Integrating Social Networking Technologies in Education: A Case Study of a Formal Learning Environment. In: 8th IEEE Int. Conference on Advanced Learning Technologies, pp. 529–533. IEEE (2008)
10. McLoughlin, C., Lee, M.J.W.: Social Software and Participatory Learning: Pedagogical Choices with Technology Affordances in the Web 2.0 Era. In: Ascilite Singapore 2007, pp. 664–675 (2007)
11. Misko, J.: Combining Formal, Non-formal and Informal Learning for Workforce Skill Development. NCVER, Adelaide (2008)
12. Spencer, D.H., Hiltz, S.R.: A Field Study of Use of Synchronous Chat in Online Courses. In: Proc. of the 36th Hawaii Int. Conference on System Sciences, pp. 1–10. IEEE (2003)
13. Tynjälä, P., Häkkinen, P.: E-learning at work: theoretical underpinnings and pedagogical challenges. The Journal of Workplace Learning 17(5/6), 318–336 (2005)
14. Warne, L., Ali, I.M., Pascoe, C., Agostino, K.A.: Holistic Approach to Knowledge Management and Social Learning: Lessons Learnt from Military Headquarters. AJIS 9(1), 127–142 (2001)

Learning with Social Technologies: Workplace Learner Experiences of Wiki and Blog and Perceptions of PLE

Juha Leino, Erika Tanhua-Piiroinen, and Johanna Sommers-Piiroinen

The University of Tampere, School of Information Sciences/TRIM, Tampere, Finland
{Juha.Leino,Erika.Tanhua-Piiroinen,
Johanna.Sommers-Piiroinen}@uta.fi

Abstract. As social technology use is increasing in e-learning, so is the need to complement theoretical work with studies of learner experiences of the new dynamics of e-learning to guide this development. We studied how 15 learners experienced social media tools in a long continuous professional development (CPD) pilot training tailored for a large insurance company. While the training included some contact lectures, it was mainly conducted through blog, wiki, chat, and discussion forum tools. As we have already discussed forum and chat use in another paper on a shorter CPD training (with 40 learners) and this study confirmed the results, we focus here on learner experiences of wiki and blog. While the wiki process was widely misunderstood, wiki and blog experiences organically led learners to consider their uses as a personal learning environment. As to blog, the learners who saw it as a tool for self-reflection perceived it positively while others did not, underlining that the benefits and goals of using social tools need to be explicated. Furthermore, social learning process needs to be designed and maintained, as busy workplace learners tend to focus on fulfilling requirements. Simply adding social technology does not necessarily lead to social e-learning.

Keywords: E-learning, wiki, blog, PLE, workplace, social learning.

1 Introduction

Web 2.0 models and technologies have become enablers of learner-centered online learning, or social/collaborative e-learning [3]. Social media features, e.g. wikis, blogs, and chats, are increasingly part of e-learning in formal education and are also making inroads in continuous professional development (CPD) [5], [8]. Learning by constructing knowledge through social interactions instead of memorization is widely seen as having a great potential for enhancing learning [3], [8]. At the same time, however, many case studies have been less than successful (e.g. [3] and [2]) and there is an "ongoing debate about why and under what conditions cooperative peer-based learning is effective" [8]. In effect, the prevailing unsubstantiated evangelizing means that we urgently need case studies to uncover the actual dynamics of using social tools in learning context [4–5]. This need is even more pronounced in the field of continuous professional development where the ramification of using social media have been studied even to lesser degree [4].

T. Ley et al. (Eds.): OST 2012, IFIP AICT 395, pp. 59–68, 2013.

In this paper, we discuss experiences and perceptions of fifteen workplace learners who took part in an over one-year long pilot training that used wiki, blog, chat, and discussion forum for learning. While we contrast this long expert-development training (LT=long training) with a similar but shorter and more intensive training (ST=short training) for workplace trainers where relevant, we do not otherwise discuss the results from ST here, as they were reported in [10].

Both LT and ST were tailored for large Finnish insurance companies (two trainings; two companies) by a professional training organization, Financial and Insurance Institute FINVA. These pilot courses were part of FINVA's drive to develop their trainings by adding social media features to them, and as such were not designed or conducted for research purposes, thus representing the organization's actual efforts. Prior to this drive to incorporate social media, electronic systems used in trainings had offered few social aspects and had basically been used to allow learners to submit assignments and to download materials.

The largely qualitative data provides us with an in-depth look at the actual dynamics of using social media tools in CPD trainings. Since the learner experiences of chat and discussion forum in LT and ST were practically the same, we focus here on learner perceptions of wiki (DokuWiki) and blog (B2Evolution). The learners who understood blog's potential for introspection viewed it positively while those who did not see this aspect viewed it negatively. Wiki failed to engender social learning process online; learners ended up doing the assignment face-to-face and simply putting the results in the wiki. Overall, learners widely felt that social media tools had no real purpose in the training.

Simultaneously, however, blog and wiki use experiences organically led users to envision their uses as a personal learning environment (PLE). Although this study did not focus on PLE related factors *per se*, assisting workplace learners in developing PLE is a central research theme in our overall project (F-Shape[1]). Consequently, we were interested in what kinds of PLE related concepts had emerged organically from using social media tools in the training.

We first briefly review literature on PLE and e-learning uses of wiki and blog, and then describe our study method and the two trainings in more detail. After looking in detail at wiki and blog use in the training, we turn to discussing motivational and moderation-related factors and how to engender interactive learning process.

2 Background: Blogs, Wikis, and PLE

The way social media tools will be used in e-learning context will be different from their uses in other contexts [13]. Consequently, adding social media to e-learning is not so much about tools and technology but rather about "concepts, practices and attitudes" that guide incorporating social tools to be a part of e-learning [13].

While blog use is proliferating in e-learning, the number of in-depth studies of its use is still inadequate [9]. Used typically as a shared learning journal/diary, blog is seen as having potential to encourage reflective thinking [9], [14]. Feedback from peers and trainers is seen as integral to the experience, as interactivity allows for

[1] `http://fshape.wordpress.com/f-shape-2010-2011/in-english/`

coproducing knowledge [9]. In using blogs, it is important to keep the number of contributions learners are expected to read and comment reasonable to maintain (inter) activity without overwhelming learners [9–10]. While some case studies have been successful (e.g. [9]), some have been less so [14]. Experiences from these studies underline the importance of suitable group size, providing detailed guidelines, and explaining benefits [9], [14].

While blog centers on the individual, wiki is a collaboration tool designed to promote group interaction, a place where knowledge is iteratively co-constructed rather than absorbed or reproduced [15-16]. In effect, wiki provides educational affordances for both constructivist and collaborative learning approaches [3]. Still, as with blogs, research into using wikis in e-learning is "in its infancy" [15] and many attempts of using it have been less than successful [2-3]. Besides proficiency issues [3]—even learners with IT background and initial training have had technical proficiency problems [2]—learners have had motivational problems [2–3], [15]. Learners focus on activities that provide "the greatest perceived benefit" [3]. As currently only visible individual efforts are rewarded, promoting wiki use requires new approaches to assessment [3], [8]. Also, course contents need to be designed around wiki use to avoid an add-on perception of wiki [2–3]. Finally, learners need to be made aware of their role in the process and the benefits of using wiki—valid pedagogical reasons for engagement—need to be pointed out [2–3], [15].

Zenios and Holmes [16] furthermore suggest that wikis should not be seen as standalone collaboration tools but rather as "repository spaces for storing and sustaining shared information and collaboratively created knowledge." Their study suggests that learners do not use wiki for communication, as social dialogue necessary for knowledge co-creation needs a more direct communication tool, e.g. Skype.

Personal Learning Environment (PLE) is a concept over which there is no consensus [1], [7]. While some researchers see it as a technological system, even as a standalone application, many others consider it more of a concept or an approach [1], [7]. PLE is a learner-centric "counter-concept" to institutionally owned and controlled learning landscapes [7] that rejects the idea of one size fitting all and focuses on learner's individual needs [6]. PLE is also a recognition of the continuous nature of learning, bringing both formal and informal learning together [1]. While e.g. Downes [6] sees PLE as consisting of "a set of related concepts, each associated with the technologies and applications of Web 2.0," Fiedler and Väljataga [7] warn against the concept being reduced to a snapshot of digital artifacts available today.

3 Method, Data, and Participants

The long training (LT) lasted about one year and three months (Nov. 2010–Jan. 2012). Besides start-off and ending days, there were six 7–8 hour contact teaching days with lectures. Majority of the training, however, was carried out with social media tools: Blog (learning diary; no. of postings required not specified), discussion forum (two one-month discussions on given topics; the 1st had two threads with altogether 15 learners postings and the 2nd had three threads with altogether 5 learner and 3 trainer postings), chat (one session in small groups of 4-5), and wiki (one assignment in groups of 2–3 learners: describe customer-centricity at your unit/section).

The shorter training (ST) with forty participants, in contrast, lasted about three months and utilized chat (3 sessions), discussion forum (2 assignments), voice conferencing (2 sessions), and blog (3 assignments with one deadline). The only contact teaching days were the start-off and endings day. For details on ST research, see [10].

As social media tools in workplace e-learning represents a new field of study, studying it requires a qualitative case study approach to allow investigating complex social phenomena [12]. As a result, we collected learner input through interviews and questionnaires and observed online interactions as they took place (e.g. chats) in addition to using log data about interactions (e.g. wiki activity) and online artifacts (e.g. blog postings) as data sources. Data was collected throughout the training.

In LT, the semi-structured interviews were conducted after the training activities had ended as group interviews: Six learners (out of 15) were interviewed in two groups (G1 and G2), both consisting of three learners. The interviewed learners provide a rather comprehensive learner viewpoint of the training, as at least one of them was present as a member in every small group in the training except for one wiki group (out of the seven wiki groups) (see Table 1).

Table 1. Activity by interviewed and non-interviewed learners (*number of postings instead of learners as in others)

	Chats			Forums		Wikis						
	Group 1	Group 2	Group 3	Disc. 1*	Disc. 2*	Section 1	Section 2	Section 3	Section 4	Section 5	Section 6	Section 7
Interviewed	1	3	1	7	2	2	2	2	2	1	0	1
Non-interview	4	1	4	8	3	1	1	1	1	2	2	3
Altogether	5	4	5	15	5	3	3	3	3	3	2	4

The interview themes were selected to allow comparing the experiences in this training to other trainings we had already studied (including ST) and to plumb the wiki use and related experiences, as this is the only training we studied that used wiki. For studying PLE related factors—both not to lead learners and because the concept of PLE had not been introduced to learners—we asked open-ended questions that led learners to consider tool uses and their experiences of them in learning more widely.

Furthermore, learners were asked to blog about their perceptions of the training in the last blog posting, which thirteen learners (87%) did, thus proving us with further insight into learner experiences and perceptions of the training and the tools.

The learners' prior familiarity with social media varied. While some were very experienced chatters and had used Facebook for a long time, some others were not in Facebook and had no prior experience of chatting. Because of using Wikipedia and other wikis as information sources in everyday work, most were familiar with wikis as users. The tool training provided failed to level the skill differences; e.g. non-experienced chatters experienced the chat as too fast-paced and disjointed while experienced ones felt that chatting became something akin to exchanging group emails.

We used a typical data coding approach to analyze the qualitative data. After transcribing non-text materials, we coded them into interview themes. These themes were further coded into subcategories based on themes emerging from the material.

While other pilots that we have studied, e.g. ST [10], offer supporting evidence to many findings, case studies of actual use represent a certain set of circumstances by nature and are thus subject to contextual influences. For instance, the behavior of instructors can influence learner behavior and experience [11], as can the usability of the particular tools used; e.g. here the low usability of the wiki tool clearly influenced learner perception. Therefore, we need to exercise care in generalizing the results.

4 Blog: Perceptions and Experiences

In ST, forty people submitted each three blogs (topics selected from ten given by trainers) to a common blog, resulting in a "*gray mass*" of text that "*flooded*" in close to the one deadline, effectively "*numbing*" the learners who made practically no comments (non-compulsory). The blog ended up a system of submitting assignments.

In contrast, in LT, blogs were used more like blogs in recreational use. Learners were instructed to use them as learning diaries and consequently saw them as such. With 15 learners and no one big deadline, the number of blogs remained sensible at 61 blog postings. Although learners felt that blogs did not provide much interactivity, 22 postings (36%) still received altogether 36 comments (1–3 per posting): 19 comments (53%) were by trainers, 8 (22%) by the poster, and 9 (25%) by peer learners.

The opinions over blogs' usefulness were clearly divided between G1 and G2. G1 considered blog the best tool in the training because it caused them to "*analyze what I have learned for real,*" something that they felt would otherwise not have taken place. In contrast, G2 felt that "*there was no function, no need for writing a blog.*" G2 in fact felt that none of the social media tools contributed much to the training and considered them to have been "*glued on top*" rather artificially. G1 also felt much the same way about all the other tools but blog. The significant difference is that G1 felt blog to have a clear purpose and that it had contributed to their learning.

In effect, workplace learners are busy and have no extra time for something the function of which they do not see. Learners need to understand the benefit that using the tool brings to be motivated to use it: "*Somehow the understanding of what I benefit from this should've been communicated at the beginning—what do I benefit from writing this blog.*" Consequently, explicating the purpose and benefit of a tool can clearly spell the difference between a success and failure.

Learners felt that interactivity was "*almost entirely missing*" from blogs. With not enough comments, "*...discussion or exchanging of ideas didn't take place,*" and "*it stayed a bit diary-like.*" Learners did miss interactivity—"*it would have been nice to read comments from others and then it might've led to you commenting that*"—and were aware of blog's potential for sociality: "*...it has all these features available.*" They saw continuous, active use—"*that people would read and comment*"—as a prerequisite for interactive process and felt that some compulsoriness could have helped: "*It could be that if you had to go there,* *you might end up getting excited...*" However, learners at the same time felt that there was little encouragement for reading postings.

Learners felt that there was no culture of interactivity in their organization. Interestingly, part of the reason may be that the organization management did have a blog. Learners felt that it was "*tasteless and odorless,*" more akin to "*politically correct*" bulletin. The heavy style of informing rather than questioning or asking for opinions did not seem to invite discussion. Moreover, learners felt that since the content came from the management, "*people don't dare to go there and comment.*"

Besides self-reflection, G1 also saw other benefits in blogging. They felt that blogs offered a way to get ideas and viewpoints from others: "*...somebody who wrote about a contact day had remembered different things than I did and it was nice to read it ... it allowed exchanging benefit, you know, that's a brilliant observation, I could use it, too, or at least remember that and that theory that I could put into use at work.*"

G1 members felt that the information that ended in the blogs was different from the information that is exchanged face-to-face, partially because of the type of information and partially because in face-to-face conversation, discussion moves on and if there was no suitable opportunity to say what was on their mind, it was forgotten. Also, writing things down gave them a chance to check facts and organize their thoughts better, allowing clearer communication and, again, introspection. They also emphasized that this way of writing deepened their learning: "*...writing a blog makes you think about the subject matter and analyze it and organize what you are about to write, and that's cerebration and improves learning.*"

Both groups felt that knowing others will read the text affected their writing-style and the care put into writing: "*You do it more carefully when you remember that many will read it, and so in a way you consider more carefully your conclusions...*" This made blogging different from simply writing a learning diary on paper: "*...it was quite nice that it wasn't just a learning diary but you also wrote it for others, you took that into consideration, thought about what would be nice to read.*"

Finally, G1 expressed displeasure that some had not contributed at all or had written their blogs at very superficial level, simply fulfilling the requirement: "*...many blog postings... you didn't get inside the thoughts of the author based on them, what they had learned or what kinds of feeling at all they had about the contact days.*"

5 Wiki: Perceptions and Experiences

Wiki assignment asked learners to "form a community understanding of how customer-centricity is realized in the [organization's name] structure." Learners were divided into small groups of 2–3 to describe this at unit/department level; one unit, one wiki page. Depending on their job description, learners were involved in generating 1–4 wiki pages.

Learners uniformly saw wiki as a "*chore*" and as the worst social media tool in the training. Learners felt unmotivated to use wiki because trainers did not point out any function for it and presented it as something to try for the sake of trying. The problem was compounded by the fact that learners saw the wiki assignment as replication of a part of their intranet. Consequently, they felt their work would not be used for anything: *"...I don't know if the results are used for anything since we have better descriptions in the intra...*" It is important to have assignments that make sense to learners, that they see the benefit and purpose in what they do.

However, learner dislike of wiki here was not based on disliking or misunderstanding wiki or its purpose *per se*: *"...wiki is a fabulous tool. Plenty of great examples on the Internet...*" In fact, they constantly used various online wikis at work. Also, they were clear on the use logic: "*...anybody can go there and [fix it] if they know better.*"

Learners did not see wiki as inherently interactive: "*...if somebody does a wiki, the point is not to have a big yes-no tug-of-war happening; it's meant to be a writing that contains information.*" Also, many groups completed their wikis close to the deadline, leaving little time for interactivity even if learners had been motivated for it. Learners did feel, however, that ideally they would have read more wiki entries by others and expanded or corrected them but did not do it in this training because they felt that it was not wanted: "*...there was such a possibility and we never used it, but I don't think we were meant to, either.*" They felt that they were not even encouraged to read the contributions of others, never mind expanding or correcting them. Still, they felt that this would have made wikis more interactive and using them more meaningful.

Interestingly, small groups made their wiki contributions by getting physically together by one computer and did most of the content as group work at one sitting. The possibility of collaborating through the features offered by the wiki was not emphasized in instructions and groups ended up treating wiki as a place where to put the end-result while complaining that "*it was horribly hard for us to find common time.*"

6 PLE: Blog and Wiki as One-Stop Information Storage

When asked to think uses for social media tools for themselves, learners came up with ideas that strongly resembled the concept of PLE organically, i.e. without being introduced to the concept. Learners felt that blog could allow them to "*collect their thoughts to one place and others could then read it, too*" in addition to enabling themselves to "*follow what I have done and when.*" However, it was wiki in particular that was seen as a good tool for PLE because "*you can build out of wiki quite smartly*" a place for "*training contents... with links and everything else and so all the information would be [in one place].*" Learners said that all lecture etc. notes could be entered there directly without first writing them on paper. Wiki was also seen as offering easy building blocks: "*I'd have templates there and I'd simply have built it there.*"

Sharing and interactivity were seen as part of PLE. Learners envisioned that sharing and allowing editing for others could result in a common place for solving problems as a group and for recording the solutions.

7 Motivation, Moderation, and Activity-Cum-Interactivity

Although the organization allowed learners to use working time for the training, learners had difficulties doing so, as finding time from work was challenging and learners prioritized work over study: "*My boss said that you can use working time but [studying] took the last place because work matters were more important.*" The typical time for doing assignments at work was "*Friday afternoon*" "*when even easy things began to feel complicated … when you no longer can focus but can't go home, either…*" Also, learners typically left things close to the deadlines.

Consequently, **motivating** learners is very important. Now learners felt that social media tools were largely "*glued on top*" of the training without them having any real function or purpose. Learners felt this clearly reducing their motivation, and when asked what should be done differently, immediately emphasized giving a purpose for using social media tools: "*Well, the first thing is to consider the function, purpose, reason why … that we are just testing is not very motivating.*"

Activity at the learning environment was seen as an important motivator. Learners felt that trainers should have actively made sure that all contribute and that way started a virtuous circle of more postings and more comments, resulting in interactivity. Without activity, "*it simply dies.*" Learners felt that to engender more activity and interaction, consuming (e.g. reading) content should be encouraged and compulsoriness should be employed to keep learners returning: "*You'd have a little compulsoriness, nothing more or less, a weekly assignment to go there and have a look*" A community has to have "*a critical mass*" of activity to engender enough contributions to make going there "*worthwhile.*" Moreover, when activity was not continuous, learners had to break inertia every time they did log in: "*When you go there rarely, threshold of starting is always as high.*"

In effect, now learners described **moderation** as "*vague*" and felt that trainers should have been more active and direct in soliciting contributions. Learners wanted to have "*encouragement and prompting,*" signs of monitoring—"*tell us right from the scratch that 'we will be watching how you are doing there*"—to show that contributing was important, even if they knew that making contributions was ultimately up to them. Learners wanted clear rules instead of vague, infrequent pleas: "*…clear dates and if I haven't written by then, something to prompt, some kind of sanction or maybe carrot to start it up.*" Learners appeared to want to be shown that what they did mattered instead of feeling that any nominal, low-quality contribution was enough.

Besides stick, learners also saw need for carrot, e.g. making high-quality contributions to stand out somehow. Besides showing that contributions are read and are important, this would also have given examples of what was expected. Now some learners mentioned first looking at the content by others to understand how to approach e.g. writing wiki content. In addition, learners hoped to have indicators of how they are doing, e.g. a traffic light signal of red (not nearly enough), orange (almost there), and green (good level of contribution) to encourage contributing.

Furthermore, it is important that trainers themselves behave exemplarily; now learners felt that e.g. trainer blog with six postings (avg. 108 words; max 158 words) with one comment (by a trainer) was inactive and as such not a good example.

Without moderation engendering activity and e.g. wiki and forum activity condensing close to the deadline, learners saw the periods between contact days as "*empty.*" Social media failed to engender a feeling of continuity in the training and learners felt that they had to tune in to the training again and again: "*It didn't become a coherent package during which you could've seen an evolving whole...*" Consequently, social media tools did not integrate into the training—"*they popped up from somewhere and then went back to hiding*"—and using them became a "*chore.*"

As a solution, learners felt that instead of big deadlines, assignment should be divided into smaller deliverables with clear deadlines to engender activity, and reasonable compulsoriness should be used to engender interactivity around them. In addition, learners felt that when social media tools are to be used, learners should be preselected so that only learners "*who're really ready to use the tools*" would be selected and those "*for whom it's absolutely new and foreign*" and who have no enthusiasm for them would be offered more traditional trainings. Now the interviewed learners felt that some resisted the idea of social media which "*encumbered the whole group.*"

8 Conclusion

Social e-learning, learning together with peers that is facilitated with social media tools and, in case of formal CPD, moderated by trainers, is not about tools *per se*. It is about a learning process that needs to be designed and maintained to foster social interaction, and as such, represents a paradigm shift both for learners and trainers. In this training, social process did not emerge: "*We did it as individuals, not together—we didn't put social media into use in that sense.*" Learners did not understand their role or the role of the social media tools in the training, leading to lack of motivation. Consequently, as posited in [14–15], explicating benefits of using social media tools and approaches is essential; learners need to understand why the tools are used and how to use them to engender the value-bringing social process. Now those learners who saw introspective point in blogging liked the tool but others saw it as pointless.

Moreover, especially with asynchronous tools, e.g. wiki and blog, the process has to be designed to be continuous rather than condensing around big deadline(s) and leaving the social space otherwise dead. Furthermore, the process needs to be maintained with moderation to make sure that everybody makes quality contributions. Like Cole [3], learners in this training suggested breaking big assignments into smaller deliverables so that there would be new posting coming continuously and using judicious compulsoriness to engender interaction—commenting, correcting, and expanding—on those deliverables. This way the training/learning process could have continued between the contact days rather than learners having to re-orient to the training repeatedly.

Finally, learners organically envisioned PLE-like uses for wiki and blog. With guidance from trainers, it appears plausible that learners would be ready to start using suitable social media tools as shareable information storages where information could also be edited collaboratively, benefitting both themselves and other learners.

In summary, we need to move in our thinking further away from tool-centricity to learning process centricity, and see social media tools as means to the learning process rather than as an end onto themselves. Different tools offer different learning affordances, and while they represent an ever-changing and ever-evolving toolbox for fostering social e-learning process, they are not the process.

References

1. Attwell, G.: The Personal Learning Environments - the Future of eLearning? eLearning Papers 2(1), 1–7 (2007)
2. Choy, S.O., Ng, C.N.: Implementing Wiki Software for Supplementing Online Learning. AJET 23(2), 209–226 (2007)
3. Cole, M.: Using Wiki Technology to Support Student Engagement: Lessons from the Trenches. Computers & Education 52, 141–146 (2009)
4. Daneshgar, F., Van Toorn, C., Chan, S.C.E.: E-learning in Workplaces. In: ITI 6th Int. Conference on Information & Communications Technology, pp. 65–70. IEEE (2008)
5. Dohn, N.B.: Teaching with Wikis and Blogs: Potentials and Pitfalls. In: 7th Int. Conference on Networked Learning, pp. 142–150 (2010)
6. Downes, S.: Learning Networks in Practice. Emerging Technologies for Learning 2, 18–28 (2007)
7. Fiedler, S., Väljataga, T.: Personal Learning Environments: Concept or Technology? IJVPLE 2(4), 1–11 (2011)
8. Judd, T., Kennedy, G., Cropper, S.: Using Wikis for Collaborative Learning: Assessing Collaboration through Contribution. AJET 26(3), 341–354 (2010)
9. Ladyshewsky, R.K., Gardner, P.: Peer Assisted Learning and Blogging: A Strategy to Promote Reflective Practice during Clinical Fieldwork. AJET 24(3), 241–257 (2008)
10. Leino, J., Tanhua-Piiroinen, E., Sommers-Piiroinen, J.: Learner experiences and perceptions of using social media tools in formal workplace learning. In: Submitted to OST 2012 (2012)
11. Leino, J., Tanhua-Piiroinen, E., Sommers-Piiroinen, J.: Adding Social Media Features to Work-related Adult Learning: Educator Views, Expectations and Experiences. In: BIR 2011: Assoc. Workshops and Doctoral Consortium (Local Proc.), pp. 226–233. RTU (2011)
12. Lockyer, L., Patterson, J.: Integrating Social Networking Technologies in Education: A Case Study of a Formal Learning Environment. In: 8th IEEE Int. Conference on Advanced Learning Technologies, pp. 529–533. IEEE (2008)
13. McLoughlin, C., Lee, M.J.W.: Social Software and Participatory Learning: Pedagogical Choices with Technology Affordances in the Web 2.0 Era. In: Ascilite Singapore 2007, pp. 664–675 (2007)
14. Robertson, J.: The Educational Affordances of Blogs for Self-directed Learning. Comput.Educ. 57(2), 1628–1644 (2011)
15. Ruth, A., Houghton, L.: The Wiki Way of Learning. AJET 25(2), 135–152 (2009)
16. Zenios, M., Holmes, B.: Knowledge Creation in Networked Learning: Combined Tools and Affordances. In: Proc. 7th Int. Conference on Networked Learning, pp. 471–479 (2010)

Dialogic Leadership and ICT-Intensive Workplaces: How to Enhance Learning Potential

Sirpa Syvänen[1] and Kati Tikkamäki[2]

[1] School of Management, University of Tampere, Finland
[2] School of Information Sci ences/CIRCMI, University of Tampere, Finland
{sirpa.syvanen,kati.tikkamaki}@uta.fi

Abstract. Work organisations face demanding challenges, such as expectations to be creative, innovative, agile, competitive, efficient and adept at using employees' knowledge while understanding and taking care of employees' wellbeing. Organisations are actively implementing new ICT systems and environments because they seem to increase the effectiveness of interaction and collaboration, workplace learning and work performance. Employees are expected to learn and to innovate continuously. Thus, managers often need to be social acrobats, combining basic tasks, managing projects and creating and meeting innovative goals. Work units may be potential and versatile learning and development spaces, but at the same time, existing routines, traditions and power relations in organisations create different kinds of boundaries and conflicts. Dialogic leadership might be one of the key factors in successful modern organisations. Dialogic leadership is a prerequisite to meeting the challenges mentioned above. In this paper, we examine the potential and challenges of dialogic leadership and learning when adopting and using e-Calendar (eC) in one of the Dinno programme's professional case organisations.

Keywords: learning potential in work contexts, dialogic leadership, application of technologies, participatory action research, cooperative and dialogic development.

1 Introduction

1.1 Background: Dialogic Leadership and ICT in the Dinno Programme

Modern work organisations face demanding challenges, such as expectations to be creative, innovative, agile, competitive, efficient and adept at using employees' knowledge while taking care of employees' wellbeing. Work has become more knowledge-, professional-, network- and virtual-based in many professions. As a result of this trend, employees and managers are continuously facing new learning challenges. Managers need to be social acrobats in order to combine basic tasks, manage projects and set innovative goals [1]. They also need to be social architects in order to foster learning and innovation [2]. We suggest that dialogic leadership is the crucial factor in handling these contradictory challenges.

T. Ley et al. (Eds.): OST 2012, IFIP AICT 395, pp. 69–77, 2013.

This paper is based on the *Dialogic leadership promoting innovativeness* research programme (Dinno project 2012–2014, www.dinno.fi) funded by Tekes (the Finnish Funding Agency for Technology and Innovation). The Dinno project is a multidisciplinary programme, combining theories of creativity, innovativeness, learning, motivation and leadership [3]. Tekes funds working life development and research projects having significant novelty and research with applicable results, bringing together different research branches of science. The organisations subscribing to the programme represent both the private and public sectors. These organisations range from local government (educational, social and health sectors, municipalities) and state (professional expert organisations) organisations to private enterprises (service and professional organisations).

The research task of the programme is to determine *how dialogic leadership can enhance the creativity and innovativeness of organisations*. The programme strives to promote innovativeness, sustainability of working life, productivity and competitiveness by combining various multidisciplinary scientific and theoretical viewpoints. The main themes include: 1) dialogic leadership, power and responsibility, especially in terms of organisational restructuring, 2) *dialogic and innovative learning spaces, especially in technology-intensive work environments*, 3) dialogic skills of leaders, especially in challenging situations, 4) dialogic career management, especially downshifting and 5) dialogic development methods as sources of creativity and innovativeness.

Work processes in many sectors depend heavily on technical mediation. Technology has changed working methods, communication and knowledge management in different types of work and service units. Organisations are actively implementing new ICT (information, communication and technology) systems and environments because they believe they will increase the effectiveness of interaction and collaboration, workplace learning and work performance [4]. At the same time, routines, traditions and power relations in organisations create different kinds of boundaries and conflicts [5, 6] between various actors. This trend also challenges traditional leadership and management. In this paper, the focus is on theme two of the Dinno project. The research task is to determine *what kind of prerequisites and preconditions ICT-intensive work organisations create for dialogic leadership and innovative learning spaces*. Particular attention is paid to the challenges related to employees' skills and attitudes toward using a new application and organising work processes using that application.

1.2 Theoretical Frameworks: Dialogical Leadership and Learning

Employee participation and workplace innovations have a key role in efforts to achieve a more sustainable working life, improved performance and competitiveness for organisations. Innovativeness can be increased by wider employee participation, the sharing of knowledge and motivation [e.g. 7,8].

The Dinno project is based on theories of creativity, innovativeness, learning, motivation and leadership [e.g. 7, 8, 9, 10, 11, 12, 13]. The programme creates a multidisciplinary theoretical framework of dialogic leadership to be used in promoting workplace innovation. In addition, Dinno project combines societal, organisational, workplace and individual perspectives. The theoretical framework can be used to identify the preconditions, obstacles and catalysts of organisational creativity and innovativeness.

Dialogic leadership provides an opportunity to reconcile the needs of organisations and their employees. Its central principles are appreciative interaction, listening and the equal participation of different groups of employees in the development of activities [11, 13]. Dialogic leadership increases organisations' capacities for renewal and innovativeness, and simultaneously offers the necessary preconditions for employee wellbeing, skill development and enhancing work capability.

According to the theoretical framework, organisations are examined as potential but contradictory learning spaces [14, 15]. The main modes of organisational learning are participation, knowing, social interaction and supporting and reflecting [12, 14, 16]. All these modes take place in individual, communal and organisational contexts. Figure 1 summarises the modes of learning potential and dialogic leadership in ICT-intensive work contexts.

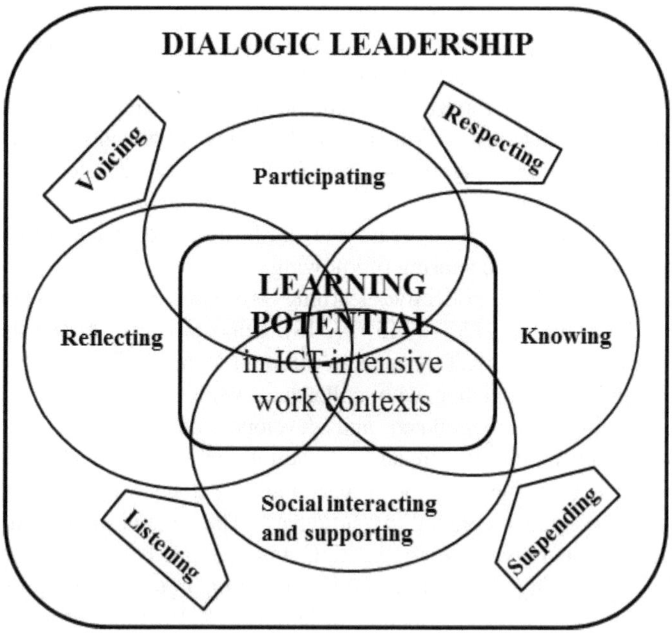

Fig. 1. Modes of learning potential and dialogic leadership [11] in ICT-intensive work contexts [modified from 14]

When implementing and using new technologies, the challenge is to recognise, coordinate and develop these modes of learning potentials. Dialogic leadership is one of the key factors in successfully meeting this challenge. The critical questions from the point of view of dialogic leadership and ICT-mediated work processes are:

- *Are the management and organisational cultures promoting participation or withdrawal?*
- *What are the possibilities and forums for participation, learning and development?*
- *How is the knowing constructed, developed and shared?*
- *What are the forms of social interaction and is there enough support?*
- *Are there possibilities for reflection?*

Implementing and using ICT systems takes place through *participation*. It is essential to coordinate the operations, interpretations and meanings in an effective way. The crucial issues are: 1) whether ICT systems promote or inhibit participation and 2) determining what kind of participation they allow. Employees can be active or passive participants, social interaction can take the form of participation or withdrawal and the organisational culture might be permissive or compulsive [14]. We believe that through dialogic leadership, it is possible to promote active participation and a permissive culture. However, we wonder whether ICT systems and technological applications promote active and meaningful participation.

In the current global economy, the generation and assimilation of knowledge would appear to be indispensable to the success of any organisation. According to Blackler [16], knowledge in organisations takes the form of *knowing*, which refers to the situated, mediated, temporary, pragmatic and contested nature of knowledge. Today, knowing is heavily ICT-mediated. Technical applications and programmes have speeded up the exchange of information, created easier access to information and allowed many people to access information simultaneously [4]. The challenge for organisations and managers is to create relevant forums and spaces for the generating, interpreting, combining and sharing of knowing.

Social interaction and collective learning processes play an important role in organisational learning [e.g. 5, 14, 15, 17, 18]. It has also been found that employees choose to learn how to use ICT systems in informal learning situations by asking peers and solving problems together with colleagues while working [4]. Individual and collective meanings are negotiated and developed during social interaction. This negotiation process might also create negative rationales for conventions and routines [5]. *Supporting* is one critical factor in meaningful interaction and learning. It includes peer support and encouragement to participate. The organisational culture may be competitive or cooperative [see cooperation strategies 5]. Dialogic leadership plays a crucial role in promoting cooperation and in supporting organisational cultures [11].

Reflective processes are key factors in learning. Reflections should take place in individual, collective and organisational contexts [14, 15, 19, 20]. Reflection means evaluating participation, which may take the form of breaking assumptions, questioning or inquiring. It is crucial to create forums and spaces for reflection, as well as to make reflection an integral part of work and development processes [5, 14, 15]. Reflection is crucial when applying and using new technical solutions. However, do ICT systems promote or inhibit reflective processes?

In this paper, we will examine the crucial modes of organisational learning and the principles of dialogic leadership, focusing on implementing and using a new ICT application in one of the Dinno project's case organisations. The focus is particularly on the challenges related to employees' attitudes and skills in using e-Calendar (henceforth eC) and on how eC enables the organising of work processes, mutual schedules and services. We will present a short case study example where the modes of participating, knowing, interacting and reflecting are challenged by a new technological application — the eC.

2 Methodological Framework: Participatory Action Research and Case Study

The research data for Dinno project is generated using both quantitative and qualitative methods, such as participatory action research and case studies, an innovativeness questionnaire, thematic seminars and workshops, individual and group interviews, letters and diaries and reflective conversation [3].

Alongside the actual research programme activities, a number of more practically oriented participatory action research projects are carried out, with a special focus on dialogic leadership, participatory and creative development methods, performance and quality of working life. The data consists of the personnel's descriptions of everyday life and activities, work and interaction in work communities. The case study discussed in this article is one of the professional case organisations in the practically oriented participatory action research project.

The case study tells about a new professional organisation that was established during one of the Dinno programme's action research project at the beginning of 2011. Arguments about the restructuring process were based on economics; a lack of resources forced five independent service units from various municipalities to join together to establish a new organisation. There had been various organisational changes during the dialogic development project. For instance, the professional organisation was divided into two functional areas, the southern and the northern areas. Two responsible managers were assigned to those geographical areas.

As is typical for action research processes, this development project was centred on the collaborative development of the practices of work communities, with the purpose of finding solutions to problems brought up by the local actors. The most important development forums and spaces for dialogue (concerning eC) have been the organisation's development group, the managers' meetings, the meetings of the southern and northern areas, the meetings of the teams and the development discussions between managers and employees.

3 Results: Challenges Related to Applying e-Calendar

In this new organisation, there was an absence of mutual forums or systems to plan and schedule services, and actions. There was also a lack of co-operation between managers and employees, both on an individual and a team level. The main challenges were focused on the great geographical distances between five service units. The organising of work processes and management could not depend on face-to-face interaction anymore. New working and communication environments necessitated the use of electronic systems to communicate and schedule mutual actions and work processes.

Two service units had previously used an eC. The challenge was to integrate the eC into a new organisation as a modern way of working and co-operating. The main challenges of the application and development processes appear in the figure below:

Attitudes, emotions, routines *"No one wants to use the new system. There is a fear of losing control and losing independence."*	**Motivation** *"It was noticed — the lack of internal motivation to learn a new system. Not everyone uses it."*
Skills and support *"I am sure that we will find internal trainers among our own staff. We must take care that they have enough time to do their jobs and support each other."*	**Principles, commitment** *"There are different ways and principles of using the eC system."* *"Not everyone puts all the relevant information in eC on time; it affects the other people badly."*
System problems *"There are many difficulties in using the new system — problems with equipment, computers, programmes and mobile phones."*	

These problematic issues concerning eC were discussed in several dialogical learning arenas and forums. Managers experienced very important to create collective principles to eC. They wanted to stress the importance of the commitment to the eC system and wanted to investigate the personnel's support needs. Managers took the problems related to the eC seriously and wanted to solve them. Based on the principles of dialogic leadership and learning, all personnel were given an opportunity to share their experiences of applying the eC. Supportive discussions occurred twice in the development group, twice in the service unit staff and once in employee – manager development discussions.

The reflections were very important because many problems emerged. The quantity of problems decreased, but the major problems remained: some of the employees did not want to use the eC system, some major mistakes had been made because of a lack of knowing and negative attitudes and a lack of commitment was reported. Some employees hid their lack of their knowledge about eC from managers and colleagues. This was the main reason they did not want to use the system. Because of this, some clients were negatively affected. For example, some appointments relating to specific services and clients vanished from the system. Some users even cancelled their own appointments. Because of these problems, people believed the whole system to be unreliable. After these reflections, agreements were made between managers supporting personnel. Each one emphasised the employer's obligation to use eC and to act according to the mutual principles. Managers stressed the commitment to eC.

From the point of view of dialogic leadership and learning, *participation* is not even possible if the solution, programmes, connections or devices do not work, or if the employees do not have the relevant skills, instructions and equipment to use them. A crucial aim is to map out and break the barriers to participation, which may be related to attitudes, motivation, a lack of skills, a lack of leadership or rigid organisational structures. It is important to notice what kind of *knowing* the participants have or should have when implementing a new technical solution. Employees also need to know the arguments for a new application. It is important to create spaces for generating and sharing knowing as well as to recognise the knowledge gaps. In our example, the employees who used the eC earlier had valuable knowledge that was used as a collective learning resource during the development process. It is also important to facilitate forums for *social interaction, support* and *dialogue*. Knowing, creation, learning processes and social support take place during social interactions. Shared meanings and understanding are crucial when developing collective work processes and operations. In the case example, the participatory action research project created a dialogic forum for different professionals and new workmates. The prerequisites for adopting new technological applications and learning new skills are the capability and possibility for *reflection*. Time and space are needed for individuals and communities to question, consider and evaluate work processes, behaviour models and habits and judgments.

When employees are expected to adopt new work tools and change their ways of thinking and acting, managers need dialogic leadership skills. They should listen to the employees, respect employees' experiences and viewpoints, suspend the self-evident ways of thinking and routines as well as voicing all the members of work community [11].

4 Conclusions

The benefits of ICT systems include speeding up the exchange of information, ensuring easy access to information, allowing many people to access information simultaneously and making it easier to reach people. However, the implementation of new ICT applications often results in problems and failures as the applications do not always work as planned [4].

The case study illuminated the learning and dialogical leadership challenges related to implementing a new technological application—the eC. ICT systems have huge potential when developing work processes and managing knowledge. However, there are also many challenges to be aware of. Based on the preliminary data and the analysis of the case example, when implementing new technical applications, the focus should be on meaningful participation, possibilities for generating and sharing knowledge, supportive interactions and spaces for reflection. Referring to Isaacs [11], dialogic leadership is carried out by listening, respecting, voicing and suspending. The development project presented in the case example is based on these principles. Participating, knowing, interacting and reflecting create potentials for learning and these potentials for learning can be achieved through dialogic leadership.

The research task for theme two is to discover the possibilities and attempt to solve the problems ICT-intensive work contexts create for dialogic leadership and dialogic learning spaces. We are at the beginning of our research journey. The next step is to generate more data via the innovativeness questionnaire to discover more about the relationship among ICT systems, dialogic leadership and learning.

Acknowledgements. This research is funded by National Funding Agency of Technology and Innovation (Tekes Finland) and supported by grants of The Finnish Work Environment Fund (TSR) and Finnish Information Processing Association (FIBA).

References

1. Ruohonen, M.: Changing Leadership Cultures. In: Zappala, S., Gray, C. (eds.) E-Commerce Service Industry. Impact of E-commerce on Consumers and Small Firms, Ashgate, London (2006)
2. Barrett, F.J.: Creating Appreciative Learning Cultures. Organization Dynamics 24(1), 36–49 (1995)
3. Syvänen, S., Kasvio, A., Loppela, K., Lundell, S., Tappura, S., Tikkamäki, K.: Dialoginen johtaminen innovatiivisuuden tekijänä. Tutkimusohjelman teoreettiset lähtökohdat, tutkimuskysymykset ja toteutus (Dialogic leadership as a factor of innovativeness. Theoretical starting points, research questions and the planned realization of a new research program), Työterveyslaitos, Helsinki (2012)
4. Korpelainen, E.: Information and Communication Technology Adoption at Work. In: Doctoral dissertations 125, Aalto University. Aalto University publication series, Unigrafia Oy, Helsinki (2011)
5. Syvänen, S.: Evil Eleven Syndrome. In: Dark Side of Workplaces. Pressures at Work and Costs of Non-interference, Doctoral dissertation, University of Tampere, School of Management. VDM Verlag Dr. Müller Aktiengesellschaft & Co., Saarbrücken (2010)
6. Hodson, R.: Disorganized, Unilateral and Participative Organizations: new insights from the ethnographical literature. Industrial Relations 40(2), 204–229 (2001)
7. Amabile, T.M.: A Model of Creativity and Innovation in Organizations. In: Staw, B.M., Cummings, L.L. (eds.) Research in Organizational Behaviour, vol. 10 (1988)
8. Whitney, D., Trosten-Bloom, A., Rader, K.: Appreciative Leadership. In: Focus on What Works to Drive Winning Performance and Build Thriving Organization, Mc Graw Hill, USA (2010)
9. Bass, B.M., Riggio, R.E.: Transformational Leadership. In: Lawrence Erlbaum Associates, Mahwah, USA (2006)
10. Deci, E.L., Ryan, R.M.: Self-determination theory and the facilitation of intrinsic motivation, social development and well-being. American Psychologist 55, 68–78 (2000)
11. Isaacs, W.: Dialogue and the Art of Thinking. In: A Pioneering Approach to Communication in Business and in Life, Currency, USA (1999)
12. Wenger, E.: Communities of Practice. In: Learning, Meaning and Identity, Cambridge University Press, New York (1999)
13. Yankelovich, D.: The Magic of Dialogue: Transforming Conflict into Cooperation. Touchstone (2001)

14. Tikkamäki, K.: Työn ja organisaation muutoksissa oppiminen - etnografinen löytöretki työssä oppimiseen (Learning in Changing Work and Organizational Contexts – Ethnographical Discovery on Workplace Learning.), Doctoral dissertation, University of Tampere, School of Education. University Press, Tampere (2006)
15. Syvänen, S.: Development Organizations and Dialogues among Services for Elderly. In: Kalliola, S., Lehtonen, J. (eds.) Dialogue in Working Life Research and Development in Finland. Labour, Education & Society. Peter Lang, New York (2008)
16. Blacker, F.: Knowledge Work and Organizations: An Overview and Interpretation. Organization Studies 16(6), 1021–1046 (1995)
17. Illeris, K.: Three Dimensions of Learning: Contemporary learning theory in the tension field between the cognitive, the emotional and the social. Paperback, Malabar (2003)
18. Wenger, E.: Communities of Practice and Social Learning Systems. In: Nicholini, D., Gherardi, S., Yanow, D. (eds.) Knowing in Organizations. A Practice-Based Approach, New York, Sharpe, pp. 77–99 (2003)
19. Raelin, J.A.: Public Reflection as the Basis of Learning. Management Learning 32, 11–30 (2001)
20. Vince, R.: Organizing Reflection. Management Learning 33, 66–78 (2002)

Learning Analytics in Higher Education

Evaluating the Practices in the E-Learning Platform from the Perspective of Knowledge Management

I-Chin Wu and Wen-Shan Chen

Department of Information Management, Fu-Jen Catholic University
No.510, Zhongzheng Rd., Xinzhuang Dist., New Taipei City 24205 Taiwan
icwu.fju@gmail.com

Abstract. A growing number of higher education institutions have adopted asynchronous and synchronous Web-based learning platforms to improve students' learning efficiency and increase learning satisfaction. To understand how students use e-learning platforms and what the implications are, we conducted an empirical study of the iCAN e-learning platform, which has been widely used in Fu-Jen Catholic University. We use the Analytic Hierarchy Process (AHP), a multi-criteria evaluation approach, to compare five practices of the teaching platform. We designed a questionnaire to measure *learners' perception of the e-learning platform* based on the theory of knowledge transforming process in knowledge management. Accordingly, the model considers functioning and objectivity in terms of the following three dimensions of learning effectiveness: *individual learning*, *group sharing* and *learning performance*. Twelve criteria with twelve evaluation items were used to investigate the effectiveness of the five practices. We also evaluated the strengths and weaknesses of the functions based on the types of courses in the iCan platform. We expect that the empirical evaluation results will provide teachers with suggestions and guidelines for using the e-learning platform effectively to facilitate their teaching activities and promote students' learning efficiency and satisfaction.

Keywords: Analytic hierarchy process, E-learning platform, Knowledge management practices, Learning analytics and modeling.

1 Introduction

The development of computer technology and the Internet has affected the most basic form of education, i.e., the traditional face-to-face teaching; therefore, leading the way of education has been influenced significantly [2]. Chen, Kinshuk & Wang (2005) [2] advanced a cyber-schooling framework that uses the familiar traditional school structure as its basis and attempts to enhance it through the use of technology to overcome the shortcomings of traditional education and study without the time and space restrictions. The traditional teaching model is based on learning in a fixed location such as a classroom, which lacks of mobility [12]. Apart from fixed locations that restrict various teaching activities, the traditional teaching model has other limitations, e.g., the tuition times are inflexible [14].

T. Ley et al. (Eds.): OST 2012, IFIP AICT 395, pp. 81–90, 2013.

Unlike traditional learning methods, e-learning platforms allow teachers to communicate with students and discuss course content anytime or anywhere. Thus, it is a very important that we determine how to combine technology and education to facilitate knowledge exchange across national boundaries without time constraints. In this study, we measured "*learners' perception of the e-learning platform*" based on the theory of knowledge transforming process in knowledge management (KM). KM is a cycle, sometimes repeated process, which generally includes creation, management and sharing activities [4]. Gray & Chan (2000) [8] advance a KM framework that seeks to categorize and integrate the creation, storage and propagation of knowledge into a single model on the view that the problem-solving process is a vehicle for connecting knowledge and performance. Knowledge can generate the value when it is used to solve problems, explore opportunities and make decisions. Therefore, many organizations adopt learning platforms to promote the inner communication of knowledge. Also, schools adopt learning platforms to enhance students' learning quality. Thus, teaching platforms are becoming important and useful tools for supporting students' learning activities.

In order to enhance the learning quality of students and encourage communication between students and teachers, many schools incorporated various kinds of teaching platforms and then counseled teachers and students on how to use them. The development of the e-learning platform paid more attention to the technology aspects than the user-centered design issues [7]. In this work, we aim to evaluate the e-learning platform from the aspect of the user's experiences. Furthermore, the evaluation of learning platforms is a multiple decision problem. A learning platform has many different functions that need to be completely considered. Therefore, we adopt the Analytic Hierarchy Process (AHP), a multi-criteria evaluation approach [15], to evaluate users' perceptions after using the learning platform. We adopted the AHP in this work because the approach was superior to traditional questionnaire methods in representing human perceptions [16]. The AHP not only gets the most important alternative but also ranks the results by conducting pair-wise comparisons for all estimated alternatives. We selected iCan as our research target, the main e-learning platform used by Fu-Jen Catholic University since 2005. To summarize, the objectives of the research are as follows:

- We adopted brainstorming approach to design a questionnaire based on the theory of knowledge transforming process. Three dimensions are considered in the questionnaire. They are individual learning, group sharing, and learning performance.
- We aim to investigate the strengths and weaknesses of different kinds of functions offered in the e-learning platform. There are five types of practices (functions) in the iCan are investigated in our questionnaire. They are homework, discussion board, material download, chat room, and learning index.
- To understand the functionalities of different practices offered in the iCan platform for types of courses, we will analyze and explain the empirical evaluation results based on the course types which are technology, and management courses.

2 Basic Concepts

2.1 Analytic Hierarchy Process (AHP)

The Analytic Hierarchy Process (AHP) is a well-known approach to resolving the decision-making problem about multiple criteria [15]. This method is an effective and practical approach that considers complex and unstructured decisions. The AHP systemically structures complex problems into a hierarchy and uses quantitative methods to evaluate alternatives that would help decision-makers choose the most appropriate solution. There are mainly three steps for considering decision problems through the AHP: constructing hierarchies, comparative judgment and synthesis of priorities. The first step is structuring the complicated problem into a hierarchy descends from an overall objective to various criteria, sub-criteria, and so on until the lowest level. The next step is determining the priorities of the elements at each level and developing the comparison matrix. The last step is synthesizing priorities from the second level down by multiplying local priorities by the priority of their corresponding criterion in the level above and adding them for each element in a level according to the criteria it effects [15].

2.2 Model Perception by Fuzzy Linguistic Approach

It is hard to assess qualitative problems by using precise values, leading to the use of the fuzzy linguistic approach [16]. The fuzzy linguistic approach is an approximating technique that could model human perception and help human decision-making. The fuzzy number plays a fundamental role in formulating the semantic meaning of the linguistic term, which represents the approximate value of each linguistic term. For assessing the relevance degree between objects (e.g., document, criteria etc.), the variable Relevance is defined and the corresponding terms–very low, low, normal, high, very high, perfect–are defined to express the context of Relevance. Notably, each linguistic variable is characterized by a quintuple (S, E(S), U, G, M) as defined in Definition I, and each linguistic term is modeled by a triangular fuzzy number (TFN) as defined in Definition II.

Definition I (Zadeh 1975) [16]: A linguistic variable is expressed as a quintuple (S, E(S), U, G, M) where S is the name of the variable; E(S) is the linguistic terms of S, that is the set of its linguistic values range over universe of discourse U; G is a syntactic rule (a grammar) that generates linguistic term set in E(S); and M is a semantic rule that assigns meaning, m(e), to each linguistic term e in E with a fuzzy set on U.

Definition II (Dubis & Prade, 1978) [5]: A fuzzy number **Z** is a "normal" and "convex" fuzzy set defined on the set **R** , and **Z** is a closed interval for every $\alpha \in (0,1]$. The membership function $f_Z(x)$ of the triangular fuzzy number (TFN) Z=(l, m, r) is given below.

$$f_{\tilde{Z}}(x) = \begin{cases} (x-l)/(m-l) & l \le x \le m \\ (r-x)/(r-m) & m \le x \le r \\ 0 & otherwise \end{cases} \tag{1}$$

This work adopts the center of area (COA) method to calculate fuzzy numbers, owing to its simplicity and practicability. The COA method calculates the fuzzy mean under uniform probability distribution assumption [85],[11]. If the fuzzy number $\tilde{U}$ is triangular, where $\tilde{U}=(l, m, r)$ the crisp rating can be derived by the equation: $CV(\tilde{U})=[(r-l)+(m-l)]/3+l$

3 The Framework

We designed three directions from the perspective of the knowledge management system. Each dimension has its own associated criteria, as shown in Table 1. We explain each dimension briefly as follows. In addition, due to the page limitation, the statements of the criterion of each dimension are summarized in Table 1.

Individual Learning: Individual learning is defined as students who can build knowledge and experience personal growth through individual reflection and through their interactions with the others and the environment [6]. In this work, we focused on how students employ the e-learning platform to achieve individual learning. For example, students can download and review the materials, deliver homework, or do the quizzes on the learning platform. Specifically, we use four criteria to evaluate the dimension of individual learning, as listed in Table 1.

Table 1. Statements of the criterion

Course types	Dimensions	Criteria	Statement
Technology and Management courses	Individual learning	Independent learning	Obtaining the ability to acquire the knowledge of courses by themselves successfully.
		Information use	Gaining the capability to apply knowledge learned from the platform.
		Finding the answers to questions	Obtaining the ability to discover answers of existing questions.
		Exploring new issue	Exploring new issues from the learning process at the learning platform.
	Group sharing	Learning support	Gaining the teaching support by communicating with instructors on the learning platform.
		Knowledge sharing	Sharing information and knowledge within the learning group in the platform. The learning contents and processes can be enriched.
		Enhancing learning attitude	Enhancing learning attitudes and enriching the learning contents by group learning processes.
		Collaboration	Improving the participation in team project.
	Learning performance	Efficiency	Increasing the efficiency because of the ease of finding the information from the platform.
		Learning achievement	Increasing the testing score and evaluation grade.
		Completeness of learning process	Achieving the completeness of learning process more easily.
		Sense of accomplishment	Obtaining a sense of achievement by resolving the problems from the learning platform.

Group Sharing: Group sharing is defined as students working in a group to complete a specific task, make decisions or solve problems. The e-learning platform is a good technology for education to facilitate communication and collaboration for better knowledge sharing [1][9]. The difference between traditional learning and e-learning is that students can talk face-to-face in traditional learning. It is synchronic. On the other hand, with e-learning, students can share their thinking via the functions in the platform; sometimes it is synchronous and other times it is asynchronous. For example, a chat room is a function that allows students to discuss to each other synchronously, while a message board helps students discuss issues asynchronously. We use four criteria to evaluate the dimension of group sharing, as listed in Table 1.

Learning Performance: Learning performance may be measured by quantitative factors such as course grades or the time to search required data, or qualitative factors such as a sense of accomplishment or achievement [13]. It is an essential part of learning, and it is quite important for students and teachers to evaluate the learning and teaching results. In this paper, we use four criteria to evaluate the dimension of learning performance. They are *efficiency*, *learning achievement*, *completeness of learning process* and *sense of accomplishment.*

4 Evaluation Setup

We adopted the AHP approach to develop the framework used to evaluate the effectiveness of functions in the iCan e-learning platform. We talked with two professors and several graduate students to design the questionnaires. We will briefly describe each investigation issue from the results of the questionnaire.

4.1 Data Collection

First, we selected the courses offered in Fu-Jen Catholic University's College of Management as the investigation target. In addition, the lecturers who are the top 50 login users of the iCan platform are another criteria used to select the target courses

Table 2. The information of the participants in technology and management courses

Return Questionnaire	Effective Questionnaire	Effective Return Rate	User Information			
			Sex		Experience	
Technology courses						
50	36	72%	Male	18	Less than 1 year	31
					1—2 years	3
			Female	18	2—3 years	2
					More than 3 years	0
Management courses						
26	24	92%	Male	17	Less than 1 year	2
					1—2 years	16
			Female	7	2—3 years	0
					More than 3 years	8

for evaluation. Finally, we selected courses offered in 2011 that belong to one of two types of courses—technology or management courses. In technology courses, we chose Java 1 and Java 2 as our investigative objects. In management courses, we chose "Special Topic on MIS" and "Knowledge Management" as our investigative objects. We adopted some rules to select the two types of courses. For technology courses, we selected programming-based courses because they are more individualistic in nature. For management courses, we selected the courses that had team work, which can stimulate knowledge sharing and collaborative activities. The number of returned questionnaires, effective questionnaires and related information for two types of courses are shown in Table 2.

4.2 Determining Evaluation Dimensions, Criteria, and Ranking Practices

We asked the participants to make pair-wise comparison estimation that compares the importance of every criterion. The questionnaire sample is shown in Figure 1.The participants check the boxes by importance. After we retrieved the completed questionnaires, we constructed a pair-wise comparison matrix and obtained the consistence index to ensure the consistency of the questionnaires. The data will show the importance of each dimension and criterion, i.e., weight; the greater the weight, the more important the dimension or criterion.

We chose five practices of iCan (homework, discussion board, material download, chat room and learning index) and adopted the fuzzy linguistic approach introduced in Section 2.2 to obtain the estimative score of each practice. The score represents the degree of each practice supporting each criterion. The five practices and statements were shown in Table 3. Based on the result of the previous questionnaire, we can get the score of each criterion, and understand participants' viewpoints of every criterion.

AHP Questionnaire Sample

1. Please rank the importance of the three dimensions at first.

☆________Individual learning (**IL** for short)
☆________Group sharing (**G** for short)
☆________Learning performance (**LP** for short)

2. Please make pair-wise comparisons

	Absolute		Very-strong		Strong		Moderate		Eqivalent	Moderate		Strong		Very-strong		Absolute		
	9 : 1	8 : 1	7 : 1	6 : 1	5 : 1	4 : 1	3 : 1	2 : 1	1 : 1	1 : 2	1 : 3	1 : 4	1 : 5	1 : 6	1 : 7	1 : 8	1 : 9	
IL																		G
IL																		LP
G																		LP

Fig. 1. The AHP questionnaire sample

Table 3. The evaluation practices of iCan learning platform

Practice	Statement
Homework	Deliver homework: Students can upload their homework before the deadline. Homework observation: Students can inspect and learn from each other's homework.
Discussion board	Students and teachers can communicate with each other on the discussion board.
Material download	Students can download the course material.
Chat room	Students can communicate just-in-time in chat room.
Learning index	It shows the learning history on the platform, including the log-in times, the summary of discussion and material download and the situation of the homework delivering.

5 Evaluation Results

5.1 Determining Evaluation Criteria Weight: Results and Discussions

The following section will show and describe the evaluation results.

Discussion of Evaluation the Weight of Dimensions: We used the data collected to calculate the weight of the three dimensions of evaluation the effectiveness of the platform, as shown in Table 4. For technology courses, the most important dimension is individual learning (C_1). That is, they think obtaining the ability and learning by themselves from the iCan learning platform is the most important dimension in technology courses. For management courses, the most important dimension is group sharing (C_2). Thus, they emphasize the knowledge or skill sharing in team work and expect that the learning contents and processes can be enriched by group sharing from the platform.

Discussion of Evaluation the Weight of Criterions: Table 5 shows the criteria with the associated weights of the two types of courses. For technology courses, information use (C_{12}) and independent learning (C_{11}) are the most two important criteria. The results show that users expect to gain the ability to apply the knowledge learned from the platform, and to acquire that knowledge successfully by themselves. In addition, they think enhancing learning attitude (C_{23}), and collaboration (C_{24}) are not very important in technology courses. For management courses, knowledge sharing (C_{22}) and learning support (C_{21}) are the most important criteria. Users expect they can share information and knowledge within the learning group in the platform, and gain the ability to apply the knowledge learned from the platform. In addition, they think obtaining a sense of achievement (C_{34}) by resolving problems from the learning platform and improving participation (C_{22}) in team projects are not very important

Table 4. The weight of each dimension of four courses for the evaluating e-learning platform

	Dimensions	Technology courses	Management courses
C_1	Individual learning	**0.46(1)**	0.35(2)
C_2	Group sharing	0.20(3)	**0.36(1)**
C_3	Learning performance	0.34(2)	0.29(3)

Table 5. The weight of each criterion of four courses for evaluating e-learning platform

	Criteria	Technology courses	Management courses
C_{11}	Independent learning	**0.144(2)**	0.088(7)
C_{12}	Information use	**0.145(1)**	**0.110(3)**
C_{13}	Finding the answers to questions	0.115(4)	0.091(5)
C_{14}	Exploring new issues	0.055(9)	0.063(8)
C_{21}	Learning support	0.084(5)	**0.113(2)**
C_{22}	Knowledge sharing	0.051(10)	**0.121(1)**
C_{23}	Enhancing learning attitude	0.029(12)	0.045(10)
C_{24}	Collaboration	0.038(11)	0.080(11)
C_{31}	Efficiency	0.126(3)	0.098(4)
C_{32}	Learning achievement	0.068(7)	0.089(6)
C_{33}	Completeness of learning process	0.077(6)	0.052(9)
C_{34}	Sense of accomplishment	0.068(7)	0.050(12)

Note: * The numbers in ( ) mean the order of each course.

criteria in management courses. Interestingly, users regard collaboration is not an important criteria for two types of courses. It indicates it is not effective to improve the participation in team project via the e-learning platform.

5.2 Rank Practices in E-Learning Platforms by Fuzzy Scores

Herein, we combined the crisp rating of each dimension or criterion (i.e., perception of usage experiences) with the associated weight (i.e., perception of importance) to calculate the fuzzy score for ranking practices in E-learning platforms. The crisp rating is derived from the fuzzy linguistic rating according to the COA method in Section 2.2.

Technology Courses. Based on the previous results, information use (C_{12}) and independent learning (C_{11}) are the most two important criteria for technology courses. Table 6 shows that the practices of downloading materials and homework support these two criteria. Notably, homework, discussion boards, and downloading materials are practices that all enhance learning support (C_{21}). On average, downloading materials performed best in each category. Moreover, we found that the scores of the chat room and learning index practices were not high, which might be the case because students seldom use them in technology courses. Interestingly, the criteria of finding the answers to questions (C_{13}) and learning achievement (C_{32}) were not ranked in the top 3 criteria supporting each practice. This indicates that the platform lacks a function to help participants discover answers to existing questions.

Management Courses. Knowledge sharing (C_{22}) and learning support (C_{21}) are the most two important criteria for management courses. Table 6 shows that the practices of downloading materials and using discussion boards support these two criteria. On average, downloading materials performed best in each category. Notably, we found that the score of the chat room practice is lower than other practices. According to our preliminary observations, users seldom use the function; this may due to its low quality. Finally, only the criterion finding the answers to questions (C_{13}) was not ranked in the top 3 criteria supporting each practice.

Table 6. Combining fuzzy scores to rank practices (technology and management courses)

	C_{11}	C_{12}	C_{13}	C_{14}	C_{21}	C_{22}	C_{23}	C_{24}	C_{31}	C_{32}	C_{33}	C_{34}
Technology courses												
Homework	69.6	71.4 (2)	67.5	61.4	72.4 (1)	71.2 (3)	63.2	68.1	71.2	70.3	69.2	67.8
Discussion board	60.7	63.4	68.6	66.4	73.1 (1)	70.8 (2)	64.2	64.7	70.8 (3)	67.9	66.7	61.0
Material download	**82.0 (3)**	**82.7 (2)**	79.6	70.4	**83.3 (1)**	73.5	64.0	66.0	80.7	74.8	79.5	68.1
Chat room	45.0	43.2	43.0	47.4 (3)	46.1	46.3 (4)	49.1 (2)	52.2 (1)	45.1	44.7	45.2	44.3
Learning index	59.2 (3)	56.3	56.3	56.0	58.5	53.1	53.0	55.2	54.4	54.3	59.7 (1)	59.3 (2)
Management courses												
Homework	78.6	82.0	79.7	79.2	71.5	**84.6 (2)**	73.9	81.1	82.3 (3)	87.7 (1)	80.6	79.9
Discussion board	74.2	79.2	82.4	83.8 (2)	80.9	**86.0 (1)**	77.7	82.6 (3)	81.2	82.2	79.3	76.7
Material download	86.6 (3)	87.3 (1)	84.9	80.4	**87.1 (2)**	85.1	72.7	72.2	83.7	80.9	85.5	69.6
Chat room	57.1	57.8	56.3	54.2	58.7	60.4 (3)	62.1 (1)	58.6	62.0 (2)	55.7	57.8	53.1
Learning index	71.8	64.3	64.9	60.8	65.3	65.8	73.3 (2)	60.3	71.5	62.5	72.2 (3)	73.4 (1)

6 Conclusion and the Future Work

We have several interesting findings and their implications from the survey results of this research. Basically, different types of courses need different kinds of practices to achieve the goals of the course. For example, for technology-based courses, learning performance is the most important dimension, and group sharing is the most important dimension for management courses. In addition, our preliminary results show that the iCan platform cannot satisfy the needs of the type of management course. Furthermore, students think information use is very important in technology courses. Thus, teachers should refer the results to refine the courses and to help students achieve the object of information usage much easier by using the e-learning platform. We expect that our empirical evaluation results will provide teachers with suggestions and guidelines for using the e-learning platform effectively to facilitate their teaching activities, and promote students' learning efficiency and satisfaction. Ćukušić et al. (2010)[3] pointed out that a clear link exists between planning and controlling of the e-learning process and its learning outcomes. Accordingly, we will consider how to refine the usage condition of each function in the e-learning platform to help teachers achieve their teaching goals and assist students to attain the learning outcomes they expect. In the future, we expect to extend the types of courses to understand of the effectiveness of the practices in the e-learning platform for different kinds of courses. We also continue using an auxiliary questionnaire to understand the users' using experiences of the e-learning platform to assist us have a further investigation.

References

1. Beckman, M.: Collaborative Learning: Preparation for the Workplace and Democracy. College Teaching 38(4), 128–133 (1990)
2. Chen, N.S., Kinshuk, Wang, Y.H.: Cyber Schooling Framework: Improving Mobility and Situated Learning. International Journal of Engineering Education 23(3), 423–431 (2005)
3. Ćukušić, M., Alfirević, N., Granić, A., Garača, Ž.: E-Learning Process Management and the e-Learning Performance: Results of a European Empirical Study. Computers & Education 55(2), 554–565 (2010)
4. Davenport, T.H., Prusak, L.: Working Knowledge–How Organizations Manage What They Know. Harvard Business School Press, Boston (1998)
5. Dubis, D., Prade, H.: Operations on Fuzzy Numbers. International Journal of Systems Science 9(3), 613–626 (1978)
6. Forcheri, P., Molfino, M.-T., Quarati, A.: ICT Driven Individual Learning: New Opportunities and Perspectives. Educational Technology & Society 3(1), 51–61 (2000)
7. Granić, A., Ćukušić, M.: Usability Testing and Expert Inspections Complemented by Educational Evaluation: A Case Study of an e-Learning Platform. Educational Technology & Society 14(2), 107–123 (2011)
8. Gray, P.H., Chan, Y.E.: Integrating Knowledge Management Practices Through a Problem Solving Framework. Communications of the AIS 4(12) Article 12 (2000)
9. Johnson, D.W., Johnson, R.T., Smith, K.A.: Cooperative Learning: Increasing College Faculty Instructional Productivity. ASHE-FRIC Higher Education Report 4, George Washington University, Washington, DC (1991)
10. Lee, E.S., Li, R.L.: Comparison of Fuzzy Number based on the Probability Measure of Fuzzy Events. Computer and Mathematics with Applications 15, 887–896 (1988)
11. Liu, D.R., Wu, I.C., Yang, K.S.: Task-based K-Support System: Disseminating and Sharing Task-relevant Knowledge. Expert Systems with Applications 29(2), 408–423 (2005)
12. Norris, C., Soloway, E., Sullivan, T.: Log on Education: Examining 25 Years of Technology in U.S. Education. Communications of the ACM 45(8), 15-18 (2002)
13. Patterson, F., Hobley, S.: A New Way To Evaluate Learning and Training? KM Review 6(3), 20–23 (2003)
14. Riffell, S.K., Sibley, D.F.: Student Perceptions of a Hybrid Learning Format: Can Online Exercises Replace Traditional Lectures? Journal of College Science Teaching 32, 394–399 (2003)
15. Saaty, T.L.: A Scaling Method for Priorities in Hierarchical Structure. Journal of Mathematical Psychology 15(3), 234–281 (1977)
16. Sato, Y.: Questionnaire Design for Survey Research: Employing Weighting Method. In: VII International Symposium on the Analytic Hierarchy Process, Honolulu, Hawaii (2005)
17. Zadeh, L.A.: The Concept of a Linguistic Variable and Its Application to Approximate Reasoning. Information Science 8(4), 199–249 (1975)

Designing Dippler — A Next-Generation TEL System

Mart Laanpere, Hans Põldoja, and Peeter Normak

Tallinn University, Institute of Informatics, Narva mnt 25, 10120 Tallinn, Estonia
{mart.laanpere,hans.poldoja,peeter.normak}@tlu.ee

Abstract. This paper discusses the conceptual design of Digital Learning Ecosystems, which, as we argue, are becoming the foundation of next-generation Technology-Enhanced Learning systems (TEL systems). We illustrate our argument by a case study on design and development of a Dippler ecosystem. First, the framework for identifying the generations of TEL systems is described and expectations towards next generation of TEL systems are drawn from the literature review. After that, the dialectics of ongoing mainstream discourse (LMS vs PLE) is analysed and platform for reaching the synthesis is drawn. As we argue, the next-generation TEL systems are better understood if not referred as "learning environments", but rather as Digital Learning Ecosystems. Finally, process and results of a design-based research on Digital Learning Ecosystem called Dippler is described and discussed.

Keywords: learning environment, socio-technical transition, digital learning ecosystem, design-based research.

1 Socio-Technical Transitions and Software System Generations

In the scope of this study, we refer to various types of software application with educational purpose as Technology-Enhanced Learning systems (TEL systems). We are focusing at major shifts in technological platforms of TEL systems across the last 50 years, but also in the ways teachers and students have been using them. As we are interested not only in the structure and design of learning-related software systems, but also their implementation patterns, we decided to set a wider perspective on TEL system as a complex socio-technical system, involving various political, economical, academic and technological aspects.

There is a solid academic foundation for studying socio-technical transitions, starting from Schumpeter [1] who interpreted technological discontinuities as creative destruction, which is a natural part of multi-dimensional innovation process involving changes in products, production processes, markets, supplies and organisations. Christensen [2] has shown that evolution within a technology generation is taking the form of a S-shape curve (see Fig. 1). Ansari & Garud [3] have used Christensen's approach to explore inter-generational transitions in the context of mobile service generations, where changes in transmission speed within a mobile service generation took a form of S-shape curve.

T. Ley et al. (Eds.): OST 2012, IFIP AICT 395, pp. 91–100, 2013.

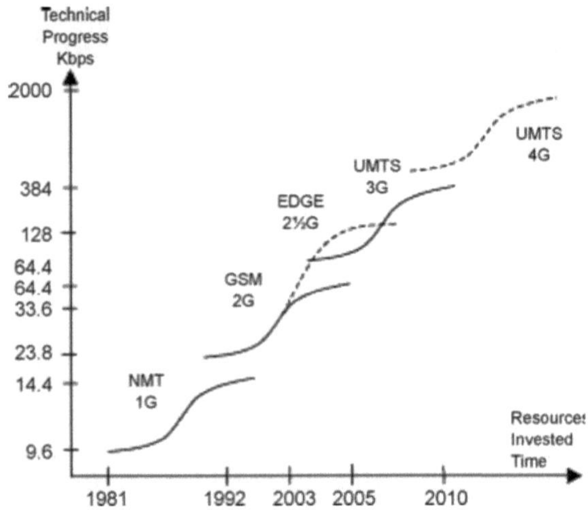

Fig. 1. S-shapes in mobile service generations [2]

Although the concept of Web 2.0 as the next generation of the WWW has been critically disputed [4], it illustrates well the fact that sometimes the reason for claims of a new generation comes mainly from the social context (incl. the radical change in technology usage patterns) and not from emergence of disruptive technology.

While it is evidently much easier to identify technology generations in case of mobile services than in case of learning-related software applications, we argue that it makes sense to conceptualise generation changes also in case of TEL systems. We believe that the era of LMS is coming to its end. Figure 2 below illustrates (yet, does not prove) our claim by showing the stagnation in the number of Moodle instances around the world. However, an increasing number of authors [5, 6, 7] argue for emergence of next generation TEL systems, which will replace traditional Learning Management Systems.

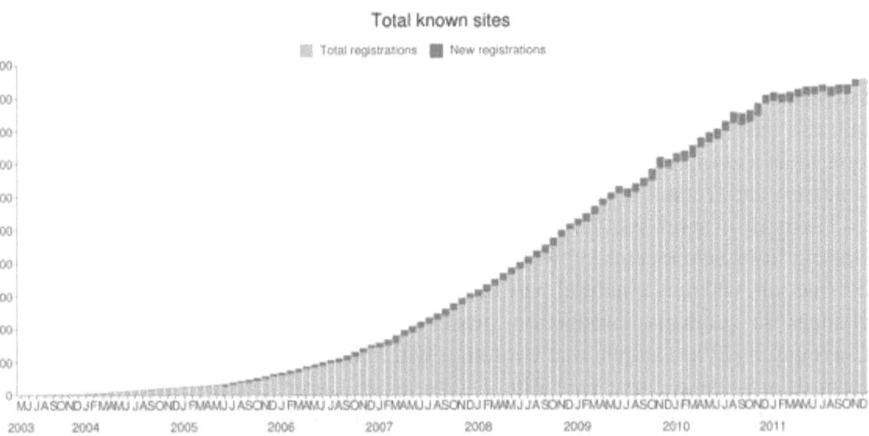

Fig. 2. S-shape curve illustrating the end of growth in Moodle installations worldwide [8]

Our aim is to provide a justification and a new conceptual framework for next-generation TEL system so it could be coherent with digital ecosystems approach.

2 Identifying the Generations of TEL Systems

Some of the key concepts in the domain ontology of Technology-Enhanced Learning (e.g. Virtual Learning Environment, Learning System, e-learning platform, educational software) are not defined by the TEL community in a consistent and consensus-based manner. The reason for this peculiarity could be that TEL domain is not yet mature, or, due to its inter-disciplinary character, it is open to discourses and vocabularies which are taken over from other domains.

In this paper, we tried to establish a sound system of concepts, which is coherent with both existing TEL practices and theories, as well as with our proposed framework of digital learning ecosystems. Venn diagram on the Figure 3 below illustrates the proposed set of concepts for domain ontology of TEL systems.

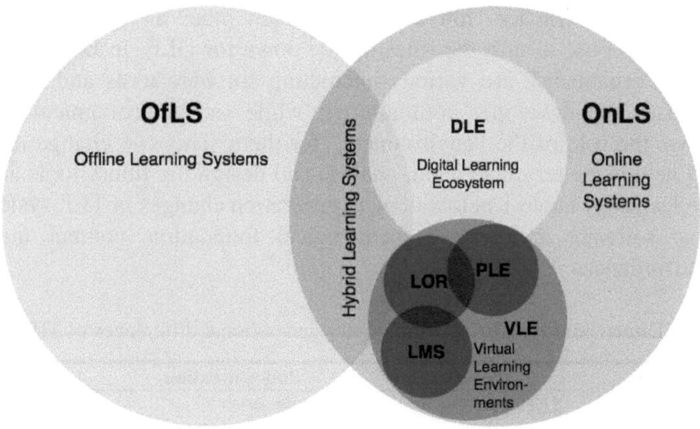

Fig. 3. Inter-relation of key concepts in the domain of TEL systems

First, TEL systems are either offline or online learning systems. Offline learning systems (e.g. desktop software used for learning and teaching, drill programs, multimedia textbooks on CD-s) can be seen as the first generation of TEL systems. The second generation of TEL systems (Virtual Learning Environments, VLE) appeared with the emergence of WWW and online learning systems. Virtual Learning Environment is defined as "a software system that combines a number of different tools that are used to systematically deliver content online and facilitate the learning experience around that content" [9]. The most prominent type of VLE are Learning Management Systems (LMS; can be also called Course Management Systems), which became the mainstream among second-generation TEL systems. LMS is defined as "a wide range of systems that organise and provide access to online learning services for students, teachers, and administrators" [10]. In parallel with LMS, Learning Object Repositories (LOR) appeared as the content was separated from the software and made reusable. Some LMSs also include a built-in LOR, thus a slight overlap on Fig. 3. We argue that the rise of Personal Learning Environments (PLE) was scaling up since 2008 as a form of democratic reaction and dialectic anti-thesis against closed and rigid nature of LMS. PLE is still a kind of VLE, but it is not (in most cases) especially designed for educational purposes and did not become a next-generation TEL system in itself, as it was argued by Mott [7]. A blog-based PLE causes some usability and privacy issues and together with growing tension between PLE and LMS, these two factors are creating a fruitful ground for the new generation of TEL systems: Digital Learning Ecosystems (DLE). Uden et al [11] have defined DLE as an integrated system of mutually connected/interacting digital species and their environment. However, their definition does not specify, which entities are interpreted as "biotic" (evolving, active) part of DLE and which parts are seen as "abiotic" environmental factors. To address this issue, we define DLE as an adaptive socio-technical system consisting of mutually interacting digital species (tools, services, content used in learning process) and communities of users (learners, facilitators, experts) together with their social, economical and cultural environment. While the second generation of TEL systems interpreted software systems as an environment where learners and teachers interacted with each other as well as with learning resources, we propose to turn the roles upside down for DLE. In DLE, the symbiotic "species" or "organisms" are various interacting software tools and services along with their user and developer communities, while social, economical and cultural context plays the role of the "environment" for them. This is a change of paradigm, which will help us better understand, analyse and design the future tools and services to enhance learning. Table 1 below depicts generation changes in TEL systems in four dimensions: software architecture, pedagogical foundation, content management, dominant affordances.

Table 1. Dimensions for distinguishing inter-generational differences of TEL systems

Dimension	1st generation	2nd generation	3rd generation
Software architecture	Desktop software	Single-server monolithic system	Cloud architecture, mobile clients
Pedagogical foundation	Stimulus-response-reinforcement	Pedagogical neutrality	Social constructivism, connectivism
Content management	Content was integrated	Separated from software, re-usable	Open, web-based, embeddable
Dominant affordances	Presentation, drill, test	Presentation, assignments, discussions	Reflection, sharing, remixing, tagging

Geels [12] proposes a Multi-Level Perspective (MLP) as an analytic framework for studying changes in socio-technical systems on three levels of aggregation: macro (socio-technical landscape), meso (technological regime or paradigm) and micro (niches: spaces of experimentation, protected from market pressure), see Fig.4 below. Radical innovation happens mainly on the micro level, in niches appearing outside of dominant technological paradigm, as a result of changes in macro-level landscape and influencing through dynamic interplay the meso-level technological regime. MLP suits well to analyse also the ongoing generation change in TEL systems. Current technological regime in TEL is clearly associated with the dominance of LMS, radical innovation happens in niches emerged on the Web 2.0 landscape, where increasing

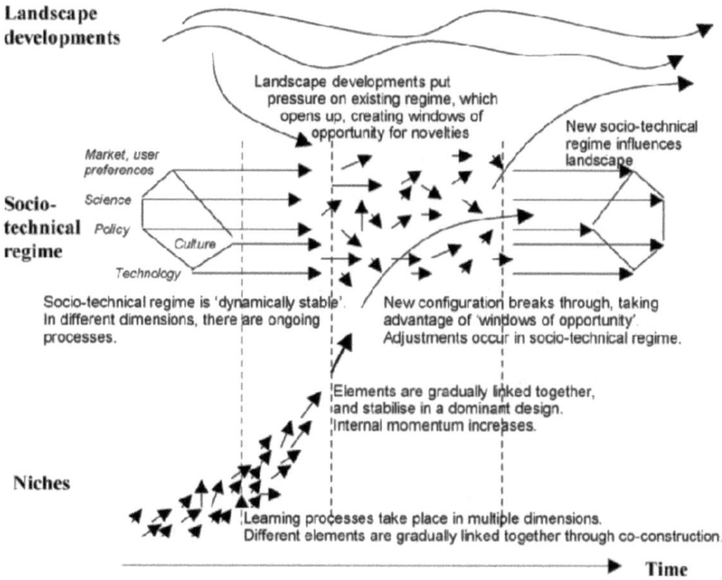

Fig. 4. A dynamic multi-level perspective on socio-technical transitions [13]

number of learners and educators find more flexible, open and social affordances to support their self-directed learning.

The number of niche-seeking experiments involving blogs and other social media tools in teaching and learning have been steadily increasing in universities, one evidence of this trend can be drawn from [14]. All together 77 academic publications from 2006 to 2011 were included in an extensive literature review on personal learning environments, involving 9 case studies from 2006, 19 from 2008 and 23 from 2010, demonstrating clearly the up-scaling of this phenomenon. While blog-based Personal Learning Environments are easy to implement on the level of single innovative teachers, these are hard to scale up to institutional level, even more difficult to integrate with existing university information systems. We argue that the next-generation TEL systems should combine the strengths of both approaches: ease of management, scalability and privacy of LMS and, on the other hand, flexibility, learner control and personalisation of PLE.

3 Methodology: Design-Based Research

The general research approach of this study was following the design-based research methodology [15]. This iterative way of doing research is increasingly used in learning sciences to design and implement pedagogical interventions and to test them in a real learning environment.

Leinonen et al [16] claim that the design of a product should communicate the theoretical findings made during the design process. For designing learning tools they propose a research-based design approach that sees final software prototype as hypothesis — potential solutions to the design challenges defined during the process. When designing Dippler as a set of software products we have followed the phases of research-based design process, which will be followed by design-based research interventions using the Dippler prototype as hypothesis.

The first phase (contextual inquiry) aimed to define the context and preliminary design challenges. The context of this study was blended learning and fully online courses in higher and vocational education. The design challenge was to combine the strengths of PLE and LMS approaches into a next generation online learning system. In the contextual inquiry phase we have conducted a number of studies on using weblogs and other social media tools in formal higher education courses [17, 18]. These studies have indicated that there is a need for a more structured online learning system that would (1) allow learners to continue using social media tools while (2) making it easier to follow and coordinate learning activities for the facilitator and (3) to manage and support the system at the institutional level. The contextual inquiry phase involved also trying out alternative approaches for managing blog-based courses. We developed two software prototypes for different course settings. LePress is a WordPress plugin that allows create courses and to manage course assignments [19]. EduFeedr is an aggregator for blog-based courses that doesn't require any plugin in a learner blog [20]. These prototypes helped us to refine the final requirements for Dippler.

The second phase of research-based design process is participatory design where important stakeholders are involved in the design process. Here we combined participatory, pedagogy-driven design with scenario-based design [21]. We prepared four scenarios that described typical use cases of Dippler: (1) facilitator sets up a course, (2) learner sets up a weblog and enrolls to the course, (3) submitting assignments and giving feedback, and (4) moving Dippler blog to another university. These scenarios were evaluated in a participatory design session involving 4 lecturers and students who had previous experience with various online learning environments.

The next phase entailed product design, aiming to define the use cases and basic interaction with the system. In that phase we wrote agile user stories [22] that were negotiated and prioritized in a web-based software project management tool Trac[1]. Various interaction design methods such as paper prototyping [23] and card sorting were used to design the user interface for Dippler.

We are currently in the final phase of research-based design process. We have produced a functional software product as hypothesis and completed pilot-testing it during four months in two MA-level courses. Feedback from these pilot courses will be used to evaluate the design decisions. Real data from actual use will help to refine the user interface details and to develop the next version of the Dippler.

4 Context of and Requirements for Dippler Project

In order to promote and develop e-learning nationwide, two consortia have been established under the lead of Estonian IT Foundation: Estonian e-University and

[1] `http://trac.htk.tlu.ee/iva2`

Estonian e-Vocational School. One example of joint efforts was that instead of acquiring by each university separately an institutional WebCT/BlackBoard licence, a country licence was bought for a central LMS server. Similarly, a number of centralised e-learning services (LOR, video-hub) were implemented or developed, including a next-generation TEL system called Dippler. Initially the following general requirements for Dippler were specified, as a result of a literature review and participatory design session:

- Use of Semantic Web and Web 2.0 technologies (RSS, folksonomies, web services, widgets, embedding, semantic annotation, ontologies).
- Modularity and open source code (GNU LGPL or BSD license), which would allow community based development.
- Different levels of use: suitable for both beginners and advanced users.
- Compatible with learning technology standards and specifications (LOM, QTI, SCORM, LD, Common Cartridge etc).
- Interoperability with other TEL tools (blogs, wikis, repositories).
- Support for Single Sign-on and authentication with OpenID and ID card.
- Multilingual and easily localized.
- Possibility to add individual tools and services, personalize the look and feel.
- Possibility to apply different business models.
- Powerful Learning Analytics possibilities.
- Compliance to general software requirements: scalable, secure, well-documented, adaptable, easy installation and administration.

Based on these requirements, the iterative design process started in 2010 and software was ready to be implemented in two pilot courses in spring term 2012.

5 Software Implementation

Dippler is implemented as a set of distributed online tools and services, not as a monolithic server software. Technical implementation of Dippler consists of three core components:

- **Back-Office Service (BOS):** a Java-based middleware application together with SOAP Web services and MySQL database that is used for storing data and communicating with other components of Dippler ecosystem,
- **Dippler Administrator (DiA):** a PHP application with institutional interface and structures (e.g. departments, curricula, domain ontologies) for setting up, managing and evaluating courses and conducting powerful learning analytics,
- **Dippler Plugin for WordPress (DiP):** which turn learners' blogs into enhanced PLEs, which communicate with BOS in order to enroll to courses, receive assignments and submit homework. Student can disconnect her blog from home institution, but all artefacts created and received during the course will remain in her Personal Learning Environment. The same blog can later be re-connected with DiA of any other university or school using Dippler.

These three core components form the heart of a larger digital learning ecosystem, where learners use their personal WordPress blogs, learning resources are stored in various Web 2.0 environments (SlideShare, YouTube, Issuu) and various social media tools can be connected with Dippler (via RSS or iFrame widgets). Dippler is also able to re-use learning objects created and/or hosted by other learning technology tools: our self-developed test authoring tool Questr, Learning Object authoring tool LeMill, and Learning Object Repository Waramu. An iPhone/iPad client for Dippler has also been developed.

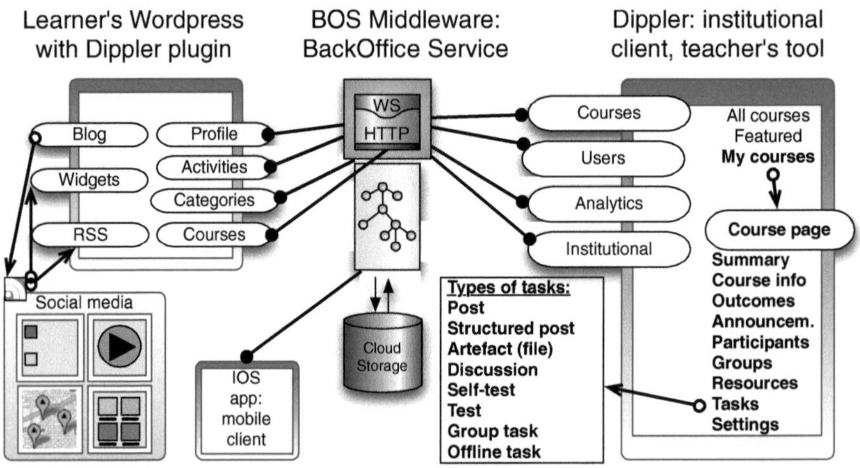

Fig. 5. Conceptual design of Dippler ecosystem

DiA acts as a catalogue of online courses and facilitators interface for managing a course. Course page is divided into 9 sections (see Fig. 5). Course feed page displays recent announcements, assignments and activity stream of the course. Learning outcomes section allows facilitator to specify learning outcomes that can be later attached to assignments, evidences in learner portfolio and other relevant objects. In the assignments section it is currently possible to create six types of tasks (free post, pre-structured post, file upload, self-test, test, group task, embedded widget), more types will be implemented in the future. In order to guide facilitators to use web-based open educational resources it is not possible to upload learning resources as files, learning resources can be only added as links or embeds. Dippler is able to retrieve learning resource metadata from YouTube or Slideshare based on URL of a resource and display the embedded resource. Both assignments and learning resources can be annotated with domain ontology concepts, which connect them to specific learning outcomes and are allowing more meaningful learning analytics.

Learners will use their WordPress blogs as personal learning portfolios. In order to connect their blog to BOS service they need to activate Dippler plugin (DiP) for WordPress. The plugin extends the blog's user interface with some new pages and widgets: course feed, assignments, learning resources, etc. Learners submit their responses to assignments as blog posts that will be copied to BOS and connected with a selected learning outcome as well as some concepts from domain ontology. Dippler plugin allows the facilitator to keep her feedback and grades private. Otherwise learners have full control over their blogs: they can change its outlook, add sidebar widgets, plugins, pages, blogroll etc.

Dippler is open-source software, distributed under Apache 2.0 license. The source code of Dippler can be downloaded from http://trac.htk.tlu.ee/iva2.

6 Conclusion and Future Research

This paper proposed a conceptual framework for next-generation TEL systems - Digital Learning Ecosystems, along with an illustrative case study on designing and developing the Dippler platform. The case study followed the participatory design-based research methodology, resulting with an innovative ecosystem of open-source tools and open learning resources, which is designed to combine the strengths of blog-based Personal Learning Environments with that of traditional Learning Management Systems.

In the next phase of our design-based research, we are planning to expand and cultivate the digital learning ecosystem of Dippler by integrating or associating it with new learning tools (e.g. concept mapping tool CMapTools, Knowledge Building tool FLE4, Twitter, Wookie widget server) and training or inviting the new groups of users, communities, educational institutions to populate the system with activities. As all activities in Dippler ecosystem leave semantically rich traces to BOS database, we foresee it as a new powerful tool for new type of learning analytics in Digital Learning Ecosystems.

Acknowledgments. This research was funded by Estonian Ministry of Education and Research, targeted research grant No. 0130159s08. Development of Dippler was funded by Estonian IT Foundation and BeST program of European Social Fund.

References

1. Schumpeter, J.A.: Business Cycles: A Theoretical, Historical and Statistical Analysis of the Capitalist Process. McGraw-Hill, New York (1939)
2. Christensen, C.M.: The Innovator's Dilemma: When New Technologies Cause Great Firms to Fail. Harvard Business Review Press, Cambridge (1997)
3. Ansari, S., Garud, R.: Inter-generational transitions in socio-technical systems: The case of mobile communications. Research Policy 38(2), 382–392 (2009)
4. Scholz, T.: Market Ideology and the Myths of Web 2.0. First Monday 13(3) (2008)
5. Rajagopal, K., Joosten-ten Brinke, D., Van Bruggen, J., Sloep, P.: Understanding personal learning networks: Their structure, content and the networking skills needed to optimally use them. First Monday 17(1) (2012)
6. Casquero, O., Portillo, J., Ovelar, R., Benito, M., Romo, J.: iPLE Network: an integrated eLearning 2.0 architecture from a university's perspective. Interactive Learning Environments 18(3), 293–308 (2010)

7. Mott, J.: Envisioning the Post-LMS Era. EDUCAUSE Quarterly 33(1) (2010)
8. Moodle Statistics, `http://moodle.org/stats`
9. Weller, M.: Virtual Learning Environments: Using, Choosing and Developing your VLE. Routledge, Oxon (2007)
10. Paulsen, M.F.: Online Education Systems: Discussion and Definition of Terms (2002), `http://nettskolen.nki.no/forskning/Definition%20of%20Terms.pdf`
11. Uden, L., Wangsa, I.T., Damiani, E.: The future of E-learning: E-learning ecosystem. In: IEEE Conf. on Digital Ecosystems and Technologies, pp. 113–117. IEEE, Cairns (2007)
12. Geels, F.W.: Technological transitions as evolutionary reconfiguration processes: a multi-level perspective and a case-study. Research Policy 31(8–9), 1257–1274 (2002)
13. Genus, A., Coles, A.-M.: Rethinking the multi-level perspective of technological transitions. Research Policy 37(9), 1436–1445 (2008)
14. Buchem, I., Attwell, G., Torres, R.: Understanding Personal Learning Environments: Literature review and synthesis through the Activity Theory lens. In: Proceedings of the The PLE Conference 2011, Southampton, UK, July 10-12 (2011)
15. The Design-Based Research Collective: Design-Based Research: An Emerging Paradigm for Educational Inquiry. Educational Researcher 32(1), 5–8 (2003)
16. Leinonen, T., Toikkanen, T., Silvfast, K.: Software as Hypothesis: Research-Based Design Methodology. In: Proceedings of the Tenth Anniversary Conference on Participatory Design 2008, pp. 61–70. Indiana University, Indianapolis (2008)
17. Väljataga, T., Pata, K., Tammets, K.: Considering Students' Perspectives on Personal and Distributed Learning Environments in Course Design. In: Lee, M.J.W., McLoughlin, C. (eds.) Web 2.0-Based E-Learning, pp. 85–107. IGI Global, Hershey (2011)
18. Väljataga, T., Põldoja, H., Laanpere, M.: Open Online Courses: Responding to Design Challenges. In: Proceedings of NBE 2011, pp. 68–75. University of Lapland, Rovaniemi (2011)
19. Tomberg, V., Laanpere, M., Lamas, D.: Learning Flow Management and Semantic Data Exchange between Blog-Based Personal Learning Environments. In: Leitner, G., Hitz, M., Holzinger, A. (eds.) USAB 2010. LNCS, vol. 6389, pp. 340–352. Springer, Heidelberg (2010)
20. Põldoja, H.: EduFeedr: following and supporting learners in open blog-based courses. In: Open ED 2010 Proceedings, UOC, OU, BYU, Barcelona (2010)
21. Carroll, J.M.: Making Use: Scenario-Based Design of Human-Computer Interactions. The MIT Press, Cambridge (2000)
22. Cohn, M.: User Stories Applied: For Agile Software Development. Addison-Wesley, Boston (2004)
23. Snyder, C.: Paper Prototyping: The Fast and Easy Way to Design and Refine User Interfaces. Morgan Kaufmann, San Francisco (2003)

Developing Learning Analytics for TUT Circle

Anne-Maritta Tervakari, Jarno Marttila, Meri Kailanto, Jukka Huhtamäki, Juho Koro, and Kirsi Silius

Hypermedia Laboratory, Department of Mathematics, Tampere University of Technology Tampere, Finland
{anne.tervakari,jarno.marttila,meri.kailanto, jukka.huhtamaki,juho.koro,kirsi.silius}@tut.fi

Abstract. In this article, we introduce the concept of learning analytics in the context of TUT Circle, a social media enhanced web service for learning in use at Tampere University of Technology. Through three case studies, we apply the methods of learning analytics for insight into the bursty nature of learning activities, procrastination, peer learning, and co-operation between two academic tribes. We found learning analytics useful in providing information to improve the pedagogical practices of online courses, as well as the quality of web-based learning in general.

Keywords: Learning Analytics, SNA, Social Media in Learning.

1 Introduction

In recent years, social media enhanced learning environments have been a topic of increasing interest, most importantly because they have been seen to promote peer learning by enhancing communication and collaboration within the student community. [1-5] Peer learning includes a selection of learning activities that are mutually beneficial and involve the sharing of knowledge, ideas, and experiences among participants. [6] The use of social media enhanced learning environments can facilitate peer learning by providing collaborative learning tools, and supporting information sharing and distribution of materials. [1-4] However, the effectiveness of the instructions and the learning interventions designed for peer learning is challenging to evaluate. [4],[5],[7] The question is, how do we determine whether, for example, the use of discussion activities has enhanced student participation in the course, or whether the use of group work truly promotes interaction and collaboration between students? [4-5]

A traditional approach for collecting information to evaluate student activity and interaction is to use evaluation surveys at the end of the course. However, these surveys only usually provide limited information for improving teaching or enhancing peer learning. Problems with the traditional approach include: the limited quantity of information collected, and the potentially large delay between the moment of answering the evaluation survey and the actualisation of the interventions, which may debase the quality of self-reported information. [7]

T. Ley et al. (Eds.): OST 2012, IFIP AICT 395, pp. 101–110, 2013.

The use of web-based learning environments provides an opportunity to collect rich data on students' communicative, collaborative, and participative actions throughout courses. However, simple participation statistics may be a poor indicator of student interaction and collaboration if considered alone. [4] The collected data analysed using sophisticated methods can provide useful information on the process of carrying out assignments, communication with other students using forums and private messages, favoured learning materials, and the evolution of the students' online community. [7]

Hypermedia Laboratory at Tampere University of Technology has conducted development projects over several years in order to design and implement a social media enhanced web service TUT Circle for supporting studying and teaching. The development and research of methods of visualisation and analysis of log data for pedagogical purposes has been a significant part of development projects of TUT Circle. The aim of this article is to describe our recent development work related to learning analytics by presenting three teaching experiments. The objectives of these experiments were to: 1) find out if the analysis and visualisations of log data provide useful information for improving pedagogical practices of online courses, and 2) collect valuable information for developing tools of learning analytics.

This study is part of a Finnish national project called Campus Conexus, which is being carried out from 2009 to 2013, and is financed by the European Social Fund. Five Finnish universities are participating in the project with an aim to study how students engage in university studies, for example by enriching learning experiences and enhancing students' personal, intellectual, collegial, and professional development. [8]

2 Learning Analytics

Learning analytics is a relatively new field of science with many definitions [9]. Buckingham Shum and Ferguson [10] state that the background of learning analytics is in web analytics and business intelligence, and that learning analytics may be understood as the use of tools to measure and advance learning and teaching. Siemens [11] defines learning analytics as "use of intelligent data, learner produced data, and analysis model to discover information and social connections and to predict and advice on learning". We see learning analytics more as a process than a set of tools, and approach the definition from the business intelligence viewpoint.

Business and Competitive Intelligence (BCI) is the process in which organisations gather systematically actionable information about competitors and the competitive environment, and ideally apply it to their planning processes and decision making, in order to improve their enterprise's performance and gain insight into externally motivated change, future developments, and their implications to the organisation [12-13]. Following the BCI definition, we define learning analytics as a process or activity in which data on teaching and learning environments is systematically gathered, processed, analysed, and evaluated to support decision making, and to gain insights on teaching and learning.

In this article, we approach the learning analytics process from the data-driven information visualisation point of view, in which data is collected and visualised to amplify users' cognition through expressive, often interactive views (cf. [14]).

Visualisation has been a key element of social network analysis and its precursor, sociometry, as a tool for exploring the structural configuration of communities, and in sharing the exploration findings to others [15]. While we do realise network visualisations are not enough for learning analytics per se, we see that they do provide a valuable viewpoint in terms of student activity.

TUT Circle, the learning platform utilised during teaching experiments, provides a good environment for applying and further developing methods of: 1) applying social media in learning, and 2) learning analytics. TUT Circle is built on Drupal[1], a content management framework. TUT Circle contains all the basic functionalities of a modern social media web service, including the possibility to publish several different types of content, e.g. wiki pages, blog posts, news items, and events. TUT Circle also promotes the networking, collaboration, and communications of small groups by allowing users to form friendships with each other, send private messages, chat, create, contribute, and comment on content, exchange opinions, and share resources within and between the groups. When compared to third-party social media platforms, a platform that is maintained by its developers enables collection of rich data as well as the development of new features on the basis of the findings. Many of the features in TUT Circle are developed by integrating and tailoring existing Drupal modules. However, development related to learning analytics has, for now, been done by implementing tailored scripts and batch processes for exporting data directly from TUT Circle database for further analysis. In addition, Google Analytics is used for support in basic Web analytics and benchmark data on TUT Circle usage.

2.1 Case 1. Interaction between Academic Tribes

In spring 2011, a cross-university course for students of two different disciplines was organised. During the course, 11 journalism and 5 hypermedia students worked together to design and implement a modern, journalistic online publication. The students were given the opportunity to experience a real-life development project, to learn how to create ideas and communicate to identify user needs, and establish requirements in a multidisciplinary environment similar to real-world design situations. The course met weekly and TUT Circle was used to support communication, collaboration, and information sharing. For example, the students reported their findings and solutions by writing blog messages or wiki pages that all students were able to edit.

Students from different disciplines learn to do things in a way that is typical to their discipline, and use language and concepts they have learned through their study path, which may cause challenges in interaction between students from different disciplines. [16] [17] The objective of this study was to uncover if students used TUT Circle for collaboration. Do students from different disciplines collaborate, or do they work entirely within their own discipline? Log data of students' reading and writing activity collected from TUT Circle was analysed and visualised to show interaction among students and content. [2].

[1] `http://drupal.org`

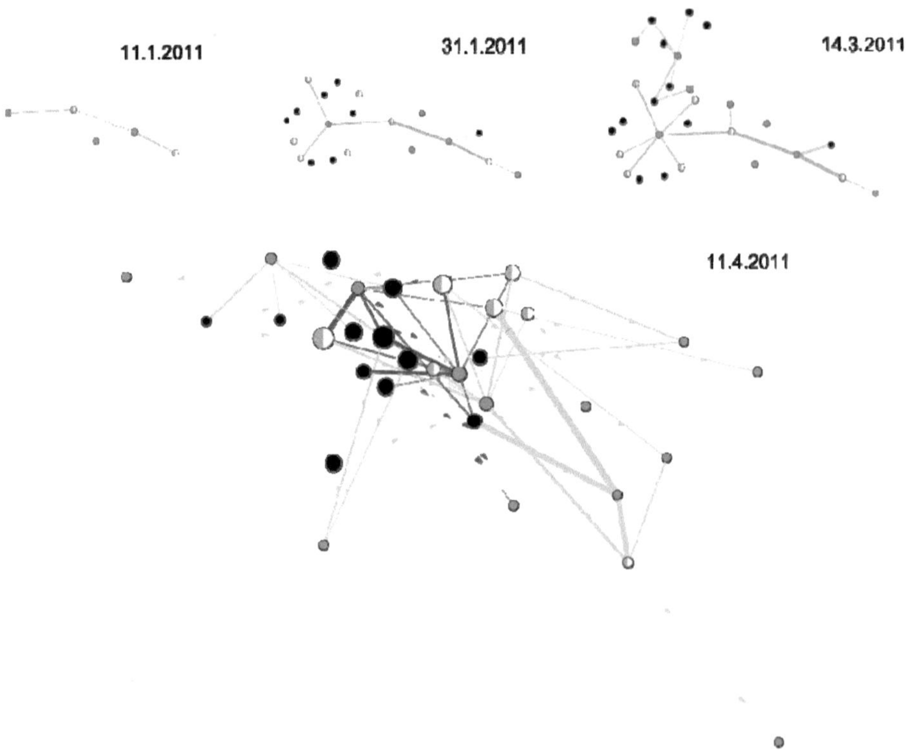

Fig. 1. Two-mode user-to-content network

The data collected from TUT Circle was visualised as a two-mode user-to-content network (See Fig. 1). The figure presents four different phases of the network evolution. The cross-discipline collaboration online started slowly, mainly only when students were asked to contribute to specific documents. Towards the end of the course, however, the cross-discipline collaboration got more intense. In the largest figure, contributions to content (light gray edges), and reading the content (dark gray edges) is visualised. Width of the edge is proportional to the amount of contributions or readings. The visualisation shows students read content produced by other students, especially from other disciplines. However, they seemed to divide into their own groups. For example, hypermedia students in particular read more content produced by journalists. This is reasonable because they need the definitions for implementation of the web-based service according to customer needs. [2]

2.2 Case 2. Peer Learning

Programming of Hypermedia is a course that aims to provide students information on different features of hypermedia and web-based services as well as their implementation. Students participating in the course had varying technical skills. It was important to offer them an opportunity to challenge their skills by allowing them to freely choose the subject and the techniques for their personal development projects. PHP and CodeIgniter were the only technologies taught during the course in spring 2011. Students were encouraged to report on their projects in TUT Circle so other students could read the reports and learn from them. Students also had opportunities to learn through passive participation, i.e through observation by reading other students' reports. [18] Thirty students reported a total of 137 feature implementations in TUT Circle. The reports were read 1189 times, excluding students reading their own reports. [1]

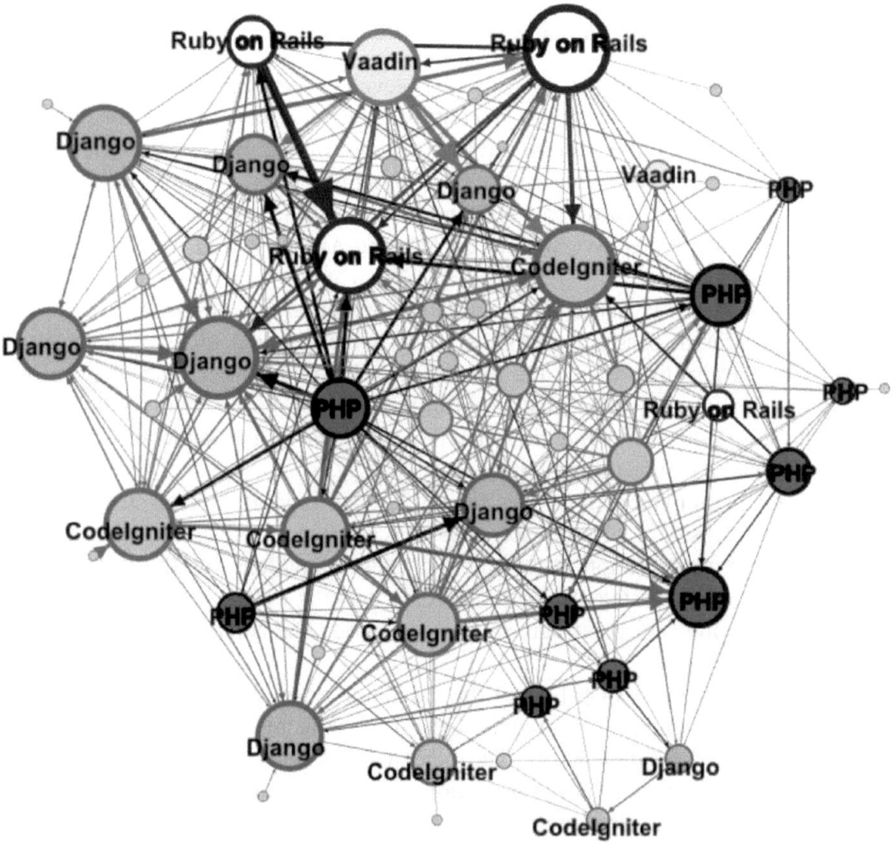

Fig. 2. Network of students in Programming of Hypermedia in spring 2011

We applied network analytics to reveal the peer learning patterns. The network in Figure 2 represents the 1-mode student-student network of students who read each others' contents on different web-programming techniques. Connections between the students are created on the basis of report reading. In the network, the weight of the connection, visualised as edge width, is equal to the number of times a student had read a report by another student. The colour corresponds to the technique the student used in his/her exercises. The network is relatively dense (0.140). Top indegree values, i.e. the number of connections pointing to a node [22], are between those using the same technologies; both PHP and alternative technologies are present. The connections between users applying different technologies also exist, but on a smaller scale. The visualisation shows that peer learning has occurred, and students have taken advantage of the opportunity to learn from other students using the same technology. With Gephi[2], a visual analytical tool for network data, the analyst is also able to explore the peer learner network in detail, including particular analysis of the evolution of peer learner network.

2.3 Case 3. Procrastination and Other Dynamics of Learning

Success in online learning requires a high level of participation and good time management skills. Particularly in university students, the main reasons for failing or dropping out from an online course are lack of time coupled with procrastination, the tendency to postpone important tasks. High procrastinators communicate less with their peers because they participate less and later than other students. A high level of procrastination has a negative impact on learning and may lead to poor academic performance. [18], [19]

In autumn 2011, Hypermedia Laboratory organised an online course for 35 students. In order to pass the course, students were required to carry out a group project with an aim to evaluate the quality of web-based service, and to contribute weekly assignments by writing messages in a discussion forum. One of the aims of the study was to monitor and describe the activities of the students in order to examine the phenomenon of participation. [3]

To reveal participation dynamics in a way that supports visual storytelling, a movie-like visualisation of user activities was created using Gource[3], a software version control visualisation tool which creates animations on the evolution of collaboratively created artefacts. With Gource, a network (or more precisely a tree) of contribution outputs, not contributors, was visualised. The contributors appear in the visualisation as they act.

Figure 3 presents two snapshots of the animation on student participation in their second weekly assignment that required them to write messages in the discussion forum (represented by dark gray). The other content shown in snapshots includes various course information and presentations of study groups. Comments written in TUT Circle discussions are represented as a tree structure under the related node. On the left side, a snapshot from Friday September 15th shows that some students had already submitted their assignments (See snapshot on the up). Most, however, submitted the exercise just before the deadline on Monday September 18th (See snapshot on the bottom). The visualisations show student participation occurred in bursts, and most of the activities took place around assignment deadlines throughout the entire course. [3]

---

[2] `https://gephi.org`

[3] `http://code.google.com/p/gource/`

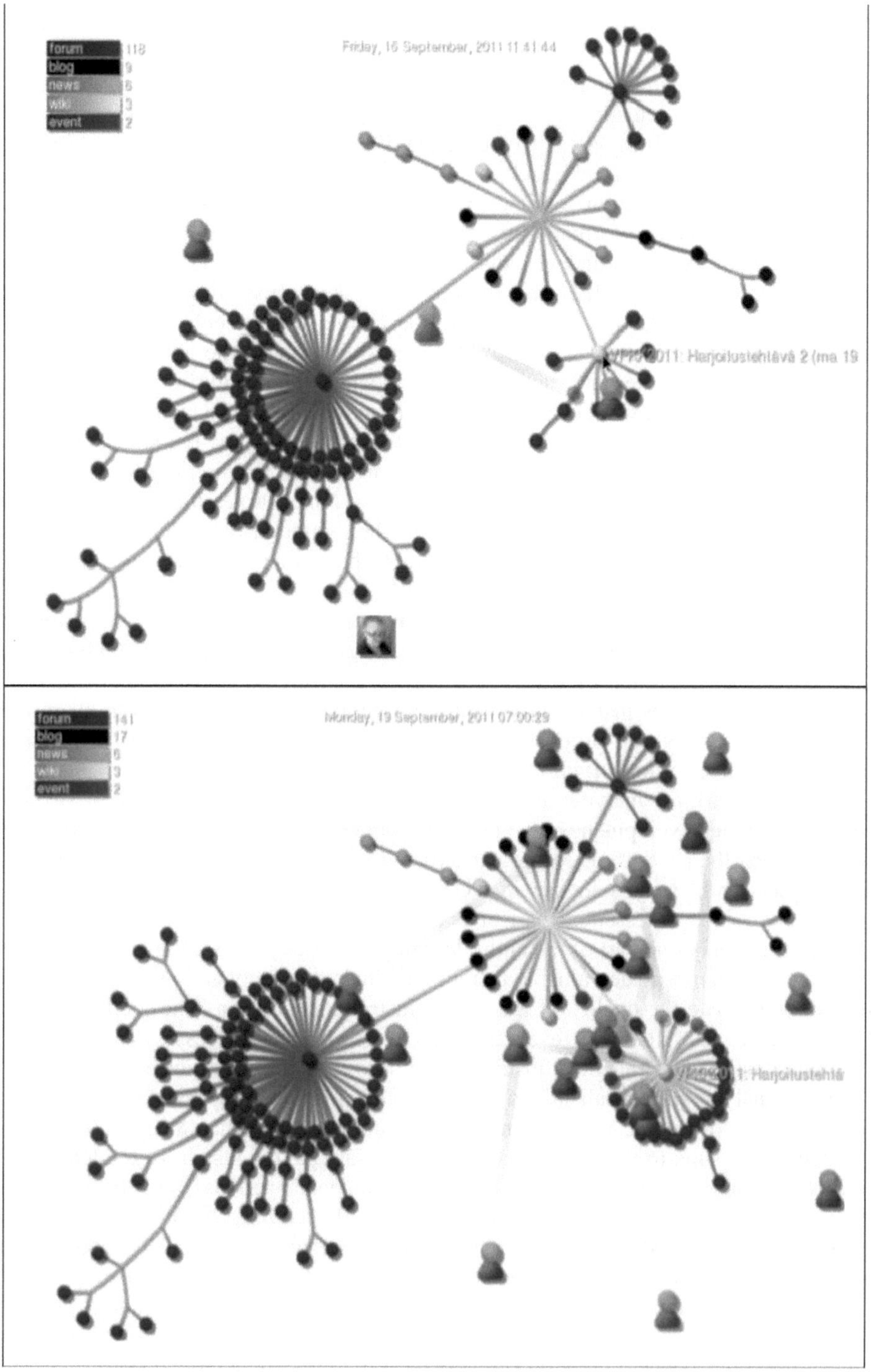

Fig. 3. Two snapshots from an animation visualising the course dynamics

3 Discussion and Conclusions

Learning analytics can be understood as a process of gathering, processing, analysing, and evaluating systematic information about teaching, learning, and learning environments. [9-11] In 2011, Hypermedia Laboratory organised three teaching experiment with an aim to: 1) find out if the analysis and visualisations of log data provided useful information for improving pedagogical practices of online courses, and 2) collect valuable information for developing tools of learning analytics.

In case 1, the analysis and visualisations of log data made the latent ties among students and contents visible, and offered the teacher possibilities to monitor the evolution of the interaction and collaboration among the students. If, for example, the students' collaboration seems to develop slowly, strategic interventions may be needed to motivate and activate the students. The static representation of the network, like in case 2, provides information about students' active and passive participation. The information may help the teacher identify active students whose reports are most read, or passive students who might have learning problems. In case 3, the animated visualisation created with Gource demonstrates the phenomenon of procrastination very clearly. Visualisations of the evolution of student participation can help teachers identify students' undesirable behaviour, and provide immediate guidance.

As the results show, learning analytics provides possibilities to verify student interaction and collaboration activities, show latent ties among students and contents, and observe the evolution of student participation. While animated visualisations of the dynamics provides insight into social configurations and the means to share the findings with others, we propose using a more traditional timeline for visualising activity over time for insight into the evolution of participation. [21]

For now, learning analytics have been applied in TUT Circle mainly to support research and the development of the platform. In the near future, we plan to take steps to fully cover the process of learning analytics by developing metrics and visual tools for students and teachers to use in TUT Circle. It's important to understand that human analysis is an essential part of learning analytics, and the tools discussed in this paper are only one part of the entire learning analytics process. For teachers, these kinds of tools can provide valuable insight into student activity and participation, and thus help evaluate the quality of a course's instructional design. The tools may also help students monitor and evaluate their performance processes and learning outcomes, and make strategic adjustments to improve their performance.

While analysis and visualisations of log data can make the actions of students more identifiable, and provide valuable information and insight, human analysis is needed to attach the results to the specific context. For example, the insight of the teacher is needed to understand connections between students' actions, and to plan the pedagogical interventions within the context of the course. Moreover, additional means are still needed to fully understand student behaviour. It is also important to realise that one crucial issue related to learning analytics is the privacy of personal information and the protection of students' identities. It is important to control access to the data collected and analysis results. There is also a need to raise important ethical questions concerning what students need to know about the data collected and analysed, and how students really benefit from being hypermonitored.

References

1. Silius, K., Tervakari, A.-M., Huhtamäki, J., Tebest, T., Marttila, J., Kailanto, M., Miilumäki, T.: Programming of Hypermedia: Course Implementation in Social Media. In: Gaol, F.L., Nguyen, Q.V. (eds.) Proc. of the 2011 2nd International Congress on CACS. AISC, vol. 144, pp. 369–376. Springer, Heidelberg (2012)
2. Silius, K., Tervakari, A.-M., Kailanto, M., Huhtamäki, J., Marttila, J., Tebest, T., Miilumäki, T.: Developing an Online Publication Collaborating among Students in Different Disciplines. In: Gaol, F.L., Nguyen, Q.V. (eds.) Proc. of the 2011 2nd International Congress on CACS. AISC, vol. 144, pp. 361–367. Springer, Heidelberg (2012)
3. Tervakari, A.-M., Silius, K., Tebest, T., Marttila, J., Kailanto, M., Huhtamäki, J.: Peer Learning in Social Media Enhanced Learning. In: 2012 IEEE Global Engineering Education Conference (EDUCON), Marrakesh, Morocco, April 17-20 (2012) (in press)
4. Soller, A.L.: Supporting Social Interaction in an Intelligent Collaborative Learning System. International J. of Artificial Intelligence in Education 12, 40–62 (2001)
5. Dawson, S.: 'Seeing' the learning community: An exploration of the development of a resource for monitoring online student networking. British J. of Educational Technology 41(5), 736–752 (2010)
6. Boud, D., Cohen, R., Sampson, J.: Peer learning and assessment. Assessment and Evaluation in Higher Education 24(4), 413–426 (1999)
7. Elias, T.: Learning Analytics: Definitions, Processes, and Potential. Creative Commons, `http://learninganalytics.net/LearningAnalyticsDefinitionsProcessesPotential.pdf`
8. Annala, J., Mäkinen, M., Svärd, M., Silius, P., Miilumäki, K.: Online community environment promoting engagement in higher education. SLS Journal - Studies for the Learning Society 2, 75–86 (2012)
9. Long, P., Siemens, S.: Penetrating the Fog: Analytics in Learning and Education. EDUCAUSE Review 46(5), 30–32 (2011)
10. Buckingham Shum, S., Ferguson, R.: Social Learning Analytics. Technical Report KMI-11-01, Knowledge Media Institute. The Open University, UK., `http://kmi.open.ac.uk/publications/pdf/kmi-11-01.pdf`
11. Siemens, G.: What are Learning Analytics? `http://www.elearnspace.org/blog/2010/08/25/what-are-learning-analytics/`
12. Fleisher, C.S., Bensoussan, B.E.: Business and Competitive Analysis: Effective Application of New and Classic Methods. FT Press, Upper Saddle River (2007)
13. Fleisher, C.S., Wright, S.: Competitive Intelligence Analysis Failure: Diagnosing Individual Level Causes and Implementing Organisational Level Remedies. J. Of Strategic Marketing 18(7), 553–572 (2010)
14. Ware, C.: Information Visualization: Perception for Design. Elsevier, San Francisco (2004)
15. Freeman, L.C.: Methods of Social Network Visualization. In: Meyers, R.A. (ed.) Encyclopedia of Complexity and Systems Science. Springer (2009)
16. Becher, T., Trowler, P.R.: Academic Tribes and Territories: Intellectual enquiry and the culture of disciplines. Open University press, Buckingham (2001)
17. Kolb, D.A.: Learning Styles and Disciplinary Differences. In: Chickering, A. (ed.) The Modern American College, Jossey-Bass Publishers, San Francisco (1981)

18. Michinov, N., Brunot, S., Le Bohec, O., Juhel, J., Delaval, M.: Procrastination, Participation, and Performance in Online Learning Environments. Computer & Education 56(1), 243–252 (2011)
19. Steel, P.U.: The Nature of Procrastination: a Meta-analytic and Theoretical Review of Quintessential Self-regulatory Failure. Psychological Bulletin 131(1), 65–94 (2007)
20. Tervakari, A.-M., Silius, K., Tebest, T., Marttila, J., Kailanto, M., Huhtamäki, J.: Peer Learning in Social Media Enhanced Learning. In: 2012 IEEE Global Engineering Education Conference (EDUCON), Marrakesh, Morocco, April 17-20 (2012) (in press)
21. Still, K., Huhtamäki, J., Isomursu, M., Lahti, J., Koskela-Huotari, K.: Analytics of the Impact of User Involvement in the Innovation Process and its Outcomes. Case study: Media-Enhanced Learning (MEL) service. In: Proceedings of the 4th World Conference on Educational Sciences, Barcelona, Spain, February 02-05 (2012)
22. Wasserman, S., Faust, K.: Social Network Analysis Methods and Applications. Cambridge University Press, New York (1994)

Collaborative Learning in Higher Education

Learning Outcomes for Blog-Based Courses: A Case Study

Kairit Tammets and Peeter Normak

Tallinn University, Institute of Informatics, Narva road 25,
10120, Tallinn, Estonia
{Kairit.Tammets,Peeter.Normak}@tlu.ee

Abstract. We specify the learning outcomes achieved through *blog-based* courses for students who have never experienced this type of course before. We also describe the main problems the students faced during the course, analyse the reasons for these problems and propose some scaffolding possibilities. The study relies on two consecutive presentations of the course "Intelligent Computer Use" in Tallinn University.

Keywords: Blog-based course, learning outcomes, university studies.

1 Introduction

It is commonly accepted that contemporary competitive and sustainable society is a learning society where education extends far beyond formal education. Some authors even claim that more than 80% of competences which people use in their professional activities are acquired through informal learning [12]. Learning environments and learning patterns in informal learning are mostly quite different from those traditionally used in formal classroom-based learning: informal learning takes place mainly in social networks supported by different web-based tools. Effective informal learning assumes the ability of learners to use suitable learning tools and to direct their learning in a chosen learning environment. Acquiring these skills and developing a culture of informal learning should certainly be included as tasks of formal education.

More and more university teachers are using different social media tools in teaching: social networking tools for discussions, blogs and slide repositories for presentations, e-portfolios for assessment etc. However, the extent of using social media tools in different subject areas varies greatly. For example, portfolio based assessment that is relatively widely used in teacher training is used infrequently in informatics' studies [1].

On the other hand, some critical questions can be asked. For example, how many of those teachers who extensively use social media tools in teaching are even asking themselves about the development of students' skills for informal learning? Do the teaching methods that are used support lifelong learning skills? Laurillard [2] has already stressed the need of using adequate teaching methods to keep pace with what

T. Ley et al. (Eds.): OST 2012, IFIP AICT 395, pp. 113–120, 2013.

is needed in professional life. Not only are ICT-skills necessary, such as word-processing, e-mailing, programming, using web browsers etc.; the learner should also be aware of how information and knowledge can shape their lives, their community, and the world around them [3]. This in turn assumes certain knowledge sharing and self-reflection skills. For a suitable tool for development of these skills, many authors suggest using blogs [4, 5]. Nevertheless, according to our experience, blog-based courses have not yet become established as a common practice at universities.

This paper studies the problems of implementing blog-based courses in informatics in university undergraduate studies. The goal of this study is to find answers to the following questions:

a) What competences does a blog-based course predominantly develop in a student?

b) What are the main problems that students identify when using blogs for learning purposes?

The findings are based on two consecutive case studies after conducting the course "Intelligent Computer Use" at Tallinn University.

2 Using Blogs in Educational Settings

During the first decade of the 21st century, universities started massive use of *Moodle* and *Blackboard* type of learning management systems. These systems were – and still are – institution-centred and accessible to authorized people only. The fact that students after graduation lost access to these systems erected a firm barrier between formal and informal learning. To overcome this, universities are opening up education to a wider audience by implementing personal learning environments that integrate blogs, e-Portfolios, and networking functionality [13].

Some universities started to use blogs for supporting student-centred learning a number of years ago [6]. Compared to traditional classroom learning, blogs have many advantages: students can choose the time and place for discussions, interactivity supports peer-assessment and self-assessment; students can reflect on their studies as well as develop their own writing skills etc. [7]. The importance of reflection as part of the learning process has been emphasized for decades [8, 9]. Nevertheless, blogs are mainly used for self-reflection in educational sciences and medicine and not so much in ICT studies.

On the other hand, previous studies about using blogs in teaching and learning have clearly shown that blog-based courses can be innovative, both for students and for facilitators. Study of Williams and Jacobs [18] indicated that using blogs offer for the support students' autonomy and greater interaction with peers. Ebner and Maurer [19] have claimed that using blogs in higher education settings enhances learning and teaching process in multiple ways and makes learning more student-centered. However, a blog-based course *per se* is not necessarily effective: a suitable course design and implementation that releases the full potential of a blog-based course is needed. For example, a course design should promote activities that support self-direction, sharing ideas, commenting, etc. [16, 17]. Luján-Mora & Juana-Espinosa [20] experienced in their study that there are some significant barriers in using blogs:

assessing student participation in the weblog is difficult as several indicators like group grading, individual posting, and quality of posts should be taken into account, using technology is restricted etc. Some students and teachers are reluctant to use blogs because they prefer more privacy in learning. Another concern is related with the hesitations of the public reflections process in weblogs by the facilitators [20] and students [20, 21]. Therefore, a blog-based course can be even more challenging for facilitators. Although the facilitators usually understand the potential of blog-based courses, they still have difficulties in making use of new opportunities in guiding discussions, monitoring students' contributions, leading students to suitable learning resources in an open environment and providing feedback etc. [14, 15].

3 Methodology

This study followed the case study methodology for data collection. Yin [11] has claimed: "a case study is an empirical enquiry that investigates a phenomenon within its real-life context". For the case study we chose a blog-based free elective course "Intelligent Computer Use" that was open to the students of all specialties. The course was designed and implemented in 2010 and 2011 in the Institute of Informatics at Tallinn University. As a model of delivery, rotational team-teaching was used. Rotational team-teaching means that there are a number of teachers involved in teaching the course; they instruct classes separately and attend class only when teaching their particular topic [10]. The aim of the course was to support development of students' knowledge and skills for using IT tools that support effective operation in an information society. The course curriculum included the following topics:

- The information society and its members;
- Composing and applying a personal learning environment;
- Selection and installation of IT-tools;
- Operating systems;
- Managing a personal computer, preventing and solving possible problems;
- Using mobile devices;
- Computer security issues;
- Web applications and their adoption;
- Social networks;
- Web-based collaboration tools;
- Multimedia at home;
- Digital photography;
- Copyright, licenses, open educational resources

The course had a separate blog that contained course materials and links to the personal course-related blogs of the students. Every week there was a 90-minute class on a specific topic followed by a one-week web-based study by the students. Students were expected to define their personal learning goals for the course in their personal course-related blogs, present a self-analysis and perform the following activities every week:

a) Elaborate, discuss and reflect on course materials on the topic;
b) Perform practical assignments on the topic;
c) Comment on peers' blog posts.

Students also had to select three topics during the semester and compose an essay on each of the selected topics. During the final stage of the course, groups of 3-4 students were formed for designing and presenting a course related project. The course ended with a double evaluation – textual and form-based. In the textual evaluation, the students had to assess different aspects of the course: the learning environment, topics of the course, tasks for home assignments, structure of the course, and identifying the problems they perceived. The evaluations were collected and analysed with the content analysis method.

4 Results and Discussion

Although exactly 32 students participated in the course in each year, none of them had previously experienced a blog-based course (almost all students were in the first semester of their university studies). This was a 4-credit course and therefore every student was expected to spend a total of 4x26 = 104 academic hours on the course. These were estimated to be divided as follows: 28 hours for classroom studies, 46 hours for elaborating course materials and performing practical assignments, 24 hours for composing essays and 6 hours for completing the course project. The vast majority of the students gave the course an extremely positive rating – the average score on the scale 1 - 5 was 4.9.

Based on the data collected from students' blogs, discussions and completed course feedback questionnaires, the course contributed predominantly to the development of the following competences of the students:

a) Improving written communication skills (composition of comprehensive texts)

Because the students had to present the solutions of the practical assignments in their blogs, about half of the time was spent on text composition. In fact some students probably spent even more time on writing, judging by some comments such as "*the amount of writing was not in accordance with the number of credits of the course and more credits should be provided*". On the other hand, although some students complained about the required amount of writing, the majority of blog posts were of very high quality (with the average score of 4.5 on the scale 1 - 5). One possible explanation for this high quality is that free accessibility to the blog posts motivated the students to put extra effort into elaboration and 'fine-tuning' of the texts.

b) Acquaintance with the principles of self-directed and community-based learning

The students were free to decide on the topics for essays and on the course project and they could manage their time, exchange information and discuss ideas etc. On the other hand, there were a few students who expected that the teachers should drive the whole process including student-to-student communications: "*it seemed that the goal of the tasks was just to make the students perform assignments, but not to encourage them to have discussions and learn from others or to work collaboratively*" as one student commented.

c) Gaining experience of systematic use of social media tools for learning

In addition to the blogs which the whole course was based on, using certain other social media tools was necessary for performing home assignments as well – course aggregator EduFeedr, viewing slides from Slideshare.net etc. The students considered "blogging" a very efficient tool. One said: "*updating the blog as part of the course assignments was new and interesting and I'd be glad if other courses would use the same approach*". Another added: "*I got the blogging experience that I never had*". Another opinion: "*I have never been a blogger, but now I know what a blog is and what can I do with it*". One student said: "*the most exciting thing about the course was blogging*".

d) Blog-based learning enhanced the learning skills of the students and contributed to their knowledge and skills on the topics of the course

The feedback from students proved that the course led them to a different learning style. One student said: "*I liked the structure of the course and that I had to perform individual tasks and analyse this process; it made me think more thoroughly*". Another added: "*It was good that we used blogs for assignments; therefore I discovered a lot of new solutions and tools for my everyday practices*". An additional opinion: "*Although I don't enjoy writing, these reflective tasks influenced my learning a lot and lecture subjects became clearer to me*". Reading others' blogs was considered important as well: "*peers' blogs provided me the possibility to see things from another angle and even more important – it developed my understanding of things*". Some students who were suspicious about using blogs at the beginning of the course did change their position later. One student said: "*Using a blog for presenting tasks seemed pointless at the beginning of the course, but actually it was really an interesting solution – all the course-related content is in the same place and I have access to it everywhere*". Another student claimed at the beginning of the course: "*blogging supports the individualism of learners*". At the end of the course he had a different opinion: "*social networking tools might even be better tools than blogs but I learnt a lot about how information flows between blogs and bloggers, which is extremely important and needed*".

Although the students assessed the whole course very positively, if we take into account the problems some students identified during the course, there are still some possibilities for further improvement in organizing the course. From the point of view of students, the main problems were the following:

a) Uncertainty and fear of composing low quality texts

Some students admitted that they did not like blogging – especially during the initial phase of the course – because of not having the necessary writing skills. "*I don't like public reflections, because I am afraid I can't produce texts without feeling embarrassment later"*, explained one student. Another student added: "*at first I did not like the idea of blogging because I am poor at writing, but by doing it repeatedly over weeks I started enjoying it*". How uncertain some students were in deciding on the quality of texts becomes evident from the comment of one student: "*excellent blog posts from previous years could be presented for students as examples*" (all blog posts of a previous year were freely available in the archive section). This indicates that providing some general guidelines for composing texts, as well examples of high quality blog posts would be useful. Stressing at the very beginning of the course that the focus in writing should be put on the content of the texts and not so much on the grammar, would most probably also lower the psychological barrier for some students.

b) Technical skills for effective blogging were insufficient

A few students experienced technical difficulties, mainly during the initial phase of the course. One student wrote: "*At the beginning it was technically difficult to use a blog, but this was probably caused by lack of experience"*. Another stated: "*the Wordpress service is a totally poor blogging environment, I faced problems with every blog post that I tried to publish, text-editor is horrible and I was very upset at the beginning of the course"*. A clear message is that the different features of blogging environments should be more thoroughly explained to the students at the very beginning of the course, accompanied with a number of practical exercises. Moreover, a dedicated section for discussing technical problems would be beneficial as well.

c) Irregular feedback from the teachers

Although the ten (10) teachers who were involved in the course were required to provide feedback to the students on a weekly basis, some of them did not do it properly or did not do it at all. This was clearly a non-motivating factor for students to present the tasks in time. One student said: "*the only thing that I did not like about this course was the lack of feedback – I expected that every week a teacher would comment on my blog post and if that had happened, then I would have tried harder to present my assignments on time"*. Another student complained in his blog: "*For example currently I don't know if my assignments are appropriate, because I have received no feedback"*. The last comment is very important and reveals explicitly the importance of providing feedback to students.

An additional problem came up during the study: how to motivate students to actively comment on each other's blog posts. The students were interested in getting more feedback from their fellow students while being quite modest themselves in commenting. Here is an example of a students' sentiment: "*Currently the statistics concerning my blog indicate that there are many visitors but very few comments on my blog posts. I think that more discussions should take place, but I don't know what carrot and stick should be given to students for doing it. Maybe the blog is not the right place for it? Maybe it would be even more efficient if teachers published the assignments in the course blog and students commented on them, instead of posting comments to fellow students' personal blogs?"* Another student posed the question very explicitly: "*how can we increase the traffic between peers' blogs?"*

A lesson from this is that comments on peers' blog posts could be taken into account when assessing the students.

5 Conclusion

A blog-based course offers opportunities to intensively develop some skills: communication skills, skills for self-directed and community-based learning and skills for applying social media tools in the learning process. The development of these skills is not always obvious in traditional classroom settings.

On the other hand, a blog-based course is equally challenging for learners as well as for teachers, especially for those who have not experienced this type of course before. Special attention should be paid to the following aspects:

(1) Explaining the features of blogging software and providing necessary technical assistance to both students and teachers,

(2) Students should be given regular feedback; this keeps them motivated and encourages more systematic work,

(3) Development of the culture of community-based learning assumes certain guidance on the part of the teachers: initiating discussions, providing examples and relevant web links, identifying and providing personal assistance to students not taking part in discussions etc.,

(4) Incentives are necessary for motivating students to comment and give feedback on the blog posts of their peers; for example, by placing an obligation on each student to comment on the blog posts of a selected number of their peers.

Acknowledgements. This study was partly funded by the Estonian Ministry of Education and Research grant 0130159s08.

References

1. Du Plessis, L.A., Koen, I.: Portfolio Assessment of Information Technology Students at a University of Technology: a case study. Education as Change 9(1), 19–41 (2005)
2. Laurillard, D.: Rethinking teaching for the knowledge society. Educause Review 37(1), 16–25 (2002)
3. Ezziane, Z.: Information Technology Literacy: Implications on Teaching and Learning. Educational Technology & Society 10(3), 175–191 (2007)
4. Boud, D.: Using journal writing to enhance reflective practice. In: English, L.M., Gillen, M.A. (eds.) Promoting Journal Writing in Adult Education, New Directions in Adult and Continuing Education, pp. 9–18. Jossey-Bass, San Francisco (2001)
5. Roland, J.E., Johnson, C., Swain, D.: "Blogging" As an Educational Enhancement Tool for Improved Student Performance: A Pilot Study in Undergraduate Nursing Education. New Review of Information Networking 16(2), 151–166 (2011)

6. Forster, W.P., Tam, T.: Weblogs and student-centred learning: Personal experiences in MBA teaching. Information Systems Education Journal 4(15), 1–8 (2004)
7. Chuang, H.: Weblog-based electronic portfolios for student teachers in Taiwan. Educational Technology Research and Development 58(2), 211–227 (2010)
8. Boud, D., Keogh, R., Walker, D.: Promoting reflection in learning: A model. In: Boud, D., Keogh, R., Walker, D. (eds.) Reflection: Turning Experience into Learning, pp. 18–40. Kogan Page, London (1985)
9. Moon, J.A.: Learning journals: A handbook for academics, students and professional development. Kogan Page, London (1999)
10. Normak, P., Tammets, K.: Rotational Team-Teaching of University Courses Based on the Connectivism Learning Theory (2012) (submitted)
11. Yin, R.K.: Case study research: Design and methods. Sage, Newbury Park (1984)
12. Cross, J.: Informal Learning – the other 80%. Internet Time Group (2003), `http://www.internettime.com/Learning/The%20Other%2080%25.htm`
13. Atwell, G., Bimrose, J., Brown, A., Barnes, S.-A.: Maturing Learning: Mashup Personal Learning Environments. In: Wild, F., Kalz, M., Palmér, M. (eds.) Mash-Up Personal Learning Environments. Proc. Of 1st Workshop MUPPLE 2008, Maastricht, The Netherlands, September 17. CEUR Workshop Proceedings, pp. 78–86 (2008) ISSN: 1613-0073
14. Väljataga, T.: If a student takes control: facilitator"s tasks and responsibilities. In: Spaniol, M., Li, Q., Klamma, R., Lau, R.W.H. (eds.) ICWL 2009. LNCS, vol. 5686, pp. 390–399. Springer, Heidelberg (2009)
15. Väljataga, T., Põldoja, H., Laanpere, M.: Open Online Courses: Responding to Design Challenges. In: Ruokamo, H., Eriksson, M., Pekkala, L., Vuojärvi, H. (eds.) Social Media in the Middle of Nowhere, pp. 68–75. University of Lapland, Rovaniemi (2011)
16. Tammets, K., Väljataga, T., Pata, K.: Self-directing at social spaces: conceptual framework for course design. In: Ed-Media, Vienna, June 4, vol. 30, pp. 2030–2038. AACE (July 2008)
17. Väljataga, T., Pata, K., Tammets, K.: Considering learners' perspectives to personal learning environments in course design. In: Lee, J.W., McLoughlin, C. (eds.) Web 2.0 Based E-Learning: Applying Social Informatics for Tertiary Teaching, pp. 85–108. IGI Global (2010)
18. Williams, J.B., Jacobs, J.: Exploring the use of blogs as learning spaces in the higher education sector. Australasian Journal of Educational Technology 20(2), 232–247 (2004)
19. Ebner, M., Maurer, H.: Blogging in Higher Education. In: Bastiaens, T., Carliner, S. (eds.) Proceedings of World Conference on E-Learning in Corporate, Government, Healthcare, and Higher Education 2007, pp. 767–774. AACE, Chesapeake (2007)
20. Luján-Mora, S., Juana-Espinosa, S.: The Use of Weblogs in Higher Education: Benefits and Barriers. In: Proceedings of the International Technology, Education and Development Conference (INTED 2007), IATED, Valencia, Spain, March 7-9, pp. 1–7 (2007)
21. Farmer, B., Yue, A., Brooks, C.: Using blogging for higher order learning in large cohort university teaching: A case study. Australian Journal of Educational Technology 24(2), 123–136 (2008)

Aligning Open, Physical, and Virtual Spaces in the CIS Sandbox

Mark Frydenberg

Bentley University, Computer Information Systems Department
Waltham, MA USA
mfrydenberg@bentley.edu

Abstract. As students operate increasingly in digital environments populated by social media tools, they need to leverage them effectively to access online resources and stay connected to the physical environments which they inhabit. This paper reports on a practitioner research project to reconfigure a traditional Computer Information Systems (CIS) tutoring lab at a business university into the "CIS Sandbox." The physical facility launched with an aligned online presence intended to engage students and contribute to their learning about CIS topics. The paper presents the rationale, design, and implementation of these collaborative tools, and their impact on the students' and tutors' educational experience. Qualitative analysis from interviews with Sandbox staff and quantitative analysis of data from a preliminary survey suggests that creatively drawing upon collaborative tools and methods enables the integration between physical and virtual spaces.

Keywords: Social Media, Collaborative Learning, Learning Space, Socio-Technical Systems, Computer Lab.

1 Introduction

Digital students assume unlimited online resources [1], engage with social media, and learn through collaborative and informal settings [2] [3]. They tend to mix virtual with physical spaces and need creative spaces in order to develop their own innovative and technology skills. As today's world requires reliance on social technologies and being connected to the Internet, it is important to for learning spaces to provide these online opportunities for connection to augment the physical spaces where students interact.

The opportunity to renovate a university computer lab for the first time in over a decade into a collaborative learning space also presented an opportunity to build a supporting online presence based on social media and social networking tools. This paper describes how this virtual environment complements the newly renovated physical space.

In researching the design of physical and virtual learning spaces, these questions guided this study:

T. Ley et al. (Eds.): OST 2012, IFIP AICT 395, pp. 121–130, 2013.

- What strategies may be employed to transform a computer lab to a physical and virtual collaborative learning space?
- How can social media and Web 2.0 collaboration tools create an online presence that will promote learning both within and outside a physical computer laboratory space?

2 From a Physical to a Virtual Learning Space

2.1 Rethinking Physical Learning Spaces

Figure 1 shows the former lab prior to renovations. It is approximately 900 square feet, housed 36 desktop computers around the perimeter, and a long table at the center of the room. Networking equipment is mounted on the back wall.

Fig. 1. Before the Renovation

Rebranded as the CIS Learning and Technology Sandbox, the new facility marks a transition from the individualized computer lab where students face the walls, to an informal space where learning takes place around tables or in a lounge setting. In engineering, "a sandbox environment consists of a controlled set of resources for trying … new app[lication]s without the risk of damaging critical parts of the system." [4] The new name promotes discovery, learning, and a sense of playfulness within a business context. The increasing number of students who own laptops, tablets, and other mobile devices [5] pointed to the need to provide more desk space and fewer desktop computers. The renovated facility, whose physical footprint did not increase, is shown in Figure 2.

Students gather informally in an area with comfortable seating and a Google TV(1), engage in tutoring at tables where they can share their laptop screens on a large monitor (2), work together on diagrams on the SMART board (3), project screens on the SMART board or the back wall when giving informal demos(4),

Fig. 2. After the Renovation

use networking equipment or one of twelve desktop computers with specialized software for CIS courses (5), and explore new technologies such as an early release of Windows 8 on a touch screen (6).

This design recognizes suggestions from the Joint Information Systems Committee [6] which advises that physical learning spaces be flexible, to accommodate both current and evolving pedagogies; future-proof, to enable space to be re-allocated and reconfigured; bold, to look beyond tried and tested technologies and pedagogies; creative, to energize and inspire learners and tutors; supportive, to develop the potential of all learners; and enterprising, to make each space capable of supporting different purposes. Several of these traits were also found in recently redesigned physical learning spaces at Rutgers University [7], University of South Carolina [8], University of Missouri [9] and other American universities, but none of these spaces also launched with an accompanying virtual presence to promote learning.

2.2 Creating a Virtual Presence with Social Media Tools

The CIS Sandbox is staffed by 6 graduate and 12 undergraduate students, also called tutors or lab assistants, whose responsibilities bridge supporting both the physical and virtual learning spaces. In the physical space, they perform mentoring and tutoring, and monitor equipment. Extending their roles to support a virtual space, they blog regularly, create tutorial videos, and use web-based collaboration tools to support an internal knowledge base.

The CIS Sandbox extends beyond an informal learning space located in the basement of a university classroom building; it lives online as an evolving ecosystem formed of several integrated social networking, social media and web-based collaboration tools. "Developing spaces where students can collaborate outside class provides support for an increased emphasis on teamwork, both in and outside higher education." [10] Abedin studied social patterns in computer supported collaborative learning environments and found that non-task interactions take place in computer-supported collaborative learning environments, often as the result of interacting with peers in an online social environment. [11]

Socio-technical systems consider both social and technical factors in creating evolving computer-based systems that benefit from social media and user-generated content. [12] The system includes the network of users, developers, information technology and environments in which it will be used and supported. [13] Social networks and social media tools play a significant role in the creation of socio-technical systems. Wheeler [14] uses the term "learning space mashups" to refer to the combination of Web 2.0 and social media tools to create collaborative and reflective learning spaces. This paper uses the term "socio-technical infrastructure" to describe the relationships between social media and social networking tools, shown in Figure 3, used in the daily operation of the Sandbox.

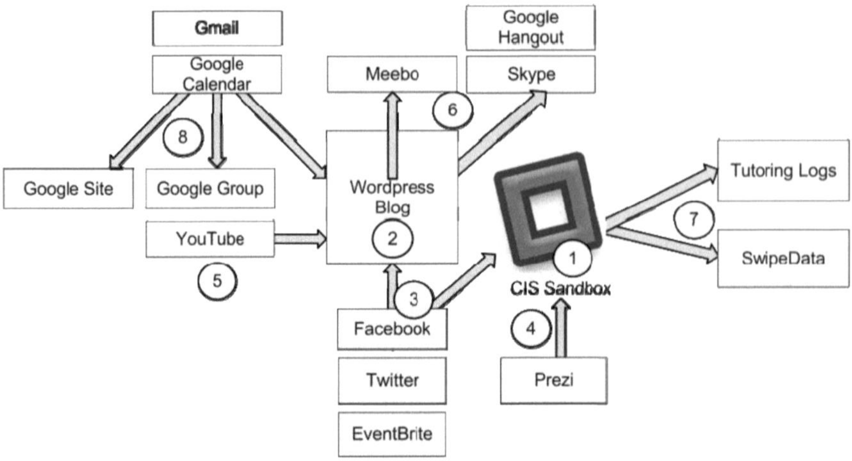

Fig. 3. Socio-Technical Infrastructure for Managing the CIS Sandbox

Each of the online tools listed promotes the physical space of the CIS Sandbox (1). The public face of the CIS Sandbox is its Wordpress blog[1] (2), shown in Figure 4. It is edited by student workers who regularly post homework tips as well as articles reflecting their own interests in information technology. Facebook status updates and Twitter posts (3) occasionally report on new blog posts or special happenings in the CIS Sandbox, and add a social dimension, as students like or follow the facility. EventBrite allows visitors to sign up for special events. Prezi (4) is used to create digital signage to draw students into the physical space.

Tutors use YouTube (5) to host their original instructional videos demonstrating explanations related to course topics. Live chat with a tutor by text with Meebo or Skype, or in a Google Hangout (6) is available via a link from the Sandbox blog, providing virtual support to off-campus students and those who are unable to visit the physical location.

Upon entering, students who visit the CIS Sandbox swipe in with their ID cards. Tutors complete an online form recording their tutoring activities with students (7). Originally the tutor form was implemented as a Google Form, and later replaced with

[1] `http://cis.bentley.edu/sandbox`

a custom web application, written by a student assistant, to automatically populate the form with the names of students who recently swiped in. These reports provide faculty with information about students in their classes who came for help and the type of questions they asked, and provide usage statistics, enabling the scheduling of more tutors at busier hours.

Google applications (8) facilitate the administrative management of the CIS Sandbox. A Google Site (wiki), shown in Figure 4, is the internal face of the CIS Sandbox. There, lab assistants contribute to an evolving knowledge base by documenting technology in the room, policies and procedures, and related information. They also share weekly status reports on their own "mini blog" pages within the wiki, describing their work on tutoring and special projects. Sharing status reports on an internal site allows their co-workers and supervisor to stay aware of what each lab assistant doing. In addition, it forms a permanent record that easily chronicle's a student worker's contribution over time.

Tutors keep their hours on a shared Google Calendar, whose collective content for all staff automatically populates the schedule page and front page sidebar of blog; a Google group encourages easy communication by email between assistants. This distribution list is often used to disseminate announcements, ask for shift coverage, and share information about Sandbox or campus happenings. Both the feed from the Google group and the calendar are embedded on the front page of the wiki for Sandbox staff to easily review.

By blogging on topics of interest to their peers, creating instructional videos, tutoring online, and sharing their activities on social media sites, CIS Sandbox staff extends the reach of the physical learning space into an online learning space.

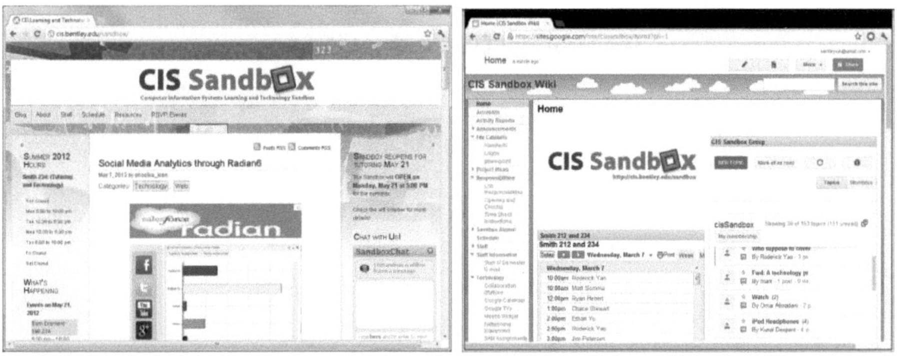

Fig. 4. The CIS Sandbox blog (left) is the public face of the CIS Sandbox. The CIS Sandbox Wiki (right) houses institutional knowledge, policies, and procedures for internal use.

3 Research Methodology

To determine the effectiveness of the physical renovation and its virtual counterpart, a voluntary online survey was offered at the end of the Fall 2011 semester to all students who had visited the CIS Sandbox at least once during its first semester of operation. 142 of the 608 students, or 23%, responded to the survey. 39% were female, 61% male.

3.1 Facility Usage

Swipe data showed that 608 unique students visited 2804 times from September to December 2011. This is more than twice the number of visits during the same semester a year earlier prior to the renovation.[2]

129 students shared how often they visited, as shown in Figure 5.

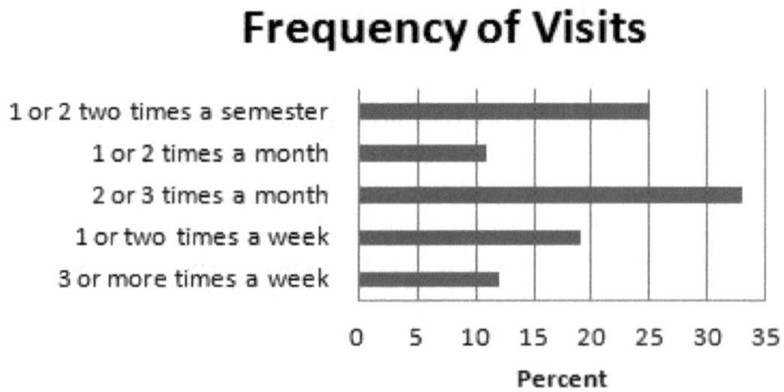

Fig. 5. Frequency of Visits to the CIS Sandbox

During its first semester, 85 of the 126 students surveyed said they had visited the blog at least once.

Figure 6 lists several technologies available in the CIS Sandbox and the number of respondents who used them during the Fall 2011 semester.

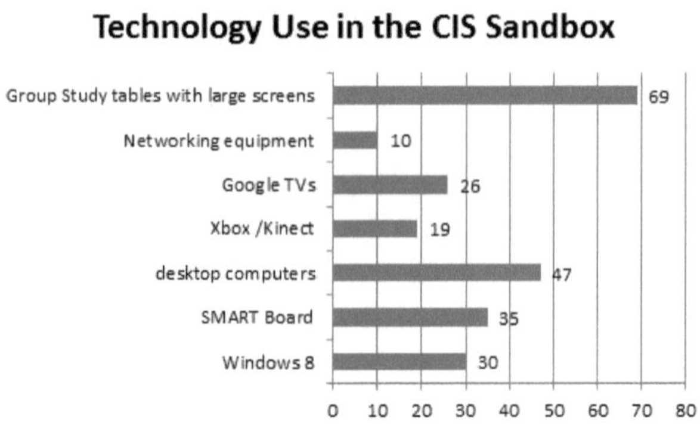

Fig. 6. Technology Use in the CIS Sandbox

Students use these technologies for both classroom and extracurricular learning. While nearly all of the students sit at the group study tables, apparently only 69 of142, or 49% use the large monitors for collaborative work. This may be due to the fact that instructors of programming courses prohibit students from displaying code on the

---

[2] Previously students signed in on paper, so this value is an estimate based on counting pages of signatures in a notebook.

large screens when getting help with homework, so other students are not able to copy it. Students generally use the wireless networking equipment when making up an assignment that their peers completed earlier in the classroom. Some sections of the introductory IT course give extra credit assignments for students who learn to use the SMART Board, Google TVs, or Windows 8 machines. Several student assistants independently explored the Microsoft Kinect SDK to configure software demos and begin to develop their own applications.

To attract advanced and interested students to the Sandbox, Microsoft evangelists offered seminars teaching students to create xBox games and mobile applications during the Fall 2011 semester. During the Spring 2012 semester, an alumnus working for Mashable, a provider of APIs for web and mobile application development, presented about the company's web services and career opportunities. These activities, many championed by the students themselves, created occasions for learning about both course-related and extracurricular topics in the CIS Sandbox, and often resulted in creating blog posts and multimedia artifacts online.

3.2 Aligning the CIS Sandbox's Physical and Virtual Spaces

Users access the CIS Sandbox virtual spaces via the Sandbox blog, chat rooms and online tutoring spaces, social networking sites, and a YouTube video channel. This section describes how each of these aligns with and extends the physical space.

The Sandbox Blog. The CIS Sandbox Wordpress blog started as a way to chronicle the renovations of the physical space online and continues to evolve as a web site to inform visitors about happenings as well as a blog where lab assistants are encouraged to post approximately twice a month about frequently asked tutoring questions, hints for students, and technology interests. For example, lab assistants learning about Windows 8, the xBox and Kinect posted about these topics. Unfortunately, there is no way to understand if these posts contributed to higher use of these technology tools by other students visiting the CIS Sandbox. Figure 7 shows the number of posts in a variety of categories during the blog's first six months.

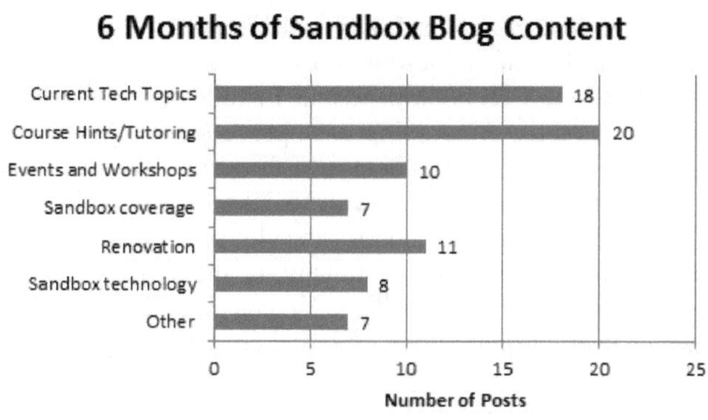

Fig. 7. Blog Posts by Category

A snapshot from Google Analytics shown in Figure 8 suggests that the blog has generated a following, with 51% of returning visitors and 48% of new visitors during its first four months. It receives on average 100 hits per day. Visits are cyclical, with fewer visitors on weekends.

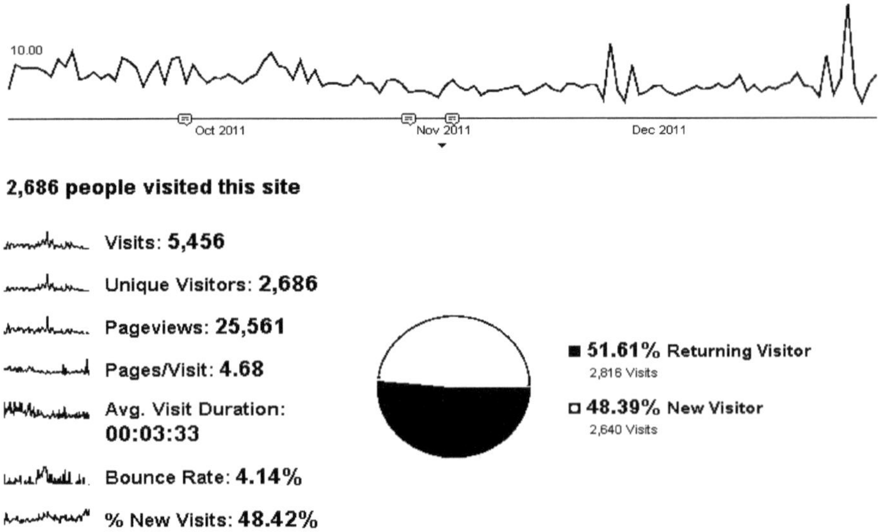

Fig. 8. Google Analytics reports on new and returning visitors

The blog is currently not open for readers to comment. Doing so would foster communication between readers and blog authors. Implementing this would require assigning a student moderator to review comments before they are posted. This change has been requested and is anticipated for a future semester.

Online Tutoring. Tutoring via Skype and screen sharing has been shown to be effective [15] [16] and the logistics of implementing this on a regular basis are currently being investigated. Several tutors have informally used these tools during the first four months of operation, and survey results suggested 62% of students surveyed would find this service useful. Social Networks. The Sandbox social media campaign got off to a slow start. Despite links on the blog to follow on Facebook and Twitter, only 34 liked the Facebook page and 14 followed @CISSandbox on Twitter during its first four months. Attempting to improve these numbers during the spring semester, some tutors encouraged students to follow the Sandbox during their tutoring sessions and distributed business cards with social media information. This raised the numbers to 115 followers on Facebook and 48 on Twitter during the following semester, but a better social media strategy is required to reach students more effectively using social networks. YouTube Videos. During the Spring 2011 semester, 4 tutors created 15 instructional videos on Excel concepts taught in an introductory IT course for which approximately 400 students are enrolled across multiple sections. Several of these videos had over 200 and as many as 255 views.[3] This suggests that at

[3] Some faculty made these videos required viewing; others did not mention them to their students.

least half of the students watched at least some of these videos. Staff also created videos of special events in the CIS Sandbox, and "how to" videos (such as how to hook up a laptop to an external monitor). All of these videos were embedded on the Sandbox blog and are available directly from the CIS Sandbox YouTube channel.

4 Conclusion

The CIS Sandbox has grown beyond a tutoring lab, to one where lab assistants and students can also explore their interests in technology in person and online. For students utilizing the services of the CIS Sandbox, learning occurred through in-person and online tutoring, and informally by reading the Sandbox blog, watching instructional videos, or attending extracurricular workshops.

For the lab staff, learning occurred not only on course subject matter that they were faced with explaining to their peers, but also through their own interactions with social media tools that make up the Sandbox's socio-technical infrastructure, and software applications and technologies that they investigated as part of special projects. 85% of the tutors surveyed commented that working in the CIS Sandbox enabled them to learn about IT trends and concepts beyond what is covered in their classes, and that they developed beneficial social media and technology skills that will help them in their future careers.

The integrated use of social media, social networking, and web-based collaboration tools as part of the CIS Sandbox's day-to-day operations provides opportunities for both lab staff and university students to interact with these applications, and prepares them to be productive contributors to the business world they are about to enter.

References

1. Tapscott, D.: Grown Up Digital: How the Net Generation is Changing Your World. McGraw Hill, New York (2008)
2. Andone, D., Dron, J., Boyne, C., Pemberton, L.: Digital Students Across Europe. In: World Conference on Educational Multimedia, Hypermedia, and Telecommunications, Florida, pp. 1741–1749 (2006)
3. Atwell, G.: Personal Learning Environments - the future of eLearning?, pp. 1–8 (2007)
4. Malizia, A.: Has Everything Been Invented? On Software Development and the Future of Apps. Computer 112, 110–111 (2011)
5. Smith, A.: Americans and their Gadgets, Washington, DC (2010), http://www.pewinternet.org/~/media//Files/Reports/2010/PIP-Americans%20and%20their%20Gadgets.pdf
6. Joint Information Systems Committee: Designing Spaces for Effective Learning: A guide to 21st century learning space design. In: Joint Information Systems Committee / Programmes/ e-Learning Innovation (2006), http://www.jisc.ac.uk/media/documents/publications/learningspaces.pdf (accessed March 2006)
7. Rutgers University: The Alcove, http://alcove.rutgers.edu/
8. University of South Carolina: Technology Lounge Dedicated at Thomas Cooper Library. Reflections (Spring) 1, 3 (2010)

9. Milne, J.: MU's Technology Lounge mimics corporate office trends. Columbia Business Times 13(25) (2007)
10. Clayton-Pederson, A., O'Neill, N.: Curricula Designed to Meet 21st Century Expectations. In: Educating the Net Generation, Educause, Boulder (2005), http://www.educause.edu/educatingthenetgen
11. Abedin, B.: Investigating the Trend of Non-Task Social Interactions in Online Collaborative Learning Environments. In: Proceedings of the 44th Hawaii International Conference on System Sciences, p. 108 (2011)
12. Baxter, G., Sommerville, I.: Socio-technical systems: From design methods to system engineering. International Journal of Human-Computer Studies, 1–33 (November 2008)
13. Scacchi, W.: Socio-Technical Design. In: The Encyclopedia of Human-Computer Interaction, Yorkshire Publishing Group, Yorkshire (2004)
14. Wheeler, S.: Learning Space Mashups: Combining Web 2.0 Tools to Create Collaborative and Reflective Learning Spaces. Future Internet, 3–13 (2009), http://www.mdpi.com/1999-5903/1/1/3/
15. Staupe, A., Kolas, L.: Online interactive learning arena over the internet. In: Proceedings of the Sixth Conference on IASTED International Conference Web-Based Education, Anaheim, vol. 2, pp. 276–281 (2007), http://dl.acm.org.ezp.bentley.edu/citation.cfm?id=1323159.1323208&coll=DL&dl=GUIDE&CFID=67263778&CFTOKEN=60224140
16. Sivula, M.: Using Skype as an Academic Tool: Lessons Learned. eLearn (7) (July 2011), http://elearnmag.acm.org.ezp.bentley.edu/archive.cfm?aid=2011843

University Students as Composers of a Digital Video

Carita Kiili[1], Merja Kauppinen[2], and Leena Laurinen[1]

[1] Department of Education
[2] Department of Teacher Education
P.O. Box 35, FI-40014 University of Jyväskylä, Finland
{carita.kiili,merja.a.kauppinen,leena.laurinen}@jyu.fi

Abstract. This paper introduces a university course in which digital video composing was used as a study method. The aim of the course was to empower future teachers to use digital and multimodal literacy practices in their own teaching. Students in education, 13 in total, participated in the course on digital literacies. The course achievement was measured with the task in which students composed a video in small-groups. The students' videos were supposed to convince a pedagogical target group about the usefulness of a teaching method or need for a reform. In the last meeting, student's videos were watched and the contents of the videos were discussed. The experiences on composing a digital video were also shared. In the last meeting, the students answered to a questionnaire on their experiences on video composing. After the course the students wrote a self-evaluation about their own learning. This paper seeks to clarify students' experiences on learning of multimodal literacy practices, ICT use and course content. Most of the students reported that they learned to create and interpret multimodal texts. New ICT-tools were also learned to use. The study showed that video composing can be used to study content knowledge at the university course.

Keywords: digital literacy, digital video composing, multimodal literacy, teacher education.

1 Introduction

Future teachers and educational professionals are in an important position when it comes to developing pupils' abilities to make meanings with different digital tools and educating digitally literate citizens. Paul Gilster [1, p. 1] was the first to introduce the term digital literacy by defining it as "the ability to understand and use information in multiple formats from a wide range of sources when it is presented via computers". Later, for example, Martin and Grudziecki [2] have defined digital literacy as awareness, attitude and ability of individuals' to use digital tools for utilizing digital sources, constructing knowledge, creating media expressions, and communicating with others in specific life situations. The sociocultural perspective on digital literacy emphasizes digital literacy as set of various social practices and prefers the use of the plural form "digital literacies" [3]. People engage in diverse digital meaning making practices, such as blogging, twittering, online discussion, to name a few. Additionally, different types of digital texts will themselves take multiple forms

T. Ley et al. (Eds.): OST 2012, IFIP AICT 395, pp. 131–140, 2013.

depending on the purpose of the text [3]. According to Gee [4] digital literacy practices are situational and socially constructed and therefore, they are best learned by participating in meaning-making activities in varying social contexts.

In this article, we concentrate on one digital literacy practice, i.e., composing a digital video, in which purposeful multimodal digital literacies are focused. We will introduce a university course for educational students in which digital video composing was used as a study method. Arranging the course was motivated by the fact that teachers in Finland still use mainly printed texts and individually-oriented literacy methods [5]. We offered students an experience of the composition of a digital video in order to empower them to use multimodal literacy practices in their forthcoming work. This paper examines students' learning experiences on engaging in multimodal literacy practices and using information and communication technology (ICT) as well as learning of the course content on digital literacies. In the present study examples are given of multimodal means that students used in their videos.

2 Multimodal Literacy Practices

Literacy and literacy education are undergoing many changes. On the Internet and other new media, knowledge is increasingly presented in multimodal forms [6]. Texts combine images, sounds, gestures, and textual elements in complex ways [7], [8]. Thus, people engage in diverse multimodal literacy practices in their free time and work life. This demands flexibility to move across different modes, genres, and discourses [9]. Bearne [6] argues that these changes influence even on that how people think.

Kress [7] illustrates changes in meaning making practices with two shifts. For writers, the change means the shift from telling the world to showing the world. Writers can combine different modalities according to the situation and purpose of the text. They can make choices between different modalities and if necessary also transform knowledge from one modality to another. For readers, the change in meaning making practices means the shift from reading as an interpretation to reading as a design. In traditional texts, the reading order is more or less fixed whereas in multimodal texts readers have to choose in what order they proceed in the text. Thus, readers create their own reading paths.

Composing multimodal texts, such as digital videos, comprise the following four aspects: materiality, framing, design, and production [10], [11]. Materiality refers to the materials and resources (e.g. images, music, concepts) that can be used to make meanings whereas framing refers to how different elements operate together and how they are connected. Design concerns how people use available resources and materials in order to create a representation. Finally, production refers to the creation of a final product (e.g. video, podcast) by using the tools needed.

Recent changes in meaning making practices suggest that a wide spectrum of different kinds of texts should be used in classrooms. However, Luukka and her colleagues [12] found that Finnish teachers in mother tongue and foreign languages use digital texts quite seldom. Reasons for this might be that teachers see literacy in a quite narrow way or they do not feel themselves confident with digital tools [13].

Earlier studies have shown that a lack of confidence on own abilities, i.e. low self-efficacy, concerning technological skills is related to teachers' low use of digital tools in their classroom [14], [15].

Experiences on digital video composing might lower future teachers' threshold to use digital and multimodal literacy practices in their own teaching. Digital video composing provides teachers with opportunities to orchestrate visual, auditive, kinesthetic, and textual modes by applying computer software, such as Movie Maker or iMovie [13]. The aim of the present teaching experiment was both to offer knowledge on digital literacies and to provide learning experiences on digital video composing. We studied what kinds of learning experiences educational students had when they studied digital literacies with composing a video.

3 Methods

3.1 Participants

The course concerning digital literacies was arranged in one Finnish faculty of Education. Students (n=13; 11 females and 2 males; 9 teacher students and 4 educational students) who participated in the course, aged from 22 to 43. The course was taught by two teachers who also acted as researchers.

3.2 Task

The course achievement was measured with a task in which the students were asked to compose a digital video, five minutes in duration, in four small-groups with 2–4 students. The students utilized Movie Maker -program in their video composing. They were asked to choose a teaching method or a reform concerning digital literacies and name a pedagogical target group for their video. The purpose of the video was to convince the target group about the usefulness of the teaching method or need for the reform. The students were also asked to include some pedagogical implications into their video. Students' creativity was encouraged.

3.3 Procedure

The course consisted of four meetings that contained two lectures on digital literacies. In the beginning of the first lesson, the students answered to a questionnaire on their use of ICT. In the third meeting, the students prepared for video composing after which the student groups composed a traditional short essay as a theoretical background for their digital videos and composed their videos with Movie Maker. In the last meeting, all four videos were watched in the class after which the students discussed how their groups had created meanings in their videos. The students also evaluated how convincing the videos were in the point of view of the target group. Finally, students shared their experiences on learning of multimodal literacy practices. In the end of the last meeting the students answered to a questionnaire on their experiences of video composing. After the course the students wrote a self-evaluation about their learning and group work.

3.4 Data Sources and Data Analyses

The data consisted of the classroom discussion arranged during the last meeting, digital videos (n = 3) composed by the groups, students' self-evaluations (n = 11) and answers to the questionnaire on their ICT use and on their experiences of video composing (n = 12). The questions on students' ICT use contained 19 Likert-scale items (a five point scale ranging from totally agree to totally disagree). The items concerned acquiring information, sharing information, and creating knowledge both in social networks and in public Internet. The questions on students' experiences on video composing contained 17 Likert-scale items. The students were asked to compare video composing with writing a traditional essay (6 items) and to assess what kinds of digital and multimodal literacy practices they learned during the course (11 items).

The duration of videos was about 5 minutes. The topics of the videos were: "Blogs should be used in the literacy class"; "Visual essay"; and "More ICTs to schools". In order to provide examples of how students created meaning in their videos we utilized the framework of multiliteracy provided by The New London Group [8]. It provides a theoretical tool to consider different meaning making modes in multimodal texts. The framework presents the following modes of meaning: linguistic, visual, audio, gestural, and spatial modes. In the framework, multimodality represents the patterns of interconnections among these five modes. The framework also specifies some design elements for each of the modes that can be used to create meanings. For example, elements of audio design include music and sound effects.

From the classroom discussion only those parts, that were relevant to this study (altogether 181 speech turns), were transcripted. From the classroom discussion and self-evaluations we selected examples that best described the students' experiences on learning of multimodal literacy practices, ICT use and course content.

The written consent to all data was sought from the students. One student did not sign the consent; therefore all data related to her was ignored, including the video of her group.

4 Results

4.1 ICT Use

The students reported that they use ICT mainly for searching information and for social networking. They use ICT far less for creating knowledge. Only few students (3) told that they have used digital tools for editing or creating videos. The students also quite seldom share knowledge with others on the Internet.

4.2 Students' Digital Videos

Table 1 provides some examples of how the students used different modes of meaning in their videos. The videos included photos, pictures, text, music, and sound effects. Students also acted in their videos (in two of them). The students combined different modes of meaning in order to create meanings in a multimodal way. For example, in one video the students had combined linguistic and visual modes when they presented the advantages of blog writing. It was told in the video that blog writing provides opportunities for problem-based learning. The words "problem-based learning", were illustrated with the photo of Rubick's cube. Later in the same video, the narrator, who is sitting in the restaurant, argues: "Blogs can be used wherever".

Table 1. Examples of the use of different modes of meaning in students' videos

Mode of meaning	Examples
Linguistic	Anagram (HOT=Higher Order Thinking); catch words; the use of questions as indicators of shifting the topic
Visual	Creating contrasts between two learning situations with colors (black-and-white vs. multicolored); visual metafora (Rubick's cube indicating problem solving); a question mark in the middle of the photo to stimulate thinking; zooming to awake attention
Audio	Making contrasts with music (joyful rhythm music vs. frightening, electronic music out of tune); silent moments as an effect; music underling a textual message
Gesture	Enthusiastic look to pronounce the message; anguished face mediating difficulties in writing; a smiling teacher is assigning a visual writing task; an offering hand movement when introducing a new writing method
Spatial	Arranging elements according to their importance; letters coming one by one upon the screen

4.3 Experiences on Learning Multimodal Literacy Practices

Most of the students (8/12) reported that they learned new multimodal means to create meanings. In Example 1, a student describes how her group combined visual and textual modes of meanings and pondered how these modes interact.

Example 1. *The text was always first. Then, the pictures gave some reasons for the text. It was a sort of dialogue between the text and picture. The purpose was to strengthen certain arguments. We stated a question at the beginning. Why? These kinds of short questions are those that one will pay attention to* (classroom discussion).

All students, except one, reported that they learned to interpret different modes of meaning during the course. The students told that they learned to see multimodal meanings during composing a digital video but also when they looked and interpreted videos composed by other students. The following example from the classroom discussion shows how the students interpreted meanings.

Example 2.

Mira: *Music varied according to the theme or topic. You paid attention to it. You noticed that now it* (the theme) *really changed.*

Anna: *Time was left for thinking. I have seen a commercial like this where a similar kind of music was used in order stimulate people to think the very idea* (classroom discussion).

According to Sanders and Albers [11], composing a digital video offers opportunities to practice critical reading when students examine material choices, consider how materials are framed and designed, and how these decisions are realized and situated within the composer's beliefs. In Example 3, a student ponders how different modes of meaning were combined for creating stereotypes in the video composed by another student group.

Example 3. *It was carried to extremes by using grayness when there was the boring teacher with a monotonous voice. Then there was a lovely, smiling teacher. And with these means the two stereotypes were created* (classroom discussion).

The students found discussions of each others' videos useful. When other students analyzed the video they provided new perspectives even for the composers, as reported by one student in Example 4.

Example 4. *When we discussed the videos together others noticed ideas from your video that are new to you. Then you realized that so it is (laughing). You have not realized that you have thought quite narrowly the message of your own video. Actually, it includes thousands of messages* (classroom discussion).

In general, the students experienced digital video composing as an innovative and social practice. One of the groups told that they learned that digital video composing demands a new kind of collaboration compared to traditional group writing tasks. On the contrary, there was another group who did not work collaboratively but divided the task and responsibilities among four group members. Two students of this group were not satisfied with this co-operative way of working as they experienced that they did not learn enough of multimodal literacy practices.

4.4 Experiences on Learning ICT Use

Only few students were familiar with Movie Maker -tool before the course. A little more than half of the students (7/12) reported that during the course they learned to use ICT-tools that were new to them. One of the students commented her experiences on learning the use of Movie Maker in the following way:

Example 5. *The most valuable learning experience was the practicing MovieMaker - program* (self-evaluation).

Two-thirds of the students experienced that they got more self-confidence in applying ICT. A chance to use new technologies may even affect students' attitudes, as shown below.

Example 6. *I could say that that the most important learning experience was the change in my attitudes. A computer is an opportunity not a threat, especially in my future profession as an adult educator* (self-evaluation).

Two-thirds of the students thought that they will apply their experience on digital video composing in future. During classroom discussion three students told that they will later use the digital writing method that they introduced in their video.

4.5 Experiences on Learning Content by Composing a Digital Video

One of the goals of the course was that students broaden their conception of literacy. This goal was pretty much achieved as 75% of the students reported that composing a digital video helped them to extend their understanding about literacy. Further, two-thirds of the students reported that they learned the course content as well as if they would have written a traditional essay in the course. The students did not experience that the pedagogical concepts were better concretized when composing a digital video compared to composing a traditional essay.

The following Example 7 illustrates how students can consider pedagogical issues when they compose a digital video. In their video, students wanted to discuss how boys in secondary school could be engaged in literacy. They suggested that composing a visual essay could motivate boys to write.

Example 7. *We thought recent discussions about writing difficulties of boys in the 9th grade, they cannot write very well. How could we develop their understanding of writing and increase their enthusiasm for writing? When boys can first express their ideas with a video or a picture, they could then accomplish their thoughts by writing* (classroom discussion).

When the students watched each others' videos they were able to share their pedagogical ideas, as shown in the following:

Example 8. I *liked a lot when you gave few examples how one could use it (blog) in the classroom: storytelling, interviewing one's godmother or godfather or grandparents* (classroom discussion).

5 Discussion

This study indicated that digital video composing as a study method provided educational students with opportunities to learn multimodal literacy practices, ICT use, and content knowledge on digital literacies. Most of the students reported that experiences on multimodal literacy practices broadened their conception of texts and literacy. This probably means that the students became to understand literacy not only as reading and writing linear, traditional texts but also as multimodal, digitally constructed social practice.

Majority of the students experienced that they learned new means to create and interpret different modes of meaning. Composing a digital video may also offer opportunities to become a more critical reader. When the students made their material choices and combined different modes of meaning in order to convince the pedagogical target group with their video, they became more aware of how meanings are embedded into the multimodal texts. They have also learned critical thinking when they talked about meanings included in each others' videos. Gee, Hull and Lankshear [16] stress that a way of reading a certain type of text is acquired only when it is acquired in a "fluent" or "native-like way" by one's being embedded in a social practice in which people also talk about such texts in certain ways, hold certain beliefs and values about them, and socially interact over them. These kinds of personal learning experiences on multimodal literacy practices may increase the possibility that future teachers will integrate multimodal, digital literacy practices in their own teaching and create pedagogies relevant to millennial students. However, working in a co-operative way may hinder opportunities for some students to learn multimodal literacies. If labor is divided in the group so that some group members are only responsible for providing a theoretical background for the video without participating in actual creation of the video, the learning aims concerning multimodal literacies might probably not be achieved.

Previous research among university students [17], [18] have shown that students use information and communication technology mainly for searching information and for social networking. In contrast, technology is less used for creating knowledge. In line with these results, only few students, who participated in the present study, had previous experiences on digital video composing. Many of the students experienced that they learned to use new ICT tools, and especially tools that can be applied for creating knowledge. Further, two-thirds of the students experienced that they got more self-confidence in applying ICT. The increase in self-confidence may lower teachers' threshold to use digital and multimodal literacy practices in their own teaching. Actually, two-thirds of the students reported that they could utilize the experiences on digital video composing in their future work. However, the fact that the course was part of optional studies might partly explain students' positive attitude towards implementing digital video composing in their class. It might be that the course was chosen only by those students who do not resist the use of ICT in teaching.

This study showed that digital video composing can be used to study content knowledge at the university course. The students reported that they learned the course content as well as if they had composed a traditional essay as a course assignment. One reason for this might be that in the course the traditional essay writing (a short background paper for a digital video) was combined with composing the video. This ensured that the students also familiarized themselves with relevant educational literature.

Although this study was based only on self-reported data it showed some potential benefits of using digital video composing as a study method in teacher education.

When students gain hands-on experiences on digital video composing they become more self-confident in using ICT tools in their own teaching. They learn to create meanings through combining different modalities and to ponder how meanings are made in videos. These learning experiences can be applied, for example, in media education. There is a need for a longer lasting intervention that would provide teacher students with experiences on creating knowledge with varying digital tools. A longer intervention would offer opportunities to measure intervention effects on students' self-efficacy and later use of ICT in the classroom.

References

1. Gilster, P.: Digital literacy. Wiley Computer Pub., New York (1997)
2. Martin, A., Grudziecki, J.: DigEuLit: Concepts and tools for digital literacy development (2007), `http://www.ics.heacademy.ac.uk/italics/vol5iss4/martin-grudziecki.pdf`
3. Lankshear, C., Knobel, M.: Introduction: Digital literacies – Concepts, policies and practices. In: Lankshear, C., Knobel, M. (eds.) Digital Literacies: Concept, Policies and Practices, pp. 1–16. Peter Lang, New York (2008)
4. Gee, J.P.: A situated-sociocultural approach to literacy and technology. In: Baker, E.A. (ed.) The New Literacies: Multiple Perspectives on Research and Practice, pp. 165–193. The Guildford Press, New York (2010)
5. Taalas, P., Tarnanen, M., Kauppinen, M., Pöyhönen, S.: Media landscapes in school and in free time – two parallel realities? Digital Kompetanse 4(3), 240–256 (2008)
6. Bearne, E.: Rethinking literacy: Communication, representation and text. Reading Literacy and Language 37(3), 98–103 (2003)
7. Kress, G.: Literacy in the new media age. Routledge, London (2003)
8. The New London Group: A pedagogy of multiliteracies: Designing social futures. In: Cope, B., Kalantzis, M. (eds.) Multiliteracies: Literacy Learning and the Design of Social Futures, pp. 9–38. Routledge, London (1996)
9. Stein, P.: Multimodal Instructional Practices. In: Coiro, J., Knobel, M., Lankshear, C., Leu, D.J. (eds.) Handbook of Research on New Literacies, pp. 871–898. Erlbaum, Mahwah (2008)
10. Kress, G., Jewitt, C.: Introduction. In: Jewitt, C., Kress, G. (eds.) Multimodal Literacy, pp. 1–18. Peter Lang, New York (2003)
11. Sanders, J., Albers, P.: Multimodal literacies: An introduction. In: Albers, P., Sanders, J. (eds.) Literacies, the Arts & Multimodalities, pp. 1–24. National Council of Teachers of English, Urbana (2010)
12. Luukka, M.-R., Pöyhönen, S., Huhta, A., Taalas, P., Tarnanen, M., Keränen, A.: Maailma muuttuu - mitä tekee koulu? In: Äidinkielen Ja Vieraiden Kielten Tekstikäytänteet Koulussa Ja Vapaa-Ajalla. Soveltavan kielentutkimuksen keskus, Jyväskylän yliopisto (2008)
13. Miller, S.M.: English teacher learning for new times: Digital video composing as multimodal literacy practice. English Education 40(1), 61–83 (2007)
14. Van Acker, F., van Buuren, H., Kreijns, K., Vermeulen, M.: Why teachers use digital learning materials: The role of self-efficacy, subjective norm and attitude. Education and Information Technologies (2011), doi:10.1007/s10639-011-9181-9

15. Albion, P.R.: Self-efficacy beliefs as an indicator of teachers' preparedness for teaching with technology. In: Technology and Teacher Education Annual 1999, Association for the Advancement of Computing in Education, Charlottesville (1999), http://eprints.usq.edu.au/6973/1/Albion_SITE_1999_AV.pdf
16. Gee, J.P., Hull, G., Lankshear, C.: The new work order: Behind the language of the new capitalism. Westview Press, Boulder (1996)
17. Kennedy, G., Judd, T., Dalgarno, B., Waycott, J.: Beyond natives and immigrants: Exploring types of net generation students. Journal of Computer Assisted Learning 26(5), 332–343 (2010)
18. Oliver, B., Goerke, V.: Australian undergraduates' use and ownership of emerging technologies: Implications and opportunities for creating engaging learning experiences for the net generation. Australasian Journal of Educational Technology 23(2), 171–186 (2007)

Challenging Learning Myths through Intervention Studies in Formal Higher Education

Sebastian H.D. Fiedler and Terje Väljataga

Centre for Educational Technology, Tallinn University, Tallinn, Estonia
fiedler@tlu.ee, terje.valjataga@tlu.ee

Abstract. The introduction of open and networked learning practices in formal higher education regularly collides with the personal beliefs and convictions that students hold in relation to their own capacity for learning and the structural and procedural conditions that they expect to be met in such settings. A series of systemic intervention studies at Tallinn University highlighted the disabling role that these personal learning myths can play when students are confronted with practices that promote a new culture of learning. This paper offers some selected examples from a qualitative data analysis and discusses the possibility to embrace personal learning myths as a core concept for further research and the development of more effective intervention instruments and approaches.

Keywords: learning myths, intervention, higher education, new learning culture.

1 Introduction

"*For most of the twentieth century our educational system has been built on the assumption that teaching is necessary for learning to occur*" (p. 34) [1]. In this conception teachers transfer information to students, who need to prove (usually by testing) their acquired knowledge in accordance with pre-defined standards. In general teachers control the learning activity of others and assume that a process of quality instruction actually "produces" desired outcomes on the receivers' end [2].

This dominating pattern has become deep-seated in our culture and has produced pervasive beliefs of how education in general and learning experiences in particular should be structured and organised. Throughout history these rigidly held beliefs have determined every aspect of pedagogical practice: the roles of teachers and students; teaching (learning) methods; assessment procedures, supporting environments, and so forth. The continued exposure to this type of teacher dependent learning environments throughout formal schooling leads many people to develop a set of potentially disabling beliefs and convictions that function as a personal "commentary" on their own capabilities for learning. These deeply engrained beliefs are labeled as "learning myths" [2]. They were able to show in their empirical work that such myths were regularly invoked in educational settings and influenced the capacity to learn of many adults.

T. Ley et al. (Eds.): OST 2012, IFIP AICT 395, pp. 141–146, 2013.

Professional educators also hold beliefs and prejudices about learning [2] and their students' capabilities. Their professional myths influence how educational systems and the embedded teaching and learning practices develop over time, thus contributing considerably to the acquisition of specific personal myths about learning among students [2].

Among many other researchers and educators, [1] claim that the current, mainstream educational system can't keep up with the rapid rate of change in the twenty-first century. The omnipresent and continuously expanding digital transformation requires and enables fundamental shifts and changes from old models to new approaches of learning. The process of establishing a new learning culture, however, is fundamentally restricted by the values, myths and beliefs about education and learning among the various stakeholders. Establishing innovative approaches, which are conflicting with the current traditional views and principles of formal education and learning requires not only the implementation of new technological instrumentation but also rather different mindsets, values and beliefs. The development of a new learning culture poses formidable challenges to existing learning myths, which need to be explored, elaborated, de-constructed and re-built.

2 Open and Networked Learning: Intentional Change Meets Learning Myths

Over a period of 5 years the authors of this paper have been engaged in a series of intervention studies that tried to promote a shift towards more open and networked forms of teaching and learning at Tallinn University (TLU), Estonia. One master level course administered by the Institute of Informatics at TLU has been used as an evolving test-bed for the iterative implementation and evaluation of intervention ideas and concepts related to various aspects of personal learning and its digital re-instrumentation through networked, open access and open source tools and services in formal higher education. Existing teaching and studying practices have been fundamentally re-designed to support the advancement of competencies for self-directing one's study and change in increasingly networked environments in work and education. This required a re-configuration of patterns of control and a redistribution of responsibility over instructional functions (such as setting objectives; selecting and executing appropriate actions and activities; selecting, combining, and integrating resources and technological tools and services; and defining criteria and procedures of evaluation). A learning contract procedure [3] has been adapted and used to support this shift of control and responsibility. Students have been encouraged to explore a wide range of digital instrumentation options (such as wikis, weblogs, and so forth) that fundamentally allow the opening up of networked learning activities beyond the confines of their local institutional context (for a more detailed overview of the intervention studies see [4-6]).

Observational data gathered throughout our intervention studies continuously indicated that the reconfiguration of typical patterns of control and responsibility in general, and the emphasis on the exploration of personal digital instrumentation options in particular, seemingly clashed with the learning myths of a good number of students. Those students expressed very strong beliefs on how formal educational environments should be structured and organised and what conditions need to be met to make "learning" in such settings possible for them. Furthermore, we were able to observe a reoccurring developmental trajectory among a number of students whose initial rejection of all concepts and practices that ran against their myths slowly gave way to personal experimentation and exploration, and finally resulted in the adaptation and reconstruction of their own systems of meaning.

These initial observations were extended into a more systematic review of data that could be interpreted as the expression of personal learning myths running counter to the intentional change goals promoted through our interventions. In particular, we analysed the students' written reflections on the course and on their study progress in relation to the courses from the academic years of 2009, 2010 and 2011. An initial qualitative content analysis [7] was conducted and complemented with the facilitator's observations of students' reactions, thoughts and complaints gathered during face-to-face meetings. The purpose of the content analysis was to detect students' challenges; problems and contradictions and map a range of personal learning myths. The analysis was also looking for any indication that the students claimed to have changed their personal learning myths by the end of the course.

3 Traces of Personal Learning Myths: Examples from Our Data Analysis

Being exposed to a rather different way of going about learning in a formal higher education setting immediately triggered some of the participants' resistance and protest. These adult learners had largely arrived at convictions about their own learning, their myths of themselves as learners, and the formal educational system altogether. For instance, one of the students shared her experiences: "*When I went to the first face-to-face meeting I was first pleasantly surprised about the unusual way of going about learning. In the next moment I was shocked, when I heard that there are no traditional lectures waiting for us, we have to think ourselves what we want to study and how; we are going to use weblogs. How is it possible, no lectures? How come all of the sudden I have to write down my learning objectives? Presenting my homeworks on the weblog? Where am I now...?*"

Our data analysis showed that one major issue for a number of students was the level of "openness" that was promoted within the re-designed course. Presenting course-related tasks and reflections publicly, being open for critical and constructive comments from peers and wider audience was met with surprise and resistance. Being asked to document and expose in public what had been so far a predominantly private activity challenged many students' personal learning myths. The following statements illustrate it rather well: "*In the beginning it was quite strange to share my thoughts with the whole world through my weblog, it was so unusual and produced resistance*" and the other one claimed: "*Blogging and me...totally opposite words. We'll see later whether I'll be addicted to blogging after this course or I'll turn back to my aforementioned statement*". Statements like "*I really had to work hard on myself before publishing my first homework on my weblog. I have never use it and I have some prejudices about that"* have been rather typical throughout the 5 years of intervention work carried out at TLU. Although being skeptical of sharing one's thoughts in public, students tended to enjoy reading, for example, weblog posts of their peers. One of the students admitted: *"It is exciting to read peer students opinions and be part of the other person's wisdom"*.

Research has suggested there is a difference in how openness and public weblog authoring should be interpreted in education [1]. Using weblogs in education should be understood as generating the space for a conversation to emerge [1] and a support for the construction of a community. However, this requires a give-and-take approach, adopting the idea of sharing, active engagement, and participation, instead of merely belonging. For instance, one of the students admitted: *"I didn't become a commentator. I read and explored what the others were doing, but I was too shy to comment on others' work myself"*. This leads to the next related issue, which trigged students' resistance. The notion of getting feedback from others besides the teacher or facilitator is rather contradictory to many students' ideas of learning and turned out to be challenging to accept. One student claimed: *"The thought that everybody can read my work, even comment on it and cited it, it requires a lot of courage to publish"* and another added: "*I also have to mention how HORRIBLE was to read comments, especially if the comment consisted of a poisonous remark. I guess it is a matter of one's feelings and obviously not discussed with oneself, because not everything shouldn't be taken so seriously"*. Realizing that this approach not only allows learning from each other but also learning *with* others [1] takes time. Obviously the myth that a lot of knowledge exists in a rather fixed form and needs to be provided by a teacher is still a rather dominating conception among students.

Taking control and responsibility (setting objectives; finding the right strategies and resources; and defining the desired outcome) is not a common occurrence within a traditional way of learning in formal educational settings. This is expressed in statements of the following kind: "*I have never created something like this [learning contract] for myself or thought about my learning objectives*". Such statements demonstrate what students tend to perceive as the typical roles and responsibilities of teachers and students alike.

In addition, the students also expressed their resistance in relation to technology and the exploration of digital instrumentation options for their purposes. One of the students shared her preferences: "*I would rather like an environment like Moodle or Blackboard, where everything is in one place and I don't have to learn and fiddle with different tools*" and the other one added: *"Jumping into an unknown situation, the speed, new information and tools, made me feel I am drowning, chronic lack of time, feeling stupid...I could continue with this list endlessly. I am never able to learn how to use these tools, what for? This is too much for me"*.

Although, some of the students had initial difficulties to get started within an overall system of considerably increased personal degrees of freedom and responsibility, they regularly admitted at the end of the course that their learning myths did not remain entirely stable throughout the overall educational episode. For instance, one of them said: *"I feel a bit better and more relaxed now. This kind of learning can be quite nice. Blogging is difficult, but possible to overcome, commenting is even more difficult, but I am developing. The next step is to overcome of myself and swim on the surface. I have to admit it is a very unusual situation".* The aforementioned statement can also be interpreted as the student's understanding that learning has changed and requires different ways of thinking, new attitudes and skills, yet also constant reflection on one's activities and progress. This is clearly stated by one of the students from the 2011 course, too: *"This course turned out to be a totally new experience - a weblog-based learning environment. It took me almost two months to get used to this. I still have to practice to be faster in reflecting, reading and commenting peer-students Weblogs. My understanding of learning has definitely changed - a web-based learning, working together on assignments..."*

Throughout our intervention studies we were able to collect recurrent empirical indication that personal learning myths played a key role for the individual reception of structural and procedural changes to existing teaching and studying practices among our student body. While we are currently in the process of refining our categorisation of seemingly disabling or limiting personal learning myths (as they were recorded through our data gathering efforts), we can already share that there is some indication that certain personal learning myths seem to hold some diagnostic, or even projective value, in relation to potentially problematic trajectories of adaptation (or rather objection, rejection, and resistance) in the context of decisively open and networked forms of learning practice in higher education. This preliminary insight, however, requires further analysis and more thorough empirical validation.

4 Discussion and Concluding Remarks

While we certainly cannot get into a more comprehensive exposition and discussion of our qualitative data analysis in this short paper format, we would like to argue that systemic intervention into current teaching and studying practices with the purpose to establish more open and networked learning formats can generally benefit from the exploration of students' personal learning myths and their potentially disabling influence. Students who are unable to revise their personal myths run the risk of remaining victims of their own, strongly rooted constructions [2]. This often results in low levels of motivation, performance, and commitment, if not an overall drop out from their educational endeavor [1]. Understanding their personal obstacles and beliefs, educators and teachers can better support students to overcome their difficulties while they are getting gradually immersed into a new culture of learning. Many students need to be supported while they are undergoing (an often under-estimated) process of personal transformation in which they need to adapt to the practices and conventions of open and networked learning, re-build their learning myths accordingly, and become integrated into the new culture. Although, personal myths do not tend to be changed overnight, they can be purposefully and self-critically brought into awareness [2] by consciously and systematically exploring and analyzing them. Our preliminary analysis showed that learners being imprisoned by their rather rigid personal learning myths tend to "assimilate" new practices and technologies during the early stages of adoption and attempt to replicate existing practices and trusted patterns of action. Even, if students embrace new practices by the end of a course, it is often not enough to achieve a sustainable and lasting effect on students. The new practices need to continue in the context of other course environments or educational episodes to encourage students to refine, elaborate, deconstruct and re-build personal learning myths that can be actually experienced as enabling within an increasingly networked society.

The intervention work at Tallinn University of the last 5 years has made some progress in this regard. Some of the open and networked learning practices that were established and refined within the context of our test-bed course have been expanded into other parts of the various Master curricula that are administered by the Institute of Informatics. Some of our intervention instruments (such as the personal learning contract procedure and the systematic use of individual weblog authoring) have proved to be considerably effective in eliciting qualitative material that expresses disabling personal learning myths held by our students. However, we feel that our educational intervention work could benefit from further research into the range and specific quality of personal learning myths that manifest themselves in the context of open and networked learning practices. We are thus planning to extend our data gathering with explorative interviews that are carried out at various points in time while students are attending our test-bed courses. Furthermore, we are interested in the longitudinal oriented mapping of individual trajectories of development when students are actually exposed to a whole series of educational episodes that embrace open and networked formats of learning. Fundamentally, we believe that the systematic exploration and integration of the concept of personal learning myths should enable us to develop more effective intervention instruments and strategies over time.

Acknowledgments. This research was funded by Estonian Ministry of Education and Research targeted research grant No. 0130159s08.

References

1. Thomas, D., Seely Brown, J.: A New Culture of Learning: Cultivating the Imagination for a World of Constant Change. Createspace (2011)
2. Harri-Augstein, E.S., Thomas, L.F.: Learning Conversations: the Self-organised Way to Personal and Organisational Growth. Routledge, London (1991)
3. Harri-Augstein, S., Cameron-Webb, I.M.: Learning to Change. In: A Resource for Trainers, Managers, and Learners Based on Self Organised Learning, McGraw-Hill, London (1996)
4. Fiedler, S., Väljataga, T.: Interventions for Second-order Change in Higher Education: Challenges and Barriers. Electronic Journal of e-Learning 8(2), 85–92 (2010)
5. Väljataga, T., Fiedler, S.: Supporting Students to Self-direct Intentional Learning Projects with Social Media. Journal of Educational Technology & Society 12(3), 58–69 (2009)
6. Väljataga, T.: If a Student Takes Control: Facilitator"s Tasks and Responsibilities. In: Spaniol, M., Li, Q., Klamma, R., Lau, R.W.H. (eds.) ICWL 2009. LNCS, vol. 5686, pp. 390–399. Springer, Heidelberg (2009)
7. Krippendorff, K.: Content Analysis: An Introduction to Its Methodology. Sage Publications, Inc. (2003)

Managing Open and Social Education

Educational Transformation with Open and Social Technologies in the Non-formal School Curriculum

An Analysis of Three Case Studies in the United Kingdom

Don Passey

Department of Educational Research, Lancaster University, UK
d.passey@lancaster.ac.uk

Abstract. This paper explores ways that open and social technologies relate to educational transformation, analysing three case studies of exemplar school-based projects. Schools in England have been asked to develop 'educational transformation'. Although there is no single definition, aspects of community and social interactions and networking are intended, as is development of appropriate uses of digital technologies. Managing educational transformation with digital technologies requires knowledge, levels of expertise, and willingness to manage innovation. Curriculum position and intention, management models and roles of intergenerational learning are fundamental to developments. Future implications for educational support and schools are considered.

Keywords: Educational transformation, social networking, school community developments, intergenerational learning, digital technologies.

1 Introduction

Educational transformation is of international concern at policy and practice levels. A recently published INTEL White Paper reported findings of educational transformation research in 5 countries [1], while Becta (former government agency in England for e-strategy) stated clearly its aims to provide: "strategic leadership in the innovative and effective use of ICT to enable the transformation of learning, teaching and educational organisations for the benefit of every learner" [2]. But the definition of educational transformation is unclear even at a single national level.

Educational transformation and school build and structure have been considered as related areas in England. In 2003, the government department for education announced the Building Schools for the Future (BSF) Programme, aiming to renew all 3,500 English secondary schools over a 15-year period from 2005 to 2020 [3]. The National Audit Office report stated that: "Refurbishment includes providing new [information and communications technology] ICT to recently built schools" (p.4). The Partnerships for Schools, an executive non-departmental public body responsible for the BSF programme, gave a clearer statement on its web-site [4] about intentions for ICT, stating that: "The whole process begins with the [local authority] LA and its schools drawing up a strategy for improving secondary education. This is informed by an

T. Ley et al. (Eds.): OST 2012, IFIP AICT 395, pp. 149–159, 2013.

understanding of the ways in which new technologies can improve educational provision" (n.p.). ICT is clearly seen as a means to improve education and learner outcomes. Indeed, the web-site states more precisely that ICT should be considered in terms of: "the development of real and virtual workspaces which help to make effective, personalised learning a reality for all pupils … access to high quality learning materials in a wide range of settings through as wide a range of end-user devices as possible … infrastructure which is extremely reliable and easy to use" (n.p.).

Schools and teachers have not necessarily found it an easy task, however, to use digital technologies and to bring about forms of improvement through transformation. In a speech at the UK's largest schools' ICT exhibition and conference, BETT 2012 [5], the Secretary of State for Education stated that: "The fundamental model of school education is still a teacher talking to a group of pupils." He went on to say that: "It's clear that technology is going to bring profound changes to how and what we teach. But it's equally clear that we have not yet managed to make the most of it." Most importantly, perhaps, he said that: "While things are changing so rapidly, while the technology is unpredictable and the future is unknowable, Government must not wade in from the centre to prescribe to schools exactly what they should be doing and how they should be doing it. We must work with these developments as they arise: supporting, facilitating and encouraging change, rather than dictating it." A key question for schools is, therefore, how is this achievable?

These statements advocate educational transformation, using ICT; they ask for something different, to meet tomorrow's needs rather than those of yesterday. This is not a new concern; but it appears it has not yet been achieved. In a study involving a survey of 2,611 pupils aged 12 to 13 and 14 to 15 years, and data from 60 focus groups held with some 300 learners, from 15 English schools representing a range of school types and demographic variables and from 12 schools representing school environments in which Web 2.0 activity was flourishing, Luckin, Logan, Clark, Graber, Oliver and Mee [6] concluded that: "The types of activity evidenced suggest that of the categories of user identified in the literature, there are readers, gamers, file-sharers, communicators and newscasters (in the sense of sharing experience through social networking sites) amongst study participants. However, relatively few learners are engaging in more sophisticated Web 2.0 activities such as producing and publishing their own content for wider consumption. In order to be motivated to publish content, learners must perceive that publication carries utility for the self or important others. In addition, learners may lack the technical knowledge and skills needed to publish content online" (p.3). Yet in informal settings open and social technologies can effectively support learning (see Yaşar and Karadeniz [7]). So, how can these technologies be positioned across curriculum elements – formal (in-class), non-formal (after-school and home-directed) and informal (undirected but related by the learner)?

2 Educational Transformation

How should educational transformation be conceptualised? An article exploring school design and educational transformation [8] concluded that, from a study of four case schools in Scandinavia: "underlying learning intentions and values of the schools can be successfully incorporated into, and supported by, design" (p.931). However, it would be wrong to assume that new buildings automatically generate transformation in forms intended and stated above by policy makers. Transformation at a structural level is not necessarily used by teachers, and indeed, can be ignored if teachers are more concerned with maintaining a traditional teaching approach. To bring about transformation, there needs to be full and adequate consideration of features other than structure - curriculum, content, process and outcome.

For this study and paper, a definition adopted of using ICT in educational transformation will include previously-cited key features: transformation is concerned with improving educational provision; it has a community focus (either school or wider); it integrates new ICT into its structure and practices; it uses a reliable and usable infrastructure; it offers high quality learning materials, personalised learning opportunity, real and virtual workspaces; and it offers encouragement to engage and develop 'readers, gamers, file-sharers, communicators and newscasters' including 'producing and publishing their own content for wider consumption' [6].

3 Research Approach and Method

The research approach taken in this study is a secondary analysis of findings from three projects previously evaluated by the author as case studies. The three projects all involved uses of emerging technologies including open and social technologies, and were all identified by schools and local education policy makers as being innovative and transformative (leading to improved educational provision and wider community involvement). These three projects were selected additionally on the basis of their providing evidence from a range of schools representative of a width of contexts.

The case studies here are reported using a framework suggested by Yin [9]: an overview of the case study project (its objectives, issues, and topics being investigated); field procedures (including role of the researcher, access to sites, and sources of information including documents, interviews, and direct observation); case study questions (specific questions that the investigator explored during data collection that related to the topic of this paper); and an analysis of results (in terms of relevance and relationship to the focal research questions in the secondary analysis in this paper):

- How is the project concerned with improving educational provision?
- In what way does it have a community focus (either school or wider)?
- How does it integrate new ICT into structure and practices, using a reliable and usable infrastructure?
- How does it offer high quality learning materials, personalised learning opportunity, and real and virtual workspaces?
- How does it offer encouragement to engage and develop 'readers, gamers, file-sharers, communicators and newscasters' including 'producing and publishing their own content for wider consumption'?

4 Case Study 1 – Links to Homes and Home Learning

An overview: in 2004, a project was initiated in an area in the north of Birmingham, the second largest city in England. Placed in the 10% most deprived areas in England [10], the project, called Aston Pride, involved 14,314 residents in 4,500 households. Concerned with community development and regeneration, it focused in part on aspects of education and learning, as key elements to address short and longer-term needs of the community. The education theme was implemented in three phases.

Field procedures: the author evaluated the project over 7 years [11], had access to implementation documents and to parent training attendance records, met with project managers regularly, and in the final phase gathered evidence through 812 home installation and 154 follow-up questionnaires, test data for mathematics and reading from 14 classes of 7 to 9 year old pupils, 32 teacher and 134 pupil mid-phase and 85 teacher and 20 parent late-stage questionnaires, and 20 parent interviews.

How was the project concerned with improving educational provision? The project aimed to increase quality of resources for teachers and pupils in schools and at home, as well as parent involvement with children's learning. In 2010, using standardised test comparisons over a 9 month period, with t-tests, ANOVA and multiple regression factor analyses to check significance of outcomes, positive shifts in mathematics and reading results were identified in a large population of pupils (over 500 in total). Impacts at statistically significant levels were identified: on mathematics scores for all pupils ($t=-8.58$, $p=.000$); particularly for girls in the final test ($F=4.577$, $p=.033$); on reading scores for all pupils ($t=-3.141$, $p=.002$); and particularly for boys ($t=-3.778$, $p=.000$). Teachers and parents reported widely and positively on impact; reports were supported by improvements in terms of national test and inspection scores (between 2004 and 2008 performance in English for 11 year-old pupils improved by 16%, from 50% to 66%, and in mathematics by 8%, from 56% to 64%, and by 2010 the attainment level in mathematics reached 74%, and in English 73%).

In what way did it have a community focus? The project aimed to increase access to resources in homes, and to benefit community members through training. By 2011, 2,680 computers were deployed in homes; some 60% of homes gained up-to-date ICT access, with possible leverage to almost the entire population (as family members shared facilities with other residents). At least 1,227 adults (1,171 parents, 47 school staff and 9 advanced learners) had been involved in ICT-based training run in schools.

How did it integrate new ICT into structure and practices, using a reliable and usable infrastructure? By 2008, funding enabled all 8 primary schools to put interactive whiteboards into all classrooms, personal digital assistants were trialled in 2 schools, computers in homes were deployed through one school, shared school training and support were facilitated, local community centres gained ICT facilities, a mobile ICT facility was established, and a pilot wireless network was set up. By 2010, the wireless infrastructure covered the entire locality; reports indicated that it was robust, providing high bandwidth and good coverage, with few instances of issues reported.

How did it offer high quality learning materials, personalised learning opportunity, and real and virtual workspaces? The third phase focused on aspects of learning, particularly providing home access to online learning resources (such as *Education City* and *Mathletics*). In 2010, 74 out of 85 teachers reported using online facilities to support homework activities. Most (52 out of the 85) reported that this practice had shifted types of homework activity; some teachers asked pupils to undertake tasks such as research at home, not previously demanded of them. This heralded a shift in demands on pupils outside classrooms, and was seen to change qualities of learning expected.

How did it offer encouragement to engage and develop 'readers, gamers, file-sharers, communicators and newscasters' including 'producing and publishing their own content for wider consumption'? The project developed pupils and teachers as 'readers'; pupils accessed online educational games at home, they shared files of completed homework with some teachers, and increased their communication with parents. They did not develop as 'newscasters' in this project.

5 Case Study 2 – The Focus of after-School Clubs and Group Work

An overview: in this case study pupil teams aged 11 to 14 years used Little Big Planet 2, a popular Sony PlayStation videogame, in 15 secondary and special schools in one LA. The project focused on: development of 21st century skills required by employers and trainers; widening career opportunities in the videogame industry; and 'building scenes for learning' by creating levels in the game. Using the videogame, a range of skills were brought together, some technical, but others including artistic, team working, logical thinking and planning skills, to construct 'levels'. Teachers 'advertised' the project, selected team members, provided working space and ICT resources, and facilitated the teams. Largely, they did not teach; the work was outside their experience or understanding, but they could access technical support to aid the pupils. Teams worked mostly in after-school clubs, but some in lesson times. Pupils often had specific roles (such as artistic director or lead programmer), but also worked collaboratively and flexibly to bring elements of planning and structure together.

Field procedures: the author evaluated the project over 6 months [12], had access to implementation and interim pupil notes, met with project managers regularly, interviewed teachers in 4 schools, and gathered evidence through 12 teacher and 107 pupil questionnaires at the outset, 8 teacher and 77 pupil questionnaires at a mid-stage, and 3 teacher and 42 pupil questionnaires at the end of the project.

How was the project concerned with improving educational provision? Looking at individual pupil responses, some pupils gained more in terms of skill development than did others. Across a group of 31 pupils responding in both the first and last surveys, by the end of the project 28 scored above the mid-point of 12 (on a range from -72 to 96, collating scores for 80 different elements in 16 sets of skills). Over the period of the project, 12 pupils neither increased nor decreased in terms of their self-reporting of skills, while 19 increased in this respect (an increase of up to 65 points).

In what way did it have a community focus? Involvement in after-school clubs required a high commitment from pupils, both in terms of attendance and in terms of work undertaken. Many pupils also worked on the project at home, individually or in groups. In team group activities, whether in-class or after-school, high levels of in-depth and focused discussion were generated and recognised in many instances.

How did it integrate new ICT into structure and practices, using a reliable and usable infrastructure? The videogame technologies were not widely integrated with other ICT systems. Communication between teachers and key supporters and between pupil teams happened within workshop events, while bespoke-created blogs and discussion forums were available but not used widely. Pupils used social media widely, however, to maintain contact, including using Facebook and mobile telephone messaging.

How did it offer high quality learning materials, personalised learning opportunity, and real and virtual workspaces? Pupils being immersed in planning and creating, and having direct contact with professionals, offered a way of working many had not previously experienced. This approach was widely welcomed by pupils, and teacher reports indicated that some pupils gained enormously from this aspect alone.

How did it offer encouragement to engage and develop 'readers, gamers, file-sharers, communicators and newscasters' including 'producing and publishing their own content for wider consumption'? In this project almost all pupils involved became 'readers' and 'gamers', but fewer engaged technically to create new levels. File sharing was not apparent, and communication happened largely in team meetings rather than through online means. Those teams completing levels (about half the number starting the project), were all encouraged to broadcast their games across an international user network for others to access and play.

6 Case Study 3 – The Audience and Reality of School Work

An overview: the BBC News School Report project, run since 2006, enables pupil teams to create and broadcast video, audio and text-based news reports. Teams put reports onto school websites at a particular time on a particular day (News Day); the sites are linked to the BBC News School Report website, made accessible to regional and national radio and television broadcasting teams, and to a worldwide audience.

Field procedures: the author and a colleague evaluated the project over 6 months [13], met with project managers on three occasions, gathered evidence using pre- and post-News Day online questionnaires for pupils (591 and 705 responses respectively) and teachers (142 and 135 responses respectively), observed two News Day events, and visited 25 schools to interview pupils and teachers.

How was the project concerned with improving educational provision? Many schools were involved because they felt it extended opportunities for pupils and could widen their experiences. Evidence indicated that the project supported important aspects of learning: authentic learning; understanding through discussion; internal cognitive aspects; and transfer of learning (thinking about how in the future they would use ideas they had learned, and using these at other times and in other contexts). Some schools subsequently considered longer term sustainability of the project, creating permanent teams to gather and report news from the school via the school website or intranet, for parents and the wider community to receive regularly updated news.

In what way did it have a community focus? The requirement of the project was for pupils to create real news stories, gathered from their school or wider community, to broadcast to wider communities and nation-wide. How did it integrate new ICT into structure and practices, using a reliable and usable infrastructure? Some schools used existing ICT facilities to fulfil project needs, while others needed more specialist support and resources (including video cameras, editing software, and advice on integrating items into web-sites). Pupils tended to work independently but not on their own. They often took responsibility for individual work elements (such as researcher, scriptwriter, or editor), all needing to be completed to a high quality and standard, within a strict time scale, for integration into a wider piece of group work. This was very different from working 'on their own', giving work to someone with a different form of responsibility for it. This approach made the project different, but allowed it to work with other school-based activities.

How did it offer high quality learning materials, personalised learning opportunity, and real and virtual workspaces? Pupil perceptions of their own gains were concerned with specific subject skills, and with team working, creativity, attitudes towards work, and social interactions. Differences in responses before and after News Day indicated perceived improvement (endorsed by teacher perceptions) in abilities to write an article for an audience (+10%, Z=-2.754, p=0.006), create ideas for news stories (+15%, Z=-5.262, p=0.000), negotiate a point with others (+10%, Z=-4.228, p=0.000), work hard in contributing to group endeavour (+11%, Z=-4.851, p=0.000), and meet deadlines (+14%, Z=-6.276, p=0.000). Although pupils indicated no significant change in abilities to produce a video and an audio story, teachers felt they had improved in these respects, suggesting that pupils' capabilities exceeded their teachers' expectations. Pupils indicated they had learned more about news production and jobs, and their understanding of how news was produced and about jobs in news.

How did it offer encouragement to engage and develop 'readers, gamers, file-sharers, communicators and newscasters' including 'producing and publishing their own content for wider consumption'? The project results indicated that more pupils were listening to and watching news media at the end of the project (+5%, Z=-2.443, p=0.015 for television, and +4%, Z=-5.107, p=0.000 for radio). The project did not focus on developing gamers, and some file sharing did happen, between pupils and between pupils and teachers. Communication, (working in teams), was enhanced greatly, but the major project focus was to develop broadcasters, which it clearly did.

7 Community Development and Educational Transformation

These case studies of practice are not universal but were implemented in ways suggesting wider potential adoption – the first involved all 8 primary schools in a geographical area; the second involved 15 secondary and special schools across another area; and the third involved 514 schools from across the United Kingdom.

An important point to recognise in each case is that digital expertise comes from the young people, is extended in the young people, and used in sharing activities and experiences with older people. While there is a parallel with the concept of 'digital natives' coined by Prensky [14], it should be noted that in each exemplar, while young people had some knowledge of ICT, this was extended. The extension made the difference - reaching out to others – parents, teachers, and wider community.

The integration of projects in the curriculum is worthy of consideration too. Each project fitted alongside a content-based curriculum; curriculum intentions matched project intentions. Indeed, some enabled important long-term skill developments such as group work, team work and communication skills that would benefit and support employment and training as well as further involvement in school. But projects were in some respects in conflict with the content curriculum and how it was managed, in terms of time and organisation. But schools involved did not see potential challenges as barriers; these projects worked in ways described in extended schools and extended curricula contexts [15]. Integrated projects and after-school clubs of these forms focus on important aspects of educational transformation – they demand a different form of organisation from that found in classrooms generally, putting the teacher squarely in the role of facilitator (including technological facilitation).

8 Social Networking and Digital Technologies

An important aspect highlighted by these cases is the role of networking through digital technologies. Although it could be argued that digital technologies should provide the medium for networking (and indeed social media were used by pupils in after-school clubs and at home), it is clear that in these cases important networking happened outside but was encouraged by the technological medium. Social interactions, between teachers and pupils, between parents and their children, between specialists in certain uses of technology and pupils, and between managers and teachers, were all fundamentally important in bringing about the transformations captured here.

In these cases, face-to-face interactions often flourished, but not in traditional 'apprentice-master' form. In many instances, the young were the 'masters' and the older generations (parents, teachers or managers) were the 'apprentices'. The development of intergenerational learning was important, adding to the need for teachers, parents and managers to take on facilitator roles. The roles of all professionals, those in the video games industry and broadcasters, worked complementarily, across ages. But the presence of open and social technologies in all cases was a vitally important stimulus.

From these cases, educational systems have yet to accommodate current professional and vocational needs of teachers and educationalists - highlighting and considering issues, or understanding ways to effectively integrate open and social technologies into practice. There are management implications, for those in schools, and those concerned with training and future policy. As Kane [16] concluded from four after-school programme evaluation studies in the United States: "After school programs may be unaccustomed to holding center stage in the national education policy debate, but that is unlikely to change anytime soon. Some of the evidence so far is forcing a reconsideration of the magnitude of impacts we might reasonably expect" (p.3).

9 Conclusions and Ways Forward

To successfully undertake initiatives exemplified here, teachers and schools needed to address management issues; curriculum concerns –projects did not absolutely match a content-based curriculum; guidance issues – projects were not supported by all those producing and inspecting the curriculum; practice concerns – projects were not part of the professional and continuing training practice of teachers; and structural concerns - projects did not fit into classrooms and lessons readily within a traditional timetable.

Vocational practice needs to be rethought; current and future teachers need to assimilate and revisit concepts and practices offered by educational transformation (including those integrating uses of open and social technologies) throughout their careers, exploring potentials that project, after-school and non-formal work can bring. In the past, the purpose of after-school clubs has been clear (in terms of games, hobbies and interests, for example); how teachers are currently trained in developing and considering these, and how benefits feed into the curriculum, is not so clear (see, for example, Malcolm, Wilson and Davidson [17]). Shurnow [18] suggested a need to review roles and centrality of after-school initiatives. Evidence here suggests a need to identify different forms of practice, so their places in the curriculum and potential impacts on pupils are clear, so those who guide and inspect the curriculum are clear about their legitimacy, so continuing professional development covers management as well as activity training and a focus on how digital technologies can play legitimate roles in after-school and home learning, so that structural concerns about developing skills in lessons alone can be revisited, and young people's involvement can be considered more from an intergenerational learning perspective (not just a learner-centred perspective) particularly with regard to using open and social technologies.

Is this a new scenario or situation? In some respects it is - after-school clubs do not often currently involve uses of ICT in these forms (and traditional computer clubs, for example, are often quite different in nature). Given this evolving scenario, those driving policy and supporting professional development need to review how the nature and practices of after-school clubs and non-formal and out-of-school learning are managed within the wider rather than the narrower curriculum.

If benefits of open and social technologies are to be gained by pupils, policy makers should consider: the importance of the non-formal curriculum; how effective evidence-based projects and home-link activities can be built into the non-formal curriculum; how transformational projects can support real-world community development; endorse such activities as being important; support creation of practice (placing and managing projects); how high quality learning materials are provided by professionals and ICT-based materials; and how a management focus can critically enhance the formal curriculum through longer-term needs of pupils and communities.

Similarly, curriculum developers should consider: how project-based activities can integrate open and social technologies to improve educational provision; encouraging intergenerational learning, through pupil-led and teacher-facilitated activities (allowing extensions of pupils' technical and associated skills); adopting transformational projects with a real-world community development focus; endorsing outcome-evidence-based activities; how technical and professional support can be offered; how high quality learning experiences can be integrated from professionals and from ICT-based materials; supporting non-formal activities to enhance the formal curriculum and influence longer-term needs of pupils and communities at local or regional level.

Acknowledgements. My sincere thanks to all the pupils, parents and teachers providing invaluable evidence in the originating case studies, and to the managers involved, Dave Brodie, Mike Farmer and Avtar Dhillon in Aston Pride NDfC, Jill Purcell in Wolverhampton LEP, and Andy Goff in Interactive Opportunities.

References

1. INTEL: White Paper - Intel Education Transformation Research: Lessons Learned Across Five eLearning Programs. Intel, USA (2011)
2. Educational Evidence Portal: Becta – British Educational Communications and Technology Agency. EPP Consortium, London (2009), http://www.eep.ac.uk/dnn2/Organizations/Becta/tabid/65/Default.aspx (accessed April 2012)
3. National Audit Office: Building Schools for the Future: renewing the secondary school estate. The Stationery Office, London (2009), http://www.publications.parliament.uk/pa/cm200809/cmselect/cmpubacc/274/274.pdf (accessed October 2011)
4. Partnerships for Schools: ICT, http://www.partnershipsforschools.org.uk/library/BSF-archive/BSF-ICT.html (accessed February 2012)
5. Gove, M.: Speech at the BETT Show 2012 (2012), http://www.education.gov.uk/inthenews/speeches/a00201868/michael-gove-speech-at-the-bett-show-2012 (accessed February 2012)
6. Luckin, R., Logan, K., Clark, W., Graber, G., Oliver, M., Mee, A.: Learners' use of Web 2.0 technologies in and out of school in Key Stages 3 and 4. Becta, Coventry (2008)
7. Yaşar, Ö., Karadeniz, Ş.: The power of social media in informal learning. In: Méndez-Vilas, A. (ed.) Education in a Technological World: Communicating Current and Emerging Research and Technological Efforts, Formatex, Badajoz (2011)
8. Leiringer, R., Cardellino, P.: Schools for the twenty-first century: school design and educational transformation. British Educational Research Journal 37(6), 915–934 (2011)
9. Yin, R.: Case study research: Design and methods, 2nd edn. Sage Publishing, Beverly Hills (1994)
10. Batty, E., Beatty, C., Foden, M., Lawless, P., Pearson, S., Wilson, I.: The New Deal for Communities Experience: A final assessment. The New Deal for Communities Evaluation: Final report, vol. 7. DCLG, London (2010)
11. Passey, D.: Independent Evaluation of the Aston Pride Phase 3 Computers in the Home Project (2009 to 2011): Final Report - March 2011. Lancaster University, Lancaster (2011)
12. Passey, D.: Independent evaluation of the Little Big Planet 2 project in Wolverhampton's Local Education Partnership schools: Outcomes and impacts - Final Report, Lancaster University, Lancaster (2012)

13. Passey, D., Gillen, J.: BBC News School Report 2008/2009: Independent Evaluation. BBC, London (2009)
14. Prensky, D.: Digital Natives, Digital Immigrants. On the Horizon 9(5), 1–6 (2001)
15. Barker, J., Smith, F., Morrow, V., Weller, S., Hey, V., Harwin, J.: The impact of out of school care: A qualitative study examining the views of children, families and playworkers. Department for Education and Skills, London (2003)
16. Kane, T.J.: Extracting Evaluation Lessons From Four Recent Out of School Time Program Evaluations. The Evaluation Exchange 10(1), 1–4 (2004)
17. Malcolm, H., Wilson, V., Davidson, J.: Out of School Care: A Brief Review of the Literature. The Scottish Council for Research in Education, Edinburgh (2002)
18. Shurnow, L.: Academic Effects of After School Programs. ERIC Digest ED458010 (2001)

Social Technologies in Education - An Actor-Network Analysis

Bill Davey[1] and Arthur Tatnall[2]

[1] School of Business IT and Logistics, RMIT University, Australia
[2] School of Management and Information Systems, Victoria University, Australia
Bill.Davey@rmit.edu.au, Arthur.Tatnall@vu.edu.au

Abstract. There are many opportunities for social technologies to create wider and more valuable educational communities. This paper presents an analysis of a Government initiative to create educational communities around schools in Victoria, Australia using social networking systems. The analysis, comparing several systems, shows that a number of factors, including interpretation of reactions by actors are crucial to the success of applications of social technologies in an educational setting.

Keywords: Social technologies, social networking, Ultranet, CASES, MySchool, schools, students, parents, teachers.

1 Introduction

It seems obvious that the addition of social-technology based software in an educational context would be readily adopted by schools and systems, but several studies [1, 2] have shown that this 'obviousness' should always be challenged. While several authors suggest a new digital age of well-prepared consumers [3, 4] there are findings that cast doubt on the unsupported assumption of automatic adoption of new systems [5-7]. Sappey and Relf [8 :19] believe that:

> *"Learning and teaching should be considered inseparable and always considered holistically in developing technology enhanced learning models."*

For many years computer systems in schools have been built around the need to handle the large amount of administrative data relating to individual students and student cohorts. This is collected from many formal and informal sources including: student enrolments, observational surveys, early year interviews, running records, other formal testing and anecdotal notes [9]. Other educational data relating to school and student performance is also important.

2 Three Computer Systems in Victorian School Communities

The goal of this study was to examine three computer systems in use in Victorian schools: CASES21, the Ultranet and MySchool, and to investigate whether, and if so

T. Ley et al. (Eds.): OST 2012, IFIP AICT 395, pp. 160–169, 2013.

how, they contribute to school community involvement and whether this has a beneficial effect on education.

2.1 CASES 21

In Government schools in Victoria the Department of Education mandates use of CASES21 (Computerised Administrative System Environment in Schools) for school administrative purposes. CASES21 aims to provide school administration with secure access to data entry and reporting modules that support school administration and finance functions. CASES21 has two modules [10]:

- An Administration Module to provide student administration support, including the facility to manage: student and family data; student pastoral data; medical information; attendance; achievement; discipline/welfare; accident and incident data; activities (including excursions); school management information; basic timetabling; daily organisation; and school associations (e.g. Parents Club and School Council).
- A Finance Module that aims to assist schools to create and receipt family and student invoices, manage debtors and creditors, manage the school's asset register, process and manage the school's local payroll, manage school finances and budgets and generate appropriate financial reports.

The prime purpose of CASES21 is to enable reporting from schools back to the Department of Education. It runs only on the school administrative network, and an earlier version has been in use since the late 1980s [11]. It was developed as a tool for overall school administration and as a means of reporting back from schools to the Department of Education. No consideration was given to its use in school classrooms either to support teacher administrative functions or to enhance teaching and learning [11-13].

2.2 The Ultranet

The Ultranet was designed to support knowledge sharing across the 1,555 Victorian government schools with their 540,000 students and 40,000 teachers [14, 15]. It was launched in September 2010 and designed to provide facilities for informing parents about their children as well as for curriculum delivery and online learning and teaching [16]. The Ultranet is: "*a student centred electronic learning environment that supports high quality learning and teaching, connects students, teachers and parents and enables efficient knowledge transfer.*" [17]. It has many of the features of a business extranet in that it is closed to people outside the Victorian government school community and requires a username and password to gain access. One major difference, however, is that with over half a million users, the Ultranet is larger than most business extranets [18].

The Ultranet's incorporates various Web 2.0 technologies so making it a closed, secure place on the Internet, accessible at any time by students, teachers and parents/guardians from the school community [19]. It was designed to allow students to access personalised learning activities and keep an ongoing record, allowing them to collaborate and communicate with students from their own school and from other Victorian government schools. They will be able to create learning portfolios and use online communication tools such as Wikis, blogs and discussion boards.

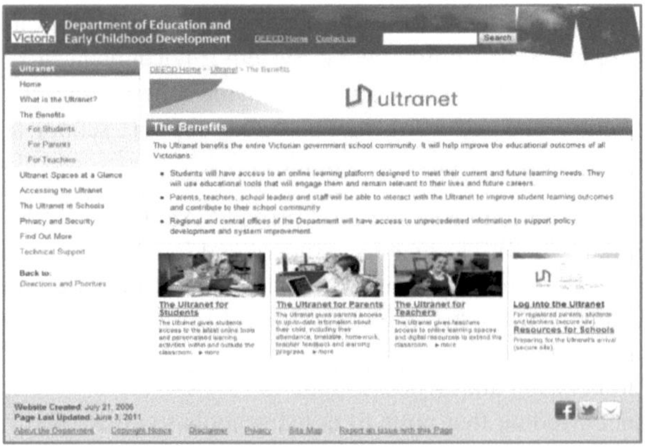

Fig. 1. The Victorian Education Ultranet (http://www.education.vic.gov.au/about/directions/ultranet/benefits/default.htm)

The idea is that, using the Ultranet, teachers will be able to create curriculum plans, collaborate with other teachers, monitor student progress and provide assessment. The Ultranet will also assist parents in gaining benefits of flexible access to student information and school resources that will help them keep up-to-date with their child's learning. This dynamic student profile will include attendance records, test results, timetables, learning progress, homework activities, tasks, and feedback so providing a way for parents to support their child. These features should strengthen and extend parental involvement in schools and will result in richer more holistic and better negotiated approaches to student learning.

2.3 MySchool

The MySchool website provides a system designed to inform parents and the community about Australian schools [20]. It was set up by the Australian Government. (Although school education in Australia is a State responsibility, the Federal Government is also a significant actor in providing information and targeted grants to schools for specific projects.) Early in 2010 the Australian Government launched this new e-government initiative [21] that contains information about each of Australia's 10,000 primary and secondary schools, including: the number of students and teachers at the school and how the school is performing in national literacy and numeracy testing. The ideas of setting up MySchool was so: "*parents and school communities would be able to compare their school's results with neighbouring schools and up to 60 statistically similar schools*" [21] to see which schools are doing well and which schools are not. Data for this comes from NAPLAN (the National Assessment Program).

MySchool is quite different to the Ultranet, however, in that it provides general information about all Australian schools, and not about particular students, to anyone who wants to see this. The aim is to allow parents to compare potential schools where they may want to send their children. MySchool also shows information on all Australian schools, both government and non-government whereas the Ultranet includes only Victorian government schools and aims to inform specific parents of their own school children.

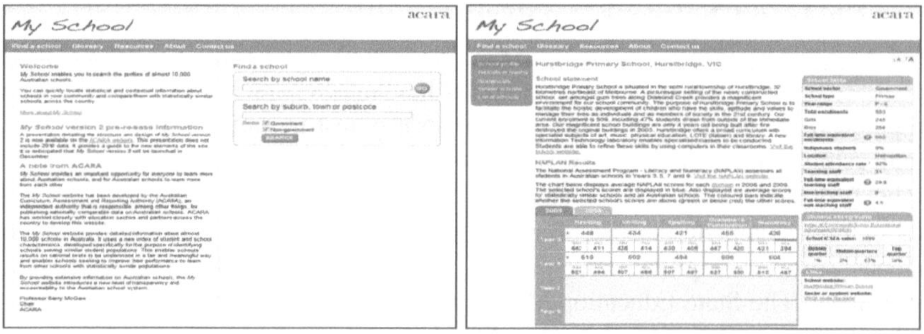

Fig. 2. MySchool website (http://www.myschool.edu.au/) showing information for Hurstbridge Primary School

3 Research Framework and Methods

Many approaches to socio-technical research treat the social and the technical in entirely different ways and as either: technologically driven or socially driven. A common approach is to focus on the technical aspects and to treat ‘the social’ as the context in which development and adoption take place. Actor-Network Theory (ANT), which originated from research in the social studies of science in the 1980s [22-24], was designed as an approach to socio-technical research that would treat the contributions of both human and non-human actors fairly and in the same way.

ANT considers the world to be full of hybrid entities containing both human and non-human elements. Questioning ‘is it social?’ or ‘is it technical?’ misses the point: the question should be ‘is this association stronger or weaker than that one?’ In this socio-technical order *nothing is purely social and nothing is purely technical.* ANT is concerned with studying the mechanics of power as this occurs through construction and maintenance of networks made up of both human and non-human actors [18]. In actor-network theory, an actor is any human or non-human entity that is able to make its presence *individually felt* by the other actors [25]. An actor is made up *only* of its *interactions* with these other actors, and a network can be hidden inside a ‘black box’ when its internal details are not under investigation.

If our research was into how students *learn* using these technologies we may have made use of a theory relating to learning with social technologies, a theory such as connectivism [26, 27]. Here, however, we are investigating adoption and use of these systems and in their use in creating educational communities, not their effectiveness in learning. For this purpose a lens that allows for contributions from both human and non-human actors is appropriate, and ANT fits well.

This research involved a study of the documentation of the three systems. A small number of people were interviewed to determine the range of relationships between the actors, including those interactions with the systems. Reports on the introduction of these systems including both official press reports and those from commentators also were used to find underlying relationships.

4 An Actor-Network Analysis

This study is especially interesting as all the human actors (schools, teachers, students and parents) are the same for each system so it is just the interactions with the non-human actors that lead to any new insights.

The first steps in any ANT analysis are to identify and 'interview' the actors. Although not complete the list of actors with significant relationships here included students, teachers, principals, parents, schools, State Government, National Government, The State Education Ministry (DEECD), the Internet and web tools and the three systems: Cases, MySchool and the Ultranet.

Table 1. CASES21, the Ultranet and MySchool

	CASES21	**The Ultranet**	**MySchool**
Purpose	School administration	Knowledge sharing	Comparison of schools
Usage	Schools must use	Encouraged	Voluntary
Year introduced	1988	2011	2010
Main human actors	Principals, school administrators, DEECD staff	Students, teachers, principals, parents	Parents, students
Main non-human actors	CASES21, school admin computers	The Ultranet, school and home computers	MySchool, schools, home computers
Sponsor	Education Department (DEECD) Victoria	Victorian government	Australian government

4.1 Relationships between Actors: Schools and Government

Schools in Victoria have had a long tradition of independence in curriculum and in the delivery of their versions of the curriculum. In the last ten years or so, attempts have been made to standardise aspects of the curriculum but these have had little effect on how it is delivered. There is a political dichotomy between making schools self-governing and having sufficient control that governments can fulfil their accountability requirements to the electorate for education expenditure. Part of the decentralisation effort of government has been to grant more power to employ individual teachers to schools, but this is constrained by budgets. This decentralisation has been accompanied by attempts to make schools accountable for performance and a number of techniques such as a National Curriculum initiative and the National Testing Plan are being employed [28]. These changes are relatively new in Australia and the relationship between government and schools is still in flux. It would be fair to say that there is not complete trust between schools and government.

4.2 Relationships between Actors: Schools and Teachers (Unions)

Teachers in Victorian state schools are represented by the Australian Education Union (AEU). One of the recent campaigns by the union is the 'Stop league tables campaign' [29], resulting in the AEU submission to the 'Senate Education Employment and Workplace Relations Committee' into the 'Administration and Reporting of NAPLAN Testing' [30]. The union campaign is directed at preventing the Government having a more intrusive influence on teaching. One effect of the MySchool website seen as being a significant problem by the union was the possibility of the school changing its delivery as a result of poor showing in the National tests. The following was used as an explanation of behaviour seen as abhorrent:

> *"Teachers have been told by the Victorian Education Department to 'explicitly teach for NAPLAN', focus on literacy and numeracy and give students a 'daily NAPLAN item' in class ... The directive has led to accusations that Victorian education authorities are pressuring schools to 'teach to the test' to lift their performance on the new website at the expense of a broader curriculum."* [31]

Significantly among their arguments is the contention that public release of information is not an absolute right of the public – presumably parents and other community interests. The AEU submission included evidence from Dr Ken Rowe of the Australian Council for Educational Research who wrote that:

> *"... it can be argued strongly that the public disclosure of information cannot be held to be an* absolute *principle."* [30 :29]

Our interviews with teachers showed that there is a general understanding that the teacher is the qualified person in the school community, but also the person with understanding of the local educational environment, and these two factors mitigate against anyone else having the right to significant input into school level decisions.

The Australian Newspaper of Dec 16th 2009 reported the desire of school principals to be given more rights to hire and fire teachers. This seems to provide evidence that teachers are seen as being antithetical to the idea of sharing power over school decisions.

The relationship between government and teachers can be seen as being instrumental in the fate of the three systems. CASES was constructed firstly to provide a single means of gathering data required by government from schools. In the knowledge that schools saw themselves as having significant data needs, the first version changes in CASES were to include modules that answered local school needs for the data being collected by government. In this way CASES began ‘co-operating’ with schools and teachers. MySchool, similarly recognised the power of teachers at the local level and completely bypassed them, communicating through the public website rather than normal communication channels, all of which required teacher involvement. The Ultranet seeks to involve teachers as part of the systems value, but has the problem of providing little help to teachers in their daily work and exposing them to local accountability that they have not experienced before. An ANT approach to this investigation considered all interactions between these actors as significant.

4.3 Relationships between Actors: Teachers and Parents

Our interviews indicated that teachers see several different types of relationships with parents. The first are with enthusiastic parents who want to be part of the school. At the primary school level these parents are involved with as many voluntary jobs as possible. These are mostly positions such as canteen worker, working bee participant and provider of reading help. A few are elected to the school council, an official, unpaid position with some governance duties for the school. The school council members do not have an easy or direct method for communicating with other parents and teachers do not see them as having the influence of an elected official with the backing of an electorate. By the secondary school level the amount of involvement of parents diminishes. There are still working bees and other volunteer jobs, but attendance involves a much lower proportion of families than for the primary level.

Secondly there are those parents who see the teachers as domain experts who take sole responsibility for student learning experiences. These parents will sign off homework and dutifully attend the occasional Parent Teacher meeting, general held once per term (semester) on a single evening for all families. These parents are happy to be directed as to what role to play and will openly become involved if they feel their ‘consumer rights’ have been infringed when their children perform less well than expected. The third parent image in the minds of teachers is of the disinterested. Teachers interviewed indicated that some parents were never seen and could not be relied upon to support teachers’ decisions.

There was no indication from any teacher interviewed that parents were seen as having any ability to contribute to education outside support for homework or a talk about “what do firemen do” (or similar). Parents felt disenfranchised by school systems. There was not a lack of support for the school but questions about their involvement in real decisions produced either incomprehension at the idea or anecdotes about ‘brick walls’ placed in their path by the school.

These relationships have a significant impact on the chances of acceptance of two of the three systems. The CASES system has an impact on parents to the extent that the system provides the school with fast access to important information (from the Education Department). A parent without visiting rights (court injunctions) will be turned away at the front desk and a student with a medical condition will be treated properly with a single CASES query. To this extent CASES supports the relationship of professional and client that teachers see as the natural state.

MySchool talks directly to parents and informs them of NAPLAN test results across their school. Teachers are armed with a number of explanations for shortfalls in performance – the problems of general statistics and such. They use these to prevent individual parent influence, but are being seen to react to MySchool in preparing students to improve results. There is no evidence outside our interviews, but it does seem that the one tactic considered by parents as a result of MySchool is to move children if the school performance is sub-par.

The Ultranet seeks to create a porous communications boundary between teachers and parents having the advantage of making the task of communicating with parents very easy for a teacher. The excuse for the 'grand occasion' parent/ teacher evening would be done away with. Teachers could become more aware of home circumstances and occurrences with little effort if parents were enticed to use the system. In our interviews teachers saw the system as being an extra workload burden in which they saw little value. Parents were not able to see anything on the system that would entice them to look, let alone contribute. This conclusion is to be doubted as the system is not fully functional as yet, but the functions that have been present for some time do seem to be ignored by both parties. The relationship between parents and teachers would lead us to conclude that the system will not progress past the present stage. It would not be in the interests of a teacher who claims absolute power over the education process to be completely candid with parents as that would presuppose parents could do something with any information they receive. Similarly a system that does not provide information is unlikely to have parents contributing. This would be especially true if they found their contributions not acted upon.

5 Conclusion

The CASES system was developed for accountability purposes to facilitate reporting from schools to the Department of Education. Its use is mandatory and it is not intended to provide support in school classrooms. The Ultranet is not just a single connection between government and the public, as is MySchool, but an attempt to create a mutually supporting educational community [19]. Its use is encouraged, but not mandated. MySchool was designed to provide information to parents about the school their children potential might attend. No regard was given to teachers as actors.

This paper has highlighted a number of important issues relating to the use of social technology in education, but we make no claim that these findings can be generalised to all other education systems. What makes a system valuable? Even systems provided available for no cost do not always persist, and the mandatory nature of some systems is not a reason for universal acceptance. When a system is seen as having value for its users it is likely to be adopted. This means we must consider that user scenarios are important when designing these systems. This paper has considered the question of who should be the actors: who should be the users of a system in a community and who should have input into its use? Should schools be regarded as central experts with no need for two way communication, or should social technology be allowed to give educational communities the opportunity to contribute?

References

1. Botto, F., Passani, A., Kiran, Y.V.: Digital Ecosystems Adoption at Local Level: A Preliminary Comparative Analysis. In: Antonio Basile Colugnati, F., Lopes, L.C.R., Barretto, S.F.A. (eds.) OPAALS 2010. LNICST, vol. 67, pp. 76–91. Springer, Heidelberg (2010)
2. Stale, G., Cakula, S.: Application of enterprise modeling method for continuing education design and development. In: Proceedings of the 3rd WSEAS International Conference on Visualization, Imaging and Simulation, pp. 86–92. World Scientific and Engineering Academy and Society (WSEAS), Faro (2010)
3. Andone, D., Robu, N., Vasiu, R.: Building a Virtual Campus for digital students. In: Global Engineering Education Conference (EDUCON). IEEE, Amman (2011)
4. Castro, M., Colmenar, A., Martin, S.: Trends of Use of Technology in Engineering Education. In: Education Engineering (EDUCON). IEEE, Madrid (2010)
5. Ouf, S., Nasr, M., Helmy, Y.: An enhanced e-learning ecosystem based on an integration between cloud computing and Web2.0. In: Proceedings of the 10th IEEE International Symposium on Signal Processing and Information Technology, pp. 48–55. IEEE Computer Society (2010)
6. Johnson, G., Broadley, T.: Learning style and digital activity: An ecological study. In: ASCILITE 2011, Hobart (2011)
7. Margaryan, A., Littlejohn, A., Vojt, G.: Are digital natives a myth or reality? University students' use of digital technologies. Computers & Education 56, 429–440 (2011)
8. Sappey, J., Relf, S.: Digital Technology Education and its Impact on Traditional Academic Roles and Practice. Journal of University Teaching & Learning Practice 7(1) (2010)
9. Tatnall, C., Tatnall, A.: Using Educational Management Systems to Enhance Teaching and Learning in the Classroom: an Investigative Study. In: Tatnall, A., Okamoto, T., Visscher, A.J. (eds.) Knowledge Management for Educational Innovation, pp. 75–82. Springer, New York (2007)
10. Department of Education and Early Childhood Development. CASES21 (2011), http://www.education.vic.gov.au/management/ictsupportservices/cases21/functionality.htm (January 2012)
11. Tatnall, A.: Information Technology and the Management of Victorian Schools - Providing Flexibility or Enabling Better Central Control? In: Barta, B.Z., Telem, M., Gev, Y. (eds.) Information Technology in Educational Management, pp. 99–108. Chapman & Hall, London (1995)
12. Davey, W., Tatnall, A.: Involving the Academic: A Test for Effective University ITEM Systems. In: Selwood, I., Fung, A.C.W., O'Mahony, C.D. (eds.) Management of Education in the Information Age: The Role of ICT, pp. 83–92. Kluwer Academic Publishers / IFIP, Assinippi Park, Massachusetts (2003)
13. Tatnall, A., Davey, W.: Open ITEM Systems are Good ITEM Systems. In: Nolan, P. (ed.) Institutional Improvement through Information Technology in Educational Management, pp. 59–69. Kluwer Academic Publishers, Dordrecht (2001)
14. Australian Bureau of Statistics. Statistics Victoria (Mar 2010), http://www.abs.gov.au/AUSSTATS/abs@.nsf/Lookup/1100.2Main+Features3Mar+2010 (November 2010)
15. Department of Education and Early Childhood Development. Summary Statistics for Victorian Schools (2010), http://www.education.vic.gov.au/about/publications/newsinfo/factsandfigures.htm (November 2010)

16. Department of Education and Early Childhood Development. Ultranet - Students@Centre Trial (2010), http://www.education.vic.gov.au/about/directions/ultranet/trial.htm (November 2010)
17. Department of Education and Early Childhood Development. Ultranet (2010), http://www.education.vic.gov.au/management/ultranet/default.htm (May 2010)
18. Tatnall, A., Dakich, E.: Informing Parents with the Victorian Education Ultranet. In: Informing Science and IT Education. Informing Science, Novi Sad (2011)
19. Tatnall, A., Dakich, E., Davey, W.: The Ultranet as a Future Social Network: An Actor-Network Analysis. In: 24th Bled eConference. University of Maribor, Bled (2011)
20. Australian Curriculum Assessment and Reporting Authority. My School (2010), http://www.myschool.edu.au/SchoolSearch.aspx (November 2010)
21. Gillard, J.: My School website launched (2010), http://www.deewr.gov.au/ministers/gillard/media/releases/pages/article_100128_102905.aspx (May 2010)
22. Callon, M.: Some Elements of a Sociology of Translation: Domestication of the Scallops and the Fishermen of St Brieuc Bay. In: Law, J. (ed.) Power, Action & Belief. A New Sociology of Knowledge? pp. 196–229. Routledge & Kegan Paul, London (1986)
23. Latour, B.: The Powers of Association. In: Law, J. (ed.) Power, Action and Belief. A New Sociology of Knowledge? Sociological Review Monograph, vol. 32, pp. 264–280. Routledge & Kegan Paul, London (1986)
24. Law, J.: The Heterogeneity of Texts. In: Callon, M., Law, J., Rip, A. (eds.) Mapping the Dynamics of Science and Technology, pp. 67–83. Macmillan Press, UK (1986)
25. Law, J. (ed.): A Sociology of Monsters. Essays on Power, Technology and Domination. Routledge, London (1991)
26. Siemens, G.: Connectivism: a Learning Theory for the Digital Age (2004), http://www.elearnspace.org/Articles/connectivism.htm (April 2012)
27. Siemens, G.: Knowing Knowledge (2006), http://www.elearnspace.org/KnowingKnowledge_LowRes.pdf (April 2012)
28. Australian Curriculum Assessment and Reporting Authority. Naplan - National Assessment Program (2010), http://www.naplan.edu.au/home_page.html (January 2012)
29. Australian Education Union. Stop League Tables (2011), http://www.aeufederal.org.au/LT/index2.html (January 2012)
30. Australian Education Union, Australian Education Union Submission to the Senate Education Employment and Workplace Relations Committee into the Administration and Reporting of NAPLAN Testing. Australian Education Union, Melbourne (2010)
31. Perkins, M.: Teach for tests, teachers told (2010), http://www.theage.com.au/national/education/teach-for-tests-teachers-told-20100204-ng6o.html (January 2012)

Evolution to Smart Learning in Public Education: A Case Study of Korean Public Education

Taisiya Kim[1], Ji Yeon Cho[2], and Bong Gyou Lee[2]

[1] Graduate School Department of Management of Technology, Yonsei University, South Korea
[2] Graduate School of Information, Yonsei University, South Korea
{lucky8619,jy.cho,bglee}@yonsei.ac.kr

Abstract. The purpose of this study is to introduce a new paradigm called "Smart Learning" in South Korea. The adoption of highly advanced Information Technology (IT) in education has been a global issue for many years. The Smart Learning paradigm in Korea is a convergence concept of Ubiquitous Learning (u-Learning) and Social Learning. This study examined the Smart Learning education system through a SWOT analysis of Korean public education. Thus, this study provides strategic implications for the countries that are in the process of promoting the Smart Learning education program.

Keywords: Smart Learning, Public Education, South Korea, SWOT analysis.

1 Introduction

Recently, the introduction of highly advanced technology to establish a new digitalized education environment has become a major global issue. Whenever new technologies emerge, many issues arise regarding how they can be introduced to support effective learning. Social technology has recently become a platform for the educational environment. In particular, many countries are currently interested in educational methods using smart devices and Social Network Services (SNS).

Advanced information technologies enable educational environment to broaden place, content, and forms of education. Digital textbooks and smart devices are replacing paper books, and the potential forms of education are becoming unlimited. For example, SNS has become an educational instrument. Consequently, telecommunication companies and portal companies are now interested in education business.

The global enterprise Apple announced plans to launch a new business in the global online education market. Apple plans to launch a digital textbook and has established a partnership with major publishers. Samsung Electronics has also announced that it will undertake an online learning service in Korea [1].

The Korean government has recognized the Electronic Learning (e-Learning) industry, the convergence industry of IT and educational services, as a fast-growing and high-value industry. In 2004 year, the government supported the policy on e-Learning industry development Act and made an investment in initiating the development of the e-Learning industry. As a result, Korea has become the leader in

T. Ley et al. (Eds.): OST 2012, IFIP AICT 395, pp. 170–178, 2013.

using e-Learning in public education, and it is developing a Smart Learning system at the moment. Smart Learning is a new concept in education, and it has recently started being used in Korea. The Korean government is now beginning to introduce a new concept of a Smart educational environment based on strong IT infrastructure and advanced social technologies.

Therefore, the objective of this study is to introduce the concept of Smart Learning by analyzing the case of Korea. This study conducted a SWOT (Strengths, Weaknesses, Opportunities, and Threats) analysis of Korean public education to analyze activating strategies for Smart Learning. Section 2 examines the concept of Smart Learning, and Korea's status in the educational market. Then, section 3 analyzes a case study regarding Smart Learning in Korean public education. Section 4 includes strategic and political implications, and the final section is the conclusion. This study can offer useful guidelines for countries that are in the process of improving their education systems with innovative technologies.

2 Smart Learning Overview

2.1 Evolution of Smart Learning

Recently, IT has been regarded as a solution for improving the quality of education. In this sense, the use of advanced technologies in the field of education has increased significantly and promoted a paradigm shift in the educational environment over the last decade [2]. Many countries expect IT to enhance the quality of education and to expand the educational industry. Therefore, the utilization and implementation of advanced technology that comprise this new learning environment is very important to the Korean government. That is why the government chose 'e-Learning' as a top priority project that will be worked on for the next few years.

In this situation, IT and the educational environment have been changing significantly, and the use of IT in education has increased rapidly for last 10 years. For example, there has been a major paradigm shift from e-Learning, which was defined as computer-based training, to Mobile Learning (m-Learning), which was driven by the advancement in mobile and wireless technologies [2], [3], [4]. m-Learning has improved a great deal more than e-Learning in terms of the flexibility of location, cost of a device, ease of use, and timely application [4]. m-Learning is very similar to e-Learning, but the only major difference is the use of mobile devices and wireless technology in the former. The development of IT has caused further changes in the educational environment, moving it away from the m-Learning environment toward the Ubiquitous Learning (u-Learning) environment. The u-Learning environment is an educational environment that allows students to study anytime and anywhere through diverse terminals, without limitations of time, place, or environment [2], [5], [6], [7]. Recently, the field of education has become interested in Social Learning, which is the use of smart devices and SNS services as educational instruments. Through social learning, students can share knowledge through their SNS and connect with teachers by tagging and sharing multimedia content that they have created. However, the adoption of social technologies in the educational system can cause privacy and copyrighting issues, among other issues. Related studies have just begun, and the effect of using social networking technologies in education is becoming an issue [8].

Recently in Korea, the Smart Learning paradigm, which combines u-Learning and social learning, has been emerging [9]. The evolution to Smart Learning is expected to improve the educational environment to advanced level regarding device, network, education program etc. However, discussions on Smart Learning have just begun in Korea, and the related studies are insufficient.

2.2 Concept of Smart Learning

So far there is no clear definition of Smart Learning. Related scholars and people who are involved with education business are discussing that the concept of Smart Learning should not be limited to just utilizing smart devices. Thus, the government, academia, and the educational industry have been working on defining and categorizing Smart Learning. At the Smart Learning Korea forum 2010 [9], a concept of Smart Learning was proposed as follows: first, it is focused on humans and content more than on devices; second, it is effective, intelligent tailored-learning based on advanced IT infrastructure [10]. Also, Kwak Duk-hoon, president and CEO of EBS (Korea's Educational Broadcasting System), said the term "Smart Learning" was first used in Korea. Then, what is the broad concept of Smart Learning in Korea?

MEST (The Korean Ministry of Education, Science and Technology) defined Smart Learning as Self-directed, Motivated, Adaptive, Resource-enriched, and Technology-embedded [11]. More information on S.M.A.R.T Learning promoted by MEST is as follows:

- S: Self-Directed, which means that the education system is progressing toward a self-learning system more than ever. Students' roles transition from knowledge adopters to knowledge creators. Also, teachers become facilitators of learning.
- M: Motivated means education becomes experience centered and involves learning by doing; creative problem solving and individualized assessment are pursued.
- A: Adaptive means strengthening of the education system's flexibility and tailoring learning for individual preference and future careers.
- R: Resource-enriched means that Smart Learning utilizes rich content based on open market, cloud education services from both public and private sectors. In other words, it expands the scope of learning resources to include collective intelligence, Social Learning.
- T: Technology-embedded means that in the Smart Learning education environment, students can learn anywhere, any time through advance technologies. Fig. 1 shows the holistic concept of SMART education in Korea.

Consequently, Smart Learning in Korea is a new paradigm using IT and network infrastructure in school education. The Smart Learning environment allows students to use all available learning devices anywhere and anytime, even social media. Students can attend courses at their own pace and are able to access only the elements of the course that pertain to them. The cutting-edge IT that is used actively in Smart

Learning is called Smart Technology. Social network computing in particular is an important factor of mutual cooperation in the learning process that compensates for the limitations of e-Learning.

But so far, the government, academia, and the educational industry have been working on defining and establishing categories for Smart Learning. The field of education needs to consider a plan of mutual study with teachers, schoolmates and efficient, phased use of social network. The technological environment is transitioning from the use of smart devices to virtual reality, and augmented reality; therefore, the government, academia, and industry research aims to find ways to converge existing technology. Also, they are currently discussing possible ways to construct the environment using high-quality content at an affordable rate [9].

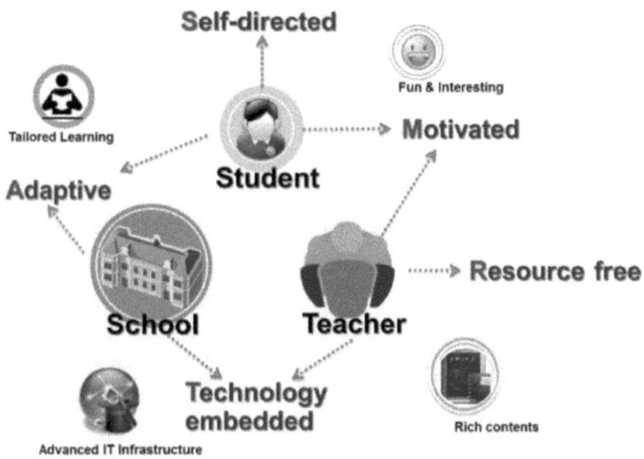

Fig. 1. SMART Education in Korea

2.3 The Current Status of IT Use in Korean Public Education

As noted, the Korean government has recently made an effort to establish an educational environment using advanced IT, such as e-Learning or u-Learning, in public education. Korea has an excellent information and communications infrastructure essential to the digitalized educational environment. High-speed internet has been installed nationwide, and there are a number of leading electronics companies in Korea like Samsung and LG that are engaged in developing smart device and telecommunication technologies. Recently, the supply of smart devices such as smartphones and smart pads has been growing rapidly, and new education paradigms like Smart Learning have been developed. This cutting-edge technological environment in Korea regarding broadband internet and devices has had a profound impact on the education industry and related policies. These are the reasons that, for the last few years, the Korean government has recognized the e-Learning education program as the future growth engine. The government's recent master plan has been focused on the evolution of Smart Learning environments and secure educational services with social technologies. The Korean government has already introduced e-Learning and u-Learning in public education and made a massive investment in that field to solve the current problems in education and to respond to the new paradigm of education environment.

As a result, Korea has already established e-Learning programs in public education since 2004. In 2009 year, about 45% of all Koreans have had the experience of using e-Learning content, and 26.2% of all educational courses have been conducted through e-Learning on more than one occasion [12]. Specifically, the Korean government is currently trying to secure national competitiveness by achieving global standardization in the digital learning environment based on outcomes from years of pilot projects. The government has consistently promoted e-Learning and devices such as digital textbooks. Now, the Smart Learning education system is being targeted as a new growth engine. Social education, related to Smart Learning, is also garnering attention, and the IPTV (Internet Protocol Television) industry is also trying to change the Smart education paradigm. The introduction of Smart Learning is attracting interest from the media and telecommunication operators. It is already having a positive impact by broadening the education industry.

3 Case Analysis of Korean Public Education

3.1 Strengths

Smart Learning consists of advanced infrastructure, and rich, fun content that can be taught in an individualized manner. The Korean educational environment has sufficient infrastructure; on average it uses 87.71% of cable, 12.08% of wireless, and 0.10% of satellite and other internet networks in public schools. From 1997 to 2008, the government invested around 3.46 billion dollars in infrastructure[11]. Also, Korea is promoting a pilot project that is focused on testing the digital textbooks used for Smart Learning. Classroom infrastructure includes an electromagnetically-induced Tablet PC with a 12-inch monitor and a computer that is installed for the teacher [2]. Remote support and management functions are included in the teacher's Tablet PC to check the students' learning activities. The school network blocks illegal access from the outside and prevent disclosure of the students' profiles.

Inside and outside the classroom, students are available to use digital textbooks; this enables them to be more active and cultivate their ability to retain information longer and enjoy classes more. Digital textbooks cover six subjects in the fifth and sixth grades (Korean, English, Mathematics, Social Studies, Science, and Music) and give students an opportunity to prepare and review the subjects without carrying a bunch of textbooks.

3.2 Weaknesses

Content area is one of the weaknesses of the Korean Smart Learning environment. Most Korean students study in private institute academies after school. In 2010, over 25,000 private institute academies registered with the Seoul Metropolitan Office of Education [13]. Every institute has its own content and knows how to teach students efficiently.

Whereas Smart Learning has to meet the demands of the systematic educational program, there is a lack of organizations to control the high quality content necessary for effective tailored learning.

The Korean digital book pilot project uses a school network that guarantees security; however, because the network has a low bandwidth, it cannot guarantee a reasonable access speed for accessing the internet. Thus, security is the most important factor for this project in public education.

However, live communication is the main factor in Smart Learning, and a school network could be too weak to support the service. Smart Learning is connected to SNS websites; therefore, it is exposed to more security risks than previous internet-based learning environments.

Historically, Korean public education had focused on the cramming method of teaching. Therefore, the social demand for Smart Learning is urgent in the Korean education market. The government is trying to increase innovation, life, and career skills in young population.

3.3 Opportunities

The supply rate of smart devices in Korea is high enough for applying Smart Learning. The Seoul Metropolitan Government predicts that the smart device supply rate in Korean will occupy almost 80% of population or even more, by 2015. In addition, people use the internet 5.4 days each week. These facts show that there are many opportunities for Smart Learning to be applied in the Korean education system.

The Korean e-Learning system is led by government organizations that see the opportunity to make a systematic investment in the Smart Learning system. Since 2007, MEST (Korean Ministry of Education, Science and Technology) and KERIS (Korea Education and Research Information Service) have promoted a new concept for a public educational environment based on advanced IT infrastructure and a u-Learning environment. MEST and KERIS have tried to introduce a successful learning environment by developing and distributing digital textbooks in line with the future education paradigm [2].

Most Korean students rely on private institute academies, and the high price of private education is a burden for parents. Also, most of the qualitative academies are decentralized in specific parts of town, leading to the falling population of young students in such academies. Generalization of Smart Learning could prevent students from having to go to the other institutes. The government will also support a nationwide open content market containing a variety of learning materials so that users may have access to high-quality educational information at a low cost.

The approach to teaching in Smart Learning provides a tailored service to suit the individual needs and level of each student. In traditional public education, it is usually difficult to teach students individually. Tailored learning is the main strength of Smart Learning, and communication with tutors continuously doubles students' motivation for learning.

3.4 Threats

The major threat of the Smart Learning system is standardization. In the process of communicating and sharing content, devices, infrastructure, and system standardization are necessary. Even though the Korean Smart Learning system is compatible with each other, new infrastructures of global enterprises could change the system. Global standardization about Smart Learning is uncertain, and changes in global market standardization can affect the Korean education market.

In addition, Korean parents are especially sensitive to their children's education, and recording students' learning abilities could increase parents' interference in a negative way. Monitoring children could result in making them more unstable rather than improving their confidence and performance in class.

There is also an expectation that private institute academies will oppose the Smart Learning system in public schools. One of the reasons is instructors unemployment. Whereas the goal of Smart Learning is to decrease the cost of private institute academies, over 25,000 of these academies are already systemized in Korea's education market. The spread of the Smart Learning system in public education programs could affect the decrease of private institute academies, and later it could cause unemployment for instructors.

4 Analysis Results and Implications

The results of the study show that the strengths of the Korean Smart Education System are its infrastructure, devices, and secured network. The implications for each result are as follows.

Table 1. SWOT analysis of the Korean Smart Education System

Strengths	***Weaknesses***
· Sufficient classroom infrastructure · Digital textbook with six public school subjects · School network to prevent disclosure of students' profiles	· Lack of high-quality content · Few content management organizations · School network has a low bandwidth for internet use · Cramming method of teaching
Opportunities	***Threats***
· High supply rate of smart devices · Government-led increases in systematic investments in Smart Education · Increased number of young students in the population · High-quality educational information at a low cost · Tailored learning service doubles the motivation of learning	· Global standardization · Parents' interference · Private institutes' oppose and instructors' unemployment

First, global companies like Samsung and LG are active in producing smart devices. The solid infrastructure and secure content controlled by the government will ensure the systematic development of Smart Learning and may eventually lead to an increase in the population of young students. In countries with expensive private education, Smart Learning is a solution with the potential to decrease the cost of after-school academies.

Second, through the cooperation of government departments, weaknesses such as a lack of quality content and management organizations could be minimized. It is important to have diverse content, but qualitative and tailored content is more important in public education. Korean EBS (Educational Broadcasting System) possesses a great deal of qualitative content and already has experience with cooperating with government organizations. EDUNET tries to create an open market in which public, private, and individual outstanding content could be used for educational purposes. Almost 6.20 million members already have joined EDUNET, and the company has around 5.5 million sources of information. Therefore, the cooperation of stakeholders like government departments, broadcasting, and telecommunications companies should lead to the creation of valuable services for the Smart Learning system.

Third, although the infrastructure is at a high level, global standardization is also an important issue, and Korean government organizations have conducted meetings on e-Learning standardization. The outcomes are going to be foundations for Smart Learning. In addition, due to the lack of high-quality content and credible organizations, parents' interference could increase and potentially threaten the Smart Learning environment. To overcome such weaknesses and threats, secured organizations that are capable of providing quality content are needed to alleviate the public's anxiety and fear of change [13].

5 Conclusion

The advancement of IT and networks has resulted in the emergence of ubiquitous computing environments and educational systems [2]. The public education system in Korea is preparing for the launch of Smart Learning educational service based on cloud computing services. Korea has been active in instituting e-Learning in public education, it is especially important to make a model of the case. To promote this new service, an analysis of possible strengths, weaknesses, opportunities, and threats, is necessary. Other countries are also planning educational programs based on social devices. However, like AT&T and Apple, which are promoting pilot project on m-Learning in ACU (Abilene Christian University), most of the projects are supported by private companies.

This study analyzed the Korean Smart Learning education system with the goal of introducing a new education paradigm. The SWOT analysis explains Korean educational environment in general as well as the specific pilot Smart Learning case. Results of the analysis show the main solutions for vitalizing Smart Learning with consideration for a prudent public or a set of content management organizations.

Such results are expected to have strategic implications for countries that are in the process of promoting the Smart Learning education system.

Acknowledgement. This research was supported by the KCC (Korea Communications Commission), Korea, under the CPRC(Communications Policy Research Center) support program supervised by the KCA (Korea Communications Agency) (KCA-2012-0902-1).

References

1. Park, S.: [MWC 2012] Samsung is going into digital textbook business... Opening 'Learning Hub Zone'. Etoday (March 20, 2012)
2. Kim, S.J.: Developing a framework of u-Learning for research and practice. Doctoral dissertation, Yonsei University (2010)
3. Lee, B.G., Kim, S.J., Park, K.C., Kim, S.J., Jeong, E.S.: Empirical analysis of learning effectiveness in u-Learning environment with digital textbook. KSII Transactions of Internet and Information Systems 6(3), 869–885 (2012)
4. Milrad, M.: How should learning activities using mobile technologies be designed to support innovative educational practices? In: Sharples, M. (ed.) Big Issues in Mobile Learning: Report of a Workshop by the Kaleidoscope Network of Excellence Mobile Learning Initiative, pp. 28–30. University of Nottingham, Nottingham (2007)
5. Chen, Y.S., Kao, T.C., Sheu, J.P., Chiang, C.Y.: Mobile Scaffolding Aid-Based Bird Watching Learning System. In: Proc. of IEEE International Workshop on Wireless and Mobile Technologies in Education (WMTE 2002), pp. 15–22 (2002)
6. Huh, H.O., Seo, S.S., Kang, E.S., Jeon, B.K., Jang, K.Y., Kye, B.K., Ko, B.S.: Research on developing a next generation learning model in a Ubiquitous computing environment. Korea Education & Research Information Service. Research report KR 2006-4 (2006)
7. Jeong, S.M., Go, B.S., Seo, J.H., Sin, S.U.: Understanding of u-Learning. Korea Education & Research Information Service. Research report RM 2005-54 (2005)
8. Lockyer, P.: Integrating social networking technologies in education: A case study of a formal learning environment. In: 8th IEEE International Conference on Advanced Learning Technologies, Santander, Spain, July 1-5 (2008)
9. Noh, K.S.: An exploratory study on concept and realization conditions of Smart Learning. The Journal of Digital Policy & Management 9(2), 79–88 (2011)
10. Gwak, D.: The meaning and predict of Smart Learning. Smart Learning Korea Proceeding. Korean e-Learning Industry Association (2010)
11. MEST: Ministry of Education, Science and Technology of the Republic of Korea, Smart education promotion strategy, President's Council on National ICT Strategies (2011)
12. Korea Institute for Electronic Commerce and Korea Ministry of Knowledge Economy: e-Learning industry status survey. Korea Institute for Electronic Commerce (2008)
13. Todd, R.W.: Fear of change impedes cloud adoption for many companies. CIO BIZ (August 8, 2011)

Doctoral Student Papers

Driving Forces behind the Development and Stabilization of Knowledge Organization Systems in Digital Environments

Jörgen Jaanus and Tobias Ley

Tallinn University, Institute of Informatics, Narva road 25,
10120, Tallinn, Estonia
{Jorgen.jaanus,tobias.ley}@tlu.ee

Abstract. The emergence of Digital Ecosystems can be endorsed by creating shared conceptualizations. Knowledge Organization Systems (KOS) form a backbone of organizing knowledge. Focusing in developing KOS and having its present and future requirements in mind would eventually support knowledge sharing and learning at collective level. Three types of KOS are distinguished: a) private level KOS; b) arbitrary KOS; c) methodic KOS. Knowledge Maturing can be described as goal-oriented learning on a collective level. In line with the knowledge maturing model, we assume that stabilizing and dynamic forces co-exist in all organizations which seek a dynamic equilibrium between further development and stabilization. Identifying and measuring these forces would help in the effective development of Knowledge Organization Systems and consequently support planning and development of information systems.

Keywords: Knowledge Organization Systems, Knowledge Maturing, Digital Ecosystems.

1 Background Concepts

Digital Ecosystems support modern networked economies being a next generation information and communications technology for ensuring that information and knowledge are shared across organizations as quickly and effectively as possible [1]. The functional characteristics relate digital ecosystems to achieving cooperation, knowledge sharing, accessing, editing and extrapolating data in order to facilitate learning, knowledge flow and information [2].

Within those ecosystems there are nodes which have their internal development mechanisms which can be described as goal-oriented learning on a collective level defined as knowledge maturing. Knowledge maturing process consists of five consecutive stages: expressing ideas, distributing in communities, formalizing, ad-hoc learning and standardization [3]. Hereby it is claimed that those stages appear in consecutive organizational settings. Ideas are typically expressed in small communities of practice while the standardization can appear at industry-wide level.

T. Ley et al. (Eds.): OST 2012, IFIP AICT 395, pp. 181–184, 2013.

Ontologies are taken as a core enabler for Digital Ecosystems which is built from the entire residing knowledge while Knowledge Organization Systems (KOS) are a development framework for that.

KOS are referred to as levels of semantics [4], maturity of knowledge organization [5], spectrum of knowledge representation [6] or just ontology spectrum [7]. The key difference in those concepts is whether ontologies are considered just formal ontologies whose concepts and relations have definitions that are stated in logic or in some computer-oriented language that can be automatically translated to logic or ontologies are considered on the broader spectrum including both formal and terminological ontologies as distinguished in [8]. There are four knowledge organization systems that can be used to model and organize concepts and to describe terms semantically: controlled vocabularies, taxonomies, thesaurus, and ontologies. [4] Controlled vocabulary is described as a weaker end of this spectrum. Adding structure, hierarchy and child-parent relationships to the controlled vocabulary taxonomy is created. Further from taxonomy thesaurus represent equivalence, homographic, hierarchical, and associative relationships. Using richer semantic relationships among terms and attributes, as well as strict rules about how to specify terms and relationships leads to ontologies. The development of those four KOS in this particular sequence is considered as semantic continuum.

KOS have an important role in each of the knowledge maturing stage. As knowledge matures, more complex structure is needed for knowledge sharing and technical interoperability at the broader scale. The concept of KOS as the core of Digital Ecosystems has shared conceptualization as an essential development mechanism. Private level KOS exist as idiosyncratic and for mainly private use. From this state KOS mature and then gain the guiding role. As an opposite to private level KOS it can be entitled public level KOS which has to distinguishable roles: arbitrary and methodic which roughly correspond to the maturing and guidance in Knowledge Maturing model.

2 Conceptual Assumptions

Hereby it is claimed that KOS develop and stabilize to the level which is optimal for knowledge sharing requirements at a given stage of knowledge maturing. Knowledge sharing takes place between individuals in communities, communities in organizations and organizations within cooperation networks. KOS are functioning as boundary objects between those functional units which enable cross-boundary flow of information and knowledge.

Boundary objects are plastic, interpreted differently across communities but with enough immutable content to maintain integrity [9]. The role of the boundary object is not the by-product of organizing knowledge but it is essential to consider KOS as artifacts becoming mediators of distributed cognition as described by Wallace and Ross [10]. This perspective has broadened the value of KOS from solely standardization and findability to coordination and sense-making, consequently fuelling the efforts to advance towards the higher end of semantic spectrum.

The table below depicts the connections between KOS and knowledge maturing stages within consecutive organizational settings.

Table 1. The congruence between KOS, Knowledge Maturing stages and structural units

Knowledge Organization Systems	Controlled Vocabulary		Taxonomy	The-saurus	Ontology
Knowledge Maturing Stages	Expres-sing ideas	Distributing in communities	Formalization	Ad-hoc training	Standardization
Structural Units	Individual ⇨	Community ⇨		Organization ⇨	Cooperation network

As knowledge maturing leads to ontology development, enterprise application software applications have to be adjusted according to the knowledge maturing requirements which consequently become the cornerstone of long-term competitiveness. For gaining anticipated functionality of any information system it has to incorporate both flexibility and strict standards for information exchange.

As a consequence of ontology development more patterns appear between nodes which makes the overall Digital Ecosystem more dynamic. According to chaos theory in an extremely dynamic organization the boarders and the identity of the organization become open and fluid and cooperative external relationships are sometimes more important than internal ones. If the speed of development is much faster outside the structural unit than inside, the organization moves from equilibrium to the edge of chaos. In this situation a self-organizing ability emerges which is capable of creating a new order [11]. The ability of the organization to adapt to its ecosystem is considerably increased. If the organizations have difficulties finding the right adjustments to their dynamic surroundings the stabilizing forces prevail and KOS have lower interoperability needs. According to Knowledge Maturing model dynamic forces appear through generating new ideas and maturing those ideas throughout the entire ecosystem. Stabilizing forces are observable through organizational guidance. There are dynamic and stabilizing forces which influence the development of KOS and Knowledge Maturing.

Research for identifying and measuring those forces would add focus and precision to the development of KOS and consequently support planning and development of information systems. The existing and anticipated connectivity between various nodes in Digital Ecosystems would be the basis of understanding and measuring those forces.

3 Research Approach

Based on this conceptual approach the next step is developing practical model which has Digital Ecosystem as the unit of analysis with three levels: a) an individual belonging to the community; b) community member belonging to the organization; c) knowledge worker as part of industry/ cooperation network.

According to the conceptual assumptions we have to investigate three different types of KOS. First, private level KOS are measured based on respondents' ability to recognize and form categories from pre-given objects. Second, arbitrary KOS is based on the questions about work processes depicting regularly appearing situations. Third, methodic KOS are derived from Enterprise Application Software applications.

The analogous research approach has been successfully used by APOSDLE in the work place learning study [12].

4 Conclusions

In this paper we have modeled and presented several concepts which provide insight to organizing knowledge. KOS develop and stabilize to the level which is optimal for knowledge sharing requirements at a given stage of knowledge maturing.

There are connections between KOS and knowledge maturing stages within consecutive organizational settings. Two forces coexist which influence development of KOS and Knowledge Maturing. Dynamic forces appear through generating new ideas and maturing those ideas throughout the Digital Ecosystem and stabilizing forces appear through organizational guidance.

The framework of Digital Ecosystems provides context for understanding and measuring those dynamic and stabilizing forces in order to support planning and development of information systems.

References

1. Price, C., Turnbull, D.: The organizational challenges of global trends. A McKinsey global survey. McKinsey Quarterly (2007)
2. Digital Business Ecosystems, Luxembourg, Office of Official Publications of European Communities (2007)
3. Maier, R., Schmidt, A.: Characterizing Knowledge Maturing. In: 4th Conference Professional Knowledge Management (WM 2007), Potsdam, Germany (2007)
4. Cardoso, J.: The Syntactic and the Semantic Web. Semantic Web Services: Theory, tools and applications. Information Science Reference, New York (2007)
5. Brun, R., Hinkelmann, K., Telesko, R., Thönssen, B.: Towards an Integrated Approach to Assess the Potential of an Enterprise to Mature Knowledge. In: WM 2009, 5th Conference of Professional Knowledge. Management, GI-Edition LNI P-145, pp. 440–444 (2009)
6. Davis, M.: Semantic Wave 2008 Report: Industry Roadmap to Web 3.0 & Multibillion Dollar Market Opportunities (2008), `http://www.project10x.com`
7. Lassila, O., McGuinness, D.: The Role of Frame-Based Representation on the Semantic Web (2002)
8. Lacasta, J., Nogueras-Iso, J., Zarazaga-Soria, F.: Terminological Ontologies (2010)
9. Star, S.L., Griesemer, J.R.: Institutional Ecology, 'Translations' and Boundary Objects: Amateurs and Professionals in Berkeley's Museum of Vertebrate Zoology (1989)
10. Wallace, B., Ross, A.: Beyond Human Error: Taxonomies and Safety Science. Ergonomics 51(9) (2006)
11. Caluwe, L., Vermaak, H.: Thinking about Change in Different Colours (2008)
12. De Hoog, R., Kooken, J., Ley, T., Kump, B., Lindstaedt, S.: Advanced Process-Oriented Self-Directed Learning Environment (2008)

Collaborative Tagging Applications and Capabilities in Social Technologies

Danel Apse and Tobias Ley

Tallinn University, Institute of Informatics, Narva road 25,
10120, Tallinn, Estonia
{danel02,tley}@tlu.ee

Abstract. With this paper we will be exploring the usage of Collaborative Tagging in administrative Information Systems of the Estonian Defence Forces (EDF), which is currently using Information Systems (IS) mainly for administrative purposes. The potentials of using Collaborative Tagging in Inter- and Intra-organizational settings for knowledge management and sharing are not well understood at present. Moreover, military applications of Collaborative Tagging have not been reported. The paper will therefore explore some initial use cases of the use of Collaborative Tagging and from these identify potentials and threats. Does collaborative tagging in semantic environment help us better organize knowledge in the EDF Information Systems? Semantics can foster to gain individual knowledge in the community.

Keywords: Collaborative Tagging (CT), Estonian Defence Forces (EDF), Knowledge Maturing, Semantic Scuttle (SSC).

1 Introduction

Collaborative tagging describes the process by which many users add freely chosen keywords (tags) to shared content (such as webpages, photos, ...) and in the last years, collaborative tagging systems emerged as a popular tool supporting knowledge workers such as researchers or students in managing their own resources and finding relevant material based on keywords assigned to them [1].

With this paper, we will be exploring the usage of Collaborative Tagging in administrative Military Information Systems. The Estonian Defence Forces (EDF) is currently using Information Systems (IS) mainly for administrative purposes.

2 Backgrounds

In order to proceed with further analyses the conceptual terms should be clarified:

- **Tags** are metadata about the resource;
- **Collaborative tagging** (CT) systems allow users to share resources in the web and to annotate them with freely chosen keywords, so called tags. The resources together with the tags are stored on a central server and can be accessed from any computer connected to the web. The term social bookmarking system often is used interchangeably for such systems.

T. Ley et al. (Eds.): OST 2012, IFIP AICT 395, pp. 185–188, 2013.

Tags, Collaborative Tagging, Taxonomy, Folksonomy - this is common terminology getting from individual knowledge sharing into group knowledge sharing in the current research.

The Concept of administrative Information Systems of EDF is based on strong Taxonomy. There are for every Information Systems platform different kind of uses cases, which describe different problems.

- EDF Information System Postipoiss (provides the possibility of managing incoming and outgoing documents during these lifecycles. Finding the specific document is time consuming. The System uses expired structure and it needs modern solutions and capabilities, which would satisfy user`s needs.);
- EDF Mil intranet (It supports transportation orders, job time schedule administration, training materials databases and a lot of other necessary possibilities);
- EDF Mil internet web page (for public gives answers to the questions: What EDF is? What the EDF tasks are?)
- ILIAS E-Learning portal (different kind of learning manuals, course papers etc.)

The problem: At the moment used Information Systems are having information overlapping – you can find the same information in different systems. Information is not managed effectively – finding exact information in different information systems can be very time consuming and problematic. One of the helpful solutions would be to start using Collaborative Tagging in the systems simultaneously with Taxonomy. How much it would help by organizing user`s knowledge during information sharing in the systems? - The empirical studies are conducted for this reason by the author.

3 Knowledge Maturing

The kind of activity and commitment which is facilitating tagging in organizational environment has to carry broader mission and goal for EDF.

Knowledge maturing is a concept which defines goal-oriented learning on a collective level. While developing collaborative tagging capabilities it thus becomes essential to evaluate the alternative solutions from knowledge maturing perspective. During the knowledge maturing process knowledge becomes less contextualized, more explicitly linked and easier to communicate. It takes place in five sequential phases defined as: expressing ideas, distributing in communities, formalization, ad-hoc learning and standardization [3]. As collective tagging reflects the process of knowledge creation from individual perspective and collective perspective then the activities within collective tagging can be connected to the knowledge maturing phases.

In order develop and maintain the credible capacity of EDF and ensure constant learning at organizational level knowledge maturing phases have to identifiable inside the collective tagging.

4 The Research Project and Methodology

In this section the Research Vision of the Knowledge Maturing in the Collaborative Tagging will be presented. The principal author of the current research paper has started from the beginning of the year 2012 the small research project by using the Semantic Scuttle (SSC) software.

SSC has been implemented based on three level layers:

1. Information Systems Layer consists of different kind of used administrative Information Systems (IS) in EDF.
2. Semantic Layer consists of used Information System called SSC. It`s goal and possibility is to combine all the coming information from IS into semantic context – every SSC user can find necessary information more efficiently and information is combined into one environment.
3. Knowledge Maturing Layer – taken into account the Knowledge Maturing theory we can improve organizational knowledge collaboration. We can use technology efficiently and organizational knowledge will be improved.

Collaborative Tagging improves Knowledge Management, because by using Tags we can prioritize most used information and knowledge. Personal Tag Clouds will be shared and it gives in community setting capability of Community Tag Cloud sharing. Finally we will have Taxonomy in Collaborative Tagging – based on common rules how to share information and knowledge will be tagging used as effective tool.

The principal author of the current paper would define research project as field experiment in Nascent Theory Research, because current research project tries to solve different kind of practical problems by using theory which has not been used in such context before [4].

The principal author would define his research steps as Traditional Field Research Process [4]:

- Identify target area of interest (Collaborative Tagging capability in EDF Information Systems);
- Reading the literature (reading about Collaborative Tagging generally)
- Develop research question (will be developed according that Knowledge not managed effectively in EDF Information Systems)
- Design a study (Interviews, observations, questionnaire produced regarding how could help EDF Information Systems users Collaborative Tagging tool Semantic Scuttle by sharing knowledge more effectively)
- Collect and analyse data (Qualitative data that need to be interpreted)
- Write up results
- Publish the research project

Research consists of 4 cycles. Every cycle starts from action planning and continues with action, action observation and finally changes will be conducted:

- I Cycle: Orientation phase goal was to understand the situation regarding information management in EST MIL information systems (domain description is the outcome). Different use cases were defined. First answers to the questionnaire.
- II Cycle: Check out phase goal will be interviews (should be recorded) with the selected interested co-workers with professional ideas how to improve the environment. Detailed description of necessary needs and their improvement with CT technology and look up in semantic layer context will be done. Analysing semantic scuttle context with selected users will be conducted.
- III Cycle: Exercising phase goal would be by summarizing previous phases improved use cases will be defined and exercises based on use cases how to improve these problems based on user's opinions by using CT technology and semantic scuttle context. All the ideas and experiences will be documented.
- IV Cycle: evaluation phase goal would be summary of the project and documented results. Results should show different final use cases and how these will be solved based on CT and Semantic layer context. Finalized will be semantic layer context regarding Knowledge Maturing (KM) processes.

Further research improvements will be taken into account during PhD studies of the paper author.

References

1. Schoefegger, K., Seitlinger, P., Ley, T.: Towards a User Model for Personalized Recommendations in Work-Integrated Learning: A Report on an Experimental Study with a Collaborative Tagging System (2010), http://www.sciencedirect.com
2. Jäschke, R.: Formal Concept Analysis and Tag Recommendations in Collaborative Tagging Systems (2011), http://www.kde.cs.uni-kassel.de/jaeschke
3. Maier, R., Schmidt, A.: Characterizing Knowledge Maturing. In: 4th Conference Professional Knowledge Management (WM 2007), Potsdam, Germany (2007)
4. Edmondson, A.C., McManus, S.E.: Methodological fit in management field research. Academy of Management Review 32(4), 1155–1179 (2007)

Privacy Awareness of Students and Its Impact on Online Learning Participation – A Case Study

Birgy Lorenz, Sonia Sousa, and Vladimir Tomberg

Tallinn University, Institute of Informatics, Narva road 25,
10120, Tallinn, Estonia
{Birgy.Lorenz,sonia.sousa,vladimir.tomberg}@tlu.ee

Abstract. This paper is based on a survey that addresses two main hypotheses - that there is a positive correlation between students' level of participation and their privacy awareness, and students with high levels of privacy awareness need to be assured that their open learning activities are protected from potential threats in order to achieve positive results. Results show that in fact there is a correlation between students' awareness of privacy and their predisposition to share and to participate in open leaning contexts. This is especially evident when students share their school assignments, grading results and teacher's feedback or even their comments with others.

Keywords: privacy, trust, e-learning, personal learning environments, LePress.

1 Introduction

Our study explores the area of privacy awareness and trust in open or semi-open learning environments. We claim that by understanding the interrelation between students' privacy awareness, their attitudes and beliefs towards sharing in an online learning environment, we will are able to contribute to the design decisions regarding the blog-based tools. The featured example of such a blog-based PLE tool is LePress[1], which is an enhancement of the most popular blog engine WordPress.

2 Background

Privacy and security researchers in the e-learning domain often focus on a technical area like logging and tracking [1], environments security (accountability, safeguards, individual access, administrative policies, disclosure, retention) [2] or sensitive data misuse, and theft [3]. Nevertheless the questions related to personal privacy have come up [4], as some researchers now included the topics of data ownership and privacy [5].

The status of e-learning in Estonia has its own clear peculiarities. At the high school level, the new National Curricula states an obligation for every school to use

[1] http://wordpress.org/extend/plugins/lepress-20/

T. Ley et al. (Eds.): OST 2012, IFIP AICT 395, pp. 189–192, 2013.

an e-learning environment [6]. At university / vocational school level, there are many open and non-open solutions to choose from, e.g. Wikiversity, Moodle, Blackboard, IVA, LeMill, WordPress, etc [7].

Burdened with new professional responsibilities, primary and secondary school teachers have raised serious questions about personal and data protection in these environments and also suggested that learning experience shouldn't be public to allow children an opportunity to make mistakes [8]. As a result, some schools have chosen closed learning environments like Moodle. At the same time closeness can be a mirage – especially when security holes are not patched and data is leaking anyway.

Thus the main aim of this study is to provide a further understanding how does the students' awareness of potential privacy threats influence students' learning experience and suggest some solution. For that we rely also on the theory about privacy by Razavi and Iverson [9], [10].

3 Methods

We carried out an empirical study among students from Pelgulinna Gymnasium and Tallinn University, with two main hypotheses: 1. There is a positive correlation between the subject's level of participation and their level of privacy awareness; 2. students with high levels of privacy awareness need to be assured that their open learning activities are protected from potential threats in order to achieve positive results.

The questionnaire was conducted by using an open source web application called LimeSurvey and used Likert scale as well as open-ended answers. Sixty-one (61) anonymous responses were collected during November 2011. The survey included 25 questions, divided into three main groups: (1) background, (2) privacy awareness, and (3) predisposition to participate in open learning activities[2].

4 Results

According to data, most participants are from Tallinn. The majority attended high school graduation level and most of them had no earlier experience with blog-based tools in learning contexts.

Regarding the first hypothesis, a positive and significant correlation was found between the subjects' predisposition to participate and their privacy awareness. More specifically, a bivariate analysis (Spearman's) showed a statistically significant correlations on the following issues: (1) those who publish often also agree that it is very easy to anonymously find information and pictures of others on the web (r=.272*, r=.267* and r=.264*); (2) those who publish often (school assignments on the web) tend also to agree that it is very easy to post comments anonymously on the web (r=.3 (Sig. (2-tailed)=.019) (3) those who publish often (something about a

[2] Please see the following address `http://goo.gl/xCTy8` for further information re-garding survey questions.

teacher or a school colleague) also agree that it is very easy to post comments about somebody (friends, teacher, school) on the web under a false name (r=.311*) and also agree that it is not easy to permanently remove content that others have posted about them on the web (r=-.319*); (4) again, those who publish often also agree that it is not safe to take part in open forum discussions (r=-.279*); but argue that it is safe to read teachers' feedback in closed learning contexts (r=.286*).

Concerning the second hypothesis, again a positive correlation was found between student's privacy awareness and the need to be assured that they are interacting in a safe place. These concerns are especially expressed by the students who believe that teachers should always *make extra efforts to provide support* to assure that their learning activities are protected from privacy threats. This issue is mostly correlated with their beliefs that (1) it is very easy to post comments in the web anonymously (r=.332**), (2) it is very easy to anonymously see their friends' information and pictures on the Facebook (r=.279*) (3), or even with their belief that an email account is a safe place to exchange messages (r=.255*); and (4) that a closed learning environment is a safe place to read teacher feedback (r=.416**); but (5) it is not safe to share (e.g. work-related resources or to exchange comments) in social e-tools like Facebook or Google+ (r=-.270*). Also, most students who agree that it is safe to read and send e-mail through an email base account claim that (1) the teacher's grading information (r=.373**), (2) homework comments (r=.284*) and (3) feedback (r=.255*) should remain private by default. Again a negative correlation was found, though between those students who believe that it is safe to share using social e-tools (work-related resources or exchange comments) and their belief that (1) teacher's feedback (r=-.253*), (2) homework submissions (-.267*) and (3) grading information (r=-.282*) should remain private by default[3].

5 Discussion

We conclude that the students who socialize the most on the Internet tend to be more aware of potential privacy threats of this communication medium and need assurance that they are interacting in a protected and secure environment. We also concluded that students in a virtual environment tend usually not to distinguish between private and educational social interactions and this might be a potential threat for their communication environment. Students don't usually filter their posts or comments when in social networks; though some of them feel that their rights and privacy may be violated if their posts or comments are open to everybody. This indicates that these matters should be addressed more at schools. Some environments convince that they store data safely, yet they may sell it to others or just have weak privacy settings.

For the future we are going to repeat the study, but also look behind of the obvious privacy needs what have come up. Unanswered questions are related to the digital divide between students and teacher changing role to provide safe learning environment.

[3] Please see the following address `http://goo.gl/xCTy8` for further information.

6 Conclusion

The main outcome of this study is that from a learners' point of view, students need to be ensured that their online learning activities are protected from potential privacy threats. Based on that knowledge we aim to implement comfortable conditions that will stimulate students for self-regulated learning. It means that from a blog-based PLE perspective (e.g. when a student uses LePress or another PLE tool) the student should be able to define access restrictions to his/her resources or information. A paramount idea is that grading, homework feedback or comments should in many cases stay private. Our study indicates that privacy is becoming more significant as schools are starting to use open and semi-open PLEs as obligatory tools to educate students. The findings of this study allow us to start a new redesign iteration of LePress software for PLE privacy needs.

References

1. May, M., Sébastien, G.: Privacy Concerns in E-learning: Is Using Tracking System a Thread? International Journal of Information and Education Technology 1(1), 1–8 (2011)
2. El-Khatib, K., Korba, L., Xu, Y., Yee, G.: Privacy and security in e-learning. International Journal of Distance Education Technologies 1(4), 1–19 (2003)
3. Hayaati, N., Alwi, M., Fan, I.-S.: Information Security Threats Analysis for E-Learning. Elearning, 285–291 (2010)
4. Next Generation Learning, Analysis of emerging trends affecting the use of technology in education. Learning (September 2008)
5. Gurses, S., Rizk, R., Gunther, O.: Privacy design in online social networks: Learning from privacy breaches and community feedback. Information Systems Journal (2008)
6. Vabariigi Valitsus, Gümnaasiumi riiklik õppekava (2011), `https://www.riigiteataja.ee/akt/114012011002`
7. Estonian Information Technology Foundation (EITF). E-Learning Development Centre Strategy, Tallinn (2012)
8. Piir, M.: Suletud ja avatud õpikeskkond, e-õppe ajakiri (2011), `http://www.etu.ut.ee/kevad-2011/opikeskkonnad/`
9. Hansen, M.: Marrying Transparency Tools with User-Controlled Identity Management. The Future of Identity in the Information Society 262, 199–220 (2008)
10. Razavi, M.N., Iverson, L.: A grounded theory of information sharing behavior in a personal learning space. In: Proceedings of the 2006 20th Anniversary Conference on Computer Supported Cooperative Work, pp. 459–468 (2006)

Towards Ways to Promote Interaction in Digital Learning Spaces

Hanna M. Olsson

Mid Sweden University, Östersund, Sweden
hanna.olsson@miun.se

Abstract. Social learning is dependent on social interactions. I am exploring ways to promote interaction in Digital Learning Spaces. As theoretical framework I use the types of interaction between learner, instructor and content. That learners feel isolated and lonely in DLSs is a problem which comes at high cost for social learning. My aim is to promote social interaction by offering the edentity: a system for making participants visible to each other by creation of a digital student identity.

Keywords: Edentity, social learning, presence, transparency, self-presentation.

1 Introduction

I am exploring ways to promote interaction in Digital Learning Spaces (DLSs). This involves testing and offering designs to make interaction more likely to occur. It seems fair to claim that in order to interact we need to know that the possibility to interact exists. A related aim is to make human resources available within DLSs. It is possible to do great things alone, but who would disagree that the result would be even greater with suitable support and contributions of others. This is in line with the ideas of Vygotsky [1] which is at base for how we picture learning today: as a social activity where a learner can reach the farthest with support of another person/other persons. Lave and Wenger [2] describe in their social theory of learning how participating in a community is at base for learning. Hence, the existence of a community should be fundamental in DLSs, why learners should first and foremost be visible to each other. Hence, the main questions of my PhD-work are:

- What is needed to promote interaction in DLSs?
- To what extent could explicitly expressed participant identities contribute to learners' motivation, experience and learning in DLSs?

To attend to those questions I will take on a design approach, and design and test **the edentity.** The edentity is my proposition of a way of making participants visual, and hence available for interaction [3, 4]. I have an overall interpretive approach towards my work. I study adult learning in diverse contexts, such as workplace and higher education, with the unifying aspect of taking place within a DLS. With DLS, I mean an interactive information space (conceptual space in 2D or 3D) used for learning-related

T. Ley et al. (Eds.): OST 2012, IFIP AICT 395, pp. 193–196, 2013.

activities, contained in a digital environment which can consist of diverse modes (i.e. text, still image, moving image, and sound).

2 Theoretical Foundations and Related Research

Moore [5] describes three types of interaction which takes place in between the three agents of learner, instructor and content. I use these types of interaction as the framework in my work. A theoretical baseline for my work is that learning is a social activity, in accordance with the theories of for example Vygotsky [1] and Lave and Wenger [2]. For social learning to at all exist, interaction is required. However, it has been argued that interaction only is not enough for learning to be successful [6]. However, when learning in DLSs it is crucial that learners perceive each other as real people, i.e. that there is social presence [7]. The DLS also need to allow transparency, so that participants can see that others are there and available for interaction [8]. Hence, designing DLSs for presence and transparency is at the base for enabling social learning in DLSs. In an environment with high presence and transparency, identity expressions are needed. I refer to identity in the terms of a subjective self-representation. I derive this way of considering identity from social sciences (see for example Hogg [9] for a theoretical discussion). Digital identity is in literature mostly treated in regard of identification in the terms of digital identity management. This way of considering digital identity is widely separated from my work on digital identity. However, some contributions can be seen from the digital identity management track, such as that digital identities must be student controlled and student owned in order to feel safe to provide personal information [10]. E-portfolios have been described as a way to construct one's digital identity (in combination with Personal Learning Environment and Social Network) [11]. I have argued that e-portfolios might be part of one's digital identity, but that it is far from enough [3]. I base this argument on the traditional use of portfolios as a way to showcase abilities, and our abilities are only a small part of our identities. For a discussion what else makes our identities I direct readers to my and PhD Thomas Persson Slumpi´s OST12 conference contribution [4].

3 Results

In figure 1, I have illustrated my work process by questions, activities and manuscripts, and how they relate to each other. The first activity that I performed was an explorative field study at a military defense academy. Supported by an instructor and two DLSs, a self-paced multimedia production and a battle simulator, soldiers were preparing for an assignment in Afghanistan. I was exploring strengths and weaknesses of DLSs, and in the studied situation the social dimension stood out as a clear asset. In the resulting manuscript 1 (m1) [12] I mapped feedback onto Moore's [5] lanes of interactions. Even though a social dimension was highly present, I judged feedback in the studied situation as incomplete. For example, feedback from the participants to the system developers was non-existent. Based on that insight I have another manuscript waiting to be written on a missing type of interaction agent, the system designer (m2).

At present, I am performing a case study with a mixed approach of user testing and interviews, in order to explore strengths and weaknesses of DLSs on a learner-content level. It is expected to result in m3 on interaction in multimedia manual.

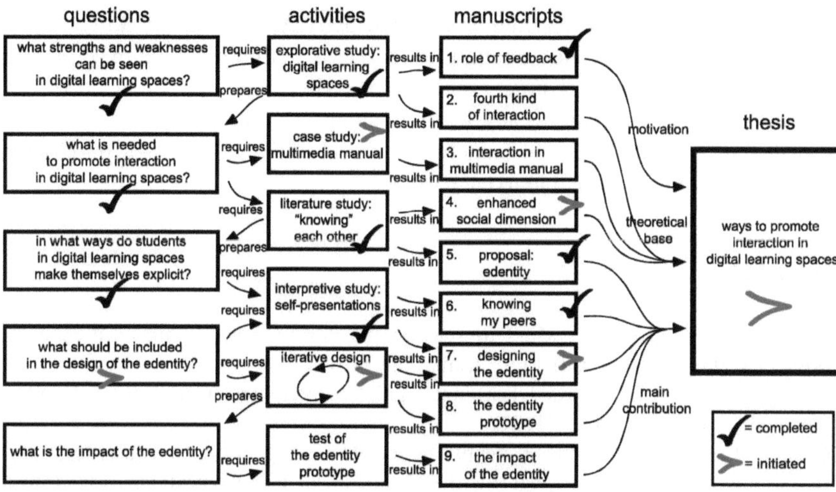

Fig. 1. Illustration of my work process

The results of the first study led me to the next question, namely: what is needed to promote interaction in DLSs? Hence, I performed a literature review on knowing each other in DLSs, resulting in the first proposal of **the edentity**: a system for making participants visible to each other by creation of a digital student identity [3] (m5). The idea of the edentity system comprises profile data, pre-knowledge, and meta-information about actions and progress, in a private, dynamic system that should be able to be migrated between all DLSs in which the student participates. Hence, it allows identity expression to be developed over time. I am also writing a more general manuscript on what is needed to create feelings of knowing each other in DLSs (m4).

This latter question was also attended to by an interpretive study where my colleague Thomas Person Slumpi and I analyzed existing self-presentations. A result of this study is m6, about knowing my peers [4]. This manuscript also addresses the question of what should be included in the design of the edentity. However, the design question is only partly answered by the study on self-presentations. The ongoing activity of iterative design of the edentity will give additional input to this question, presented in a next manuscript (m7) on designing the edentity. The iterative design activity will be ongoing during this, and the next coming year. Ultimately, it is expected to result in a testable prototype (m8), and tested in a sharp learning situation (m9), planned to be a university course given in the LMS Moodle and the prototype will then be a plug-in to Moodle. However, the aim is to make the edentity a platform independent stand alone system that will be pluggable to any DLS.

4 Concluding Remarks

What has intrigued me the most is how humans interaction in and through DLSs can be facilitated. Much research concerning DLSs is carried out, and a variety of perspectives and approaches contribute to the area. However, self-presentations in learning situations from an information systems perspective have not gotten much attention. Many agree that learning is a social activity, but only making sure that interaction takes place is not enough to make a learning situation prosperous. However, systems which obstruct social interaction just by being opaque and impersonal can be devastating to any learning situation. It is my aim to contribute to the social dimension of DLSs, ultimately by offering the edentity as a possible way for participants to become visible to each other.

References

1. Vygotsky, L.S., Cole, M.: Mind in society: the development of higher psychological processes. Harvard University Press, Cambridge (1978)
2. Lave, J., Wenger, E.: Situated learning: legitimate peripheral participation. Cambridge University Press, Cambridge (1991)
3. Olsson, H.: Proposing Learner E-dentity to social presence in digital spaces for learning. In: Asproth, V. (ed.) Challenges for the Future in an ICT Context, pp. 177–186. Mid Sweden University, Östersund (2011)
4. Olsson, H., Slumpi, T.P.: Knowing my peers - Edentity: to invite peer interaction and social learning. In: OST 2012, Tallinn (2012) (accepted)
5. Moore, M.G.: Three types of interaction. In: Harry, K., John, M., Keegan, D. (eds.) Distance Education: New Perspectives, pp. 19–24. Routledge, London (1993)
6. Garrison, D.R., Cleveland-Innes, M.: Facilitating Cognitive Presence in Online Learning: Interaction Is Not Enough. Am. J. of Distance Education 19(3), 133–148 (2005)
7. Gunawardena, C.N., Zittle, F.J.: Social presence as a predictor of satisfaction within a computer-mediated conferencing environment. Am. J. of Distance Education 11(3), 8–26 (1997)
8. Dalsgaard, C., Paulsen, M.F.: Transparency in Cooperative Online Education. The International Review of Research in Open and Distance Learning 10(3) (2009)
9. Hogg, M.A., Terry, D.J., White, K.M.: A Tale of Two Theories: A Critical Comparison of Identity Theory with Social Identity Theory. Social Psychology Quarterly 58(4), 255–269 (1995)
10. Satchell, C., Shanks, G., Howard, S., Murphy, J.: Identity crisis: user perspectives on multiplicity and control in federated identity management. Behaviour & Information Technology 30(1), 51–62 (2009)
11. Bauer, R.: Construction of One's Identity: A Student's View on the Potential of EPortfolios. Studienverlag GmbH, Wien (2009)
12. Olsson, H.M., Öberg, L.-M.: Role of feedback in uniform learning situation. In: Proceedings of the 29th ACM International Conference on Design of Communication, pp. 279–284. ACM, New York (2011)

E-Learning Using Open Source Software in African Universities

Nicholas Mavengere[1], Mikko Ruohonen[1], and Paul Nleya[2]

[1] School of Information Sciences, University of Tampere, Finland
{nicholas.mavengere,mikko.j.ruohonen}@uta.fi
[2] Educational Technology Department, University of Botswana, Botswana
nleyapt@mopipi.ub.bw

Abstract. The use of technology in education specifically for enhancing learning is of immense value for improving education delivery. This article serves to highlight the research project to be done by the University of Tampere, University of Botswana and Catholic University of Mozambique. The aim of the research is to investigate how low resourced higher education institutes could make use of free and open source technologies to enhance education delivery. The community of inquiry is used as background theory because it also seeks potential to break new ground pedagogically by addressing the challenge to scientifically explore the combination of pedagogical principles and new technology that will advance the evolution of higher education. The expected results include critical success factors in implementing learning management systems in developing countries and models of open source learning management use.

Keywords: learning management systems, open source software, low resourced education institutes, community of inquiry.

1 Introduction

The use of technology in education is of differing dimensions but however its value is equally important. For instance, in education technology can be used for storing students' records, that is university information system, and also technology can be used for learning purposes, that is, learning management systems. It is important to study the technology used for learning for several reasons, for example, it is of direct benefit to the main education stakeholders, students and also Marshall and Ruohonen [1] noted that the use of technology in classroom is still a challenge both in developed and developing countries. Therefore, it is of value to improve how to effectively and efficiently make use of technology in classroom.

Free and open source software (FOSS) is widely considered to be a tool for promoting ICT in developing countries owing mainly to advantages like reduced cost of ownership, avoidance of vendor lock-in and development of indigenous technologies [2, 3]. In other words, FOSS is a considered to be important for removing the so-called 'digital divide' between developed countries and the rest of

T. Ley et al. (Eds.): OST 2012, IFIP AICT 395, pp. 197–202, 2013.

the world. Thus, a recent trend shows that governments of developing countries, especially from Africa, are adopting FOSS over proprietary ICT. Therefore, this research seeks to utilize FOSS because of the mentioned advantages. The FOSS systems that will be used in this research are learning management systems (LMS).

This research seeks to investigate how low resourced higher education institutes could make use of free and open source technologies to enhance education delivery. The practical problem which this project seeks to solve is to reduce the impact of inadequate resources in higher education institute in developing countries. This is a common problem at most institutes in Africa. The aim of this project is to make use of free and open source technologies to reduce this problem. Technology offers a big opportunity for African education institutes to reduce the impact of lack of resources. The significance of the project is to offer sustainable solution to lack of resources at African education institutes. The research question to be addressed in this research is; ***how to make use of eLearning in African education institutes in order to foster the use of technology in higher education context?***

2 Research Background

2.1 Practical Background

Mavengere and Ruohonen [4] note five key issues in application of LMS in African universities as computer literacy, computer infrastructure, collaboration/sharing culture, human resource (IT staff) and leadership support. These are essential aspects which have to be addressed before starting a technology related project in Africa. We will briefly discuss these issues before explaining the proposed Case Studies in this research.

The main challenge for IT-enhanced education in developing countries is availability of computer infrastructure [5]. Therefore, firstly the need for computer infrastructure has to be addressed before initiating any technology related project in Africa. In this research we access the computer infrastructure availability at University of Botswana and Catholic University of Mozambique and make adequate preparations. The second step is to guarantee computer literacy, as it was noted as also an essential aspect for LMS in African universities [4]. Third aspect and related to computer literacy is availability of the required human resource expertise, such as, IT technicians and managers. This research project will incorporate student and staff exchange programmes from African universities to University of Tampere as a well to improve the human resources on IT use in education. Moreover, joint intensive courses will be done by all partner universities to share experience and learn from each other. Last, two other important aspects for application of LMS in African universities are based on organizational behaviour namely collaboration culture and leadership support. Collaboration is important especially in African education context where resources are limited in that there is mutual benefit by the sharing parties. On the other hand, leadership support is the backbone in any change initiative and use of technology is education requires support from the policy makers and administrators.

2.2 Theoretical Background

The community of inquiry framework, Figure 1, fits as the theoretical basis of this research as it also seeks potential to break new ground pedagogically by addressing the challenge to scientifically explore the combination of pedagogical principles and new technology that will advance the evolution of higher education [6]. Community of inquiry is meaningful association in addressing a problem, for instance, in the project the partners University of Botswana, Catholic University of Mozambique and University of Tampere make up the community that is multi-disciplinary and includes discourse. The philosophical basis of this research just as elaborated by the framework is collaborative constructivism. The core elements of a collaborative constructivist learning environment identified in the framework and that are required for a purposeful learning are teaching, cognitive and social presence. The first element, social presence is the participants' ability to recognize themselves as part of the community. Thus in the project we aim to make every project member and participants to identify themselves with the project and its activities as a single family. Cognitive presence, the second element of community of inquiry framework, is the degree to which learners are able to construct and verify meaning through continuous reflection and dialogue in a community of inquiry. Lastly, teaching presence includes three main responsibilities to be catered for in this project as elaborated by Garrison, Cleveland-Innes and Fung [6] "the first of the primary teaching presence responsibilities is establishing curriculum content, learning activities, and timelines. The second responsibility is monitoring and managing purposeful collaboration and reflection. The third is ensuring that the community reaches the intended learning outcomes by diagnosing needs and providing timely information and direction" (p.32).

Blended learning has transformative potential of learning in the context of the challenges facing higher education [7]. In agreement with Garrison and Kanuka [8] in simple terms blended learning "is the thoughtful integration of classroom face-to-face learning experiences with online learning experiences" (p.96). Blended learning that is the use of eLearning using open source software and face-to-face teaching will be

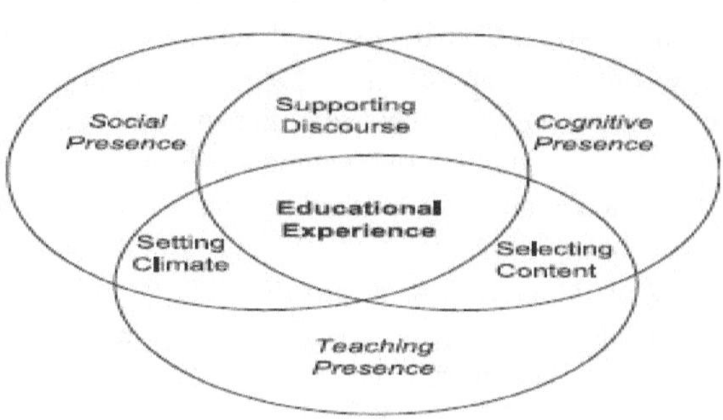

Fig. 1. Community of inquiry [9]

utilized in this project [7]. Blended learning has many advantages as noted by Garrison and Kanuka [8], such as, "effective integration of the two main components (face-to-face and Internet technology) such that we are not just adding on to the existing dominant approach or method. What makes blended learning particularly effective is its ability to facilitate a community of inquiry" (p.97).

3 Research Methodology

This article is based on a proposed research to be conducted at University of Botswana and Catholic University of Mozambique. The research project includes joint courses among the partner universities, mirror courses (same courses) done at the partner universities and exchange programs for teachers and students. The value of the exchange program is in sharing academic and professional experiences and culture. The teacher exchange will enable the visiting teacher to give classes and carry out research at the host university. The students exchange will offer students a different learning environment. The intensive courses will expose the partner universities to diverse cultures in jointly offering the courses. There will also courses on the same topic simultaneously done at the partner universities in order to share experiences. All these project activities will also be support by use of a learning management system. Case studies from each partner university will also be analysed and reported. Below is a summary from each partner university.

3.1 University of Botswana

The University of Botswana is in need of e-learning individual and institutional capacity development. This project is the right step in ensuring this as the university seeks to explore the process of eLearning integration at the UB using both proprietary (WebCT/Blackboard) and alternative Open Educational Resources (OER) (Moodle). The UB is currently using WeBCT/Blackboard for its eLearning and concurrently piloting with Moodle given that Moodle is low cost compared to WebCT/Blackboard where the UB spends $40,000 on license and service agreement fees and over $3 million for upgrades annually. There is therefore ample opportunity and relevance to explore the benefits of Moodle as a new learning management tool at the UB in the Botswana study. The University of Tampere (Finland) has expertise in the implementation of Moodle and has worked in the African context (Mozambique) assisting in the execution of Moodle OER. The Botswana case study therefore explores the process of integrating ICT into the tertiary curriculum focusing on the process of eLearning integration at the UB using identified SAM and other relevant conceptual frameworks. Therefore, the teacher and students exchange to the University of Tampere will aid in that the required expertise and experienced will be gained from the exchange program. Moreover, the university will host a joint intensive course which will provide valuable experience in its e-learning ambitions.

3.2 Catholic University of Mozambique

Catholic University of Mozambique (UCM) has recently started experimenting with aspects of an e-learning mode of delivery by being part of the African Virtual Open Initiatives and Resources (AVOIR) Network, including universities of seven countries in sub-Saharan Africa with the objective to establish a group of universities in Africa who collaboratively develop open source software (KEWL.NextGen) to promote the innovative applications of ICT in higher education. However, in 2009, a general consensus was reached on the use of Moodle as the preferred Learning Management System. The Department of Information Technology (FGTI) in Beira thus became the pioneer on the use of Moodle in UCM. The FLOSS-AHEAD project will be of immense value in developing required e-learning capabilities for UCM staff, students and the university as a whole. The exchange programs to Finland would of value as University of Tampere experience in Moodle use and moreover ICT in development in general. Therefore UCM intends to improve learning outcomes and student interest in IT in education and for development in general. Appreciation of the vast potential of Moodle is still being realized.

3.3 University of Tampere

The University of Tampere and also other universities in Finland generally use learning management systems, such as Moodle, webCT and Blackboard. However, the use of these learning management systems is very diverse with no agreed upon standards or best practices. There is room to improve the use of the learning management even though different institutes could be using different learning management system although this research advocates for FLOSS systems. Even at the same institute professors use differently technology in their classes. Thus it is motivating to draw lessons from all these different ways technology is being used and propose more efficient and effective practices that incorporate eLearning.

4 Conclusion

There is a need to be better employing the good technical facilities available to universities to provide equitable and quality education. Recent research, for example, [10, 11, 12] have noted that there is a room for improvement in the application of ICTs in classrooms. Therefore, this research project is an effort to improve the use of ICTs at universities in general and with a specific focus on improving learning and interactions between main education stakeholders, students and teachers at University of Botswana and Catholic University of Mozambique. Moreover, eLearning use with support of open source software offers a plausible channel for enhancement of higher education in developing countries. One of the greatest challenges of ICT integration in education can be summarized as limited vision, policy and leadership given that ICT is changing faster than educators ability to keep track [12]. To conclude the need to conduct evidence-led research in ICT integration in higher education is noted.

References

1. Marshall, G., Ruohonen, M.: Capacity Building for IT in Education in Developing Countries IFIP Publication. Chapman & Hall, London (1998)
2. Lerner, J., Tirole, J.: Some Simple Economics of Open Source. Journal of Industrial Economics 50(2), 197–234 (2002)
3. Camara, G., Fonseka, S.: Information Policies and Open Source Software in Developing Countries. Journal Of The American Society For Information Science And Technology 58(1), 121–132 (2007)
4. Mavengere, N.B., Ruohonen, M.J.: Using Open Source Software for Improving Dialog in Computer Science Education – Case Mozambique University. In: Tatnall, A., Kereteletswe, O.C., Visscher, A. (eds.) ITEM 2010. IFIP AICT, vol. 348, pp. 52–61. Springer, Heidelberg (2011)
5. Kumar, R.: Proceedings of World Academy of Science, Engineering and Technology, vol. 30, pp. 1307–6884 (2008)
6. Garrison, D.R., Cleveland-Innes, M., Fung, T.S.: Exploring causal relationships among teaching, cognitive and social presence: Student perceptions of the community of inquiry framework. The Internet and Higher Education 13, 31–36 (2010)
7. El-Ghalayini, H., El-khalili, N.: An approach to designing and evaluating blended courses. Edu. Inf. Tech. 17, 417–430 (2011)
8. Garrison, R., Kanuka, H.: Blended learning: Uncovering its transformative potential in higher education. Internet and Higher Education 7, 95–105 (2004)
9. Garrison, D.R., Anderson, T.: E-Learning in the 21stCentury: A Framework for Research and Practice. Routledge/Falmer, London (2003)
10. Buettner, Y.: Teaching teachers to teach ICT integration. Education and Information Technologies 11(3), 25–26 (2006)
11. Ottevanger, W.J., van den Akker, J.H., de Feiter, L.: Developing Science, mathematics, and ICT education in sub-Saharan Africa: Patterns and promising practices. World Bank Africa Region Human Development Department, Washington, D.C (2007)
12. Ruohonen, M., Mavengere, N., Nleya, P., Deodhar, S.: The Use of Free, Libre and Open Source Software (FLOSS) for African Higher Education Advancement and Development. In: Youssef, M., Anwar, S.A. (eds.) Proceedings of the 4th Conference on e-Learning Excellence in the Middle East 2011: In Search of New Paradigms for Re-engineering Education, pp. 44–54 (2011)

Discussion Groups

Organizational Learning, Agility and Social Technologies in Contemporary Workplaces

Kati Tikkamäki and Nicholas Mavengere

CIRCMI, School of Information Sciences, University of Tampere, Finland
{kati.tikkamaki,nicholas.mavengere}@uta.fi

Abstract. The contemporary workplaces face demanding challenges, such as expectations to be agile, competitive, efficient and adept to using employee knowledge. There are several required virtues in order to have a conductive workplace, for example, organizational learning and agility. The discussion forum aimed to bring out the inter-related roles of organizational learning, agility and social technologies in modern workplaces. The working methods in the discussion group consisted of brainstorming, learning café and mind mapping. Work organizations are examined as potential but contradictory learning spaces. Agility is the ability of an organization to rapidly respond to changes in demand. Organizational learning and agility are increasingly enabled by social technologies. The social technologies advances in the modern society are rigorously changing the contemporary workplaces. Social technologies include communication and interactive mechanisms embedded on the internet, such as, wikis and blogs. We suggest that organizational learning and agility might be increasingly enabled by social technologies. However, social technologies have a potential to enable and disable organizational learning. The usage of social technology and the level of agility are depending on the contextual factors like type of organization, field of profession and type of work. Different types of organizations and work have different needs for using social technologies as a driving force of organizational learning and agility.

Keywords: Organizational learning, agility, social technologies, modern workplaces, conference discussion session.

1 Introduction

This is a report of the OST´12 conference discussion session titled organizational learning, agility and social technologies in contemporary workplaces. The aim of the discussion was to bring out the inter-related roles of organizational learning, agility and social technologies in modern workplaces. The contemporary workplaces face demanding challenges, such as expectations to be agile, competitive, efficient and adept to using employee knowledge. There are several required virtues in order to have a conductive workplace, for example, organizational learning and agility. However, organizational learning and agility are intertwined in a complex way. And the complexity is even increased by the emergent of new social technologies. Moreover, both academics and practitioners have not agreed on a uniform definition

T. Ley et al. (Eds.): OST 2012, IFIP AICT 395, pp. 205–209, 2013.

of these concepts. To further explore these novice themes the discussions were guided by the following questions:

1. What is the role of social technologies in organizational learning?
2. How does organizational learning impact agility?
3. How can social technologies and organizational learning enhance agility in contemporary workplaces?

2 Working Methods of the Discussion Session

The working methods in the discussion group consisted of brainstorming, learning café and mind mapping. The number of participants were eleven of which two were also facilitators of the session. Participants of the session were: Jane Andersen (Denmark), Danel Apse (Estonia), Urmas Heinaste (Estonia), Jörgen Jaanus (Estonia), Tobias Ley (Estonia/Germany), Edmund Laugasson (Estonia), Juhani Linna (Finland), Birgy Lorenz (Estonia), Nicholas Mavengere (rapporteur, Finland), Heiki Tähis (Estonia) and Kati Tikkamäki (chair, Finland). After the introducing session (by peer interviewing) initial brainstorming took place in small workgroups. Groups defined and clarified the relationships between social technologies, organizational learning and agility by writing down the keywords and key ideas based on their knowledge and experiences. On the second day the group work was outlined by central ideas based on two scientific articles [1,2]. Then participants formulated their ideas more precisely in the Learning Café. Participants were divided into two groups and they were asked to write down on the table cloths their views about the social technologies' role in enhancing agility and organizational learning in contemporary workplaces. Groups changed the table after about 30 minutes and continued brainstorming on the table cloths. Finally, there was an open discussion where groups presented the ideas from the table cloths. On the third day we summarized the discussions by creating mind/concept maps of what we had learned about the relationships between social technologies, organizational learning and agility.

3 Organizational Learning, Agility and Social Technologies

Organizational memory is crucial concept from the point of view of organizational learning and agility. It consists e.g. of data warehousing, expert systems, best practice databases, Intranet and Internet [2]. Organizational memory includes many types of knowledge based on Blackler [3] definition like: embrained, embodied, encultured, embedded and encoded knowledge. Embrained knowledge includes parts of propositional knowledge which are internalized facts and principles. Embodied knowledge appears in forms of activity that include elements of tacit knowledge. Encultured knowledge refers to the processes of achieving shared understandings and negotiation. Embedded knowledge is situated in the products, prototypes, technologies, tools and buildings in an organization (cf. practical knowledge). Encoded knowledge is symbolic and it has usually a written nature (cf. theoretical knowledge). For example, it takes a form of instructions, handbooks, written plans or theoretical models [3]. Knowledge is encoded in symbolic forms made by human beings and embedded in concrete objects made by nature or by human beings. It is embrained and embodied in individuals and collectives and it takes the form of encultured knowledge also. Organizational memory can take a form of story, document, data base or habit/routine.

Social technologies can facilitate the access to and the usage of that memory and knowledge resources. Social technologies can be an important ingredient in the design of organizational learning infrastructure and facilitator of the learning processes like storing, accessing and revising the elements of organizational memory [2]. Social technologies are used in many contemporary professions and work contexts in communicating, finding information and collaborating. In this case social technologies are defined based on McKinsey report [4] as: "the products and services that enable social interactions in the digital realm, and thus allow people to connect and interact virtually" (pg. 4).

Organizational learning should be enhanced through systems that support communication and discourse [2]. Based on Wenger [5] communities of practice organizations can be viewed as communities of learning [6] where co-creation, sharing and negotiation of knowledge are emphasized. Social technologies may enhance these social processes by making possible to share information and tell stories with members of different communities, comparing experiences with others, building new relations and forming groups for different purposes.

Participants of the discussion group had challenges in defining the concept of agility. There exist different definitions of agility in the literature. Agility is the organization's ability to rapidly respond to changes in demand. Based on Li, Nagel and Sun [1] agility can be defined by four dimensions like social agility, organizational agility, agile communities and ecosystem agility. Social agility includes individual and team performance improvement by easier and faster interactivity on common business objectives. Organizational agility is based on the premises of boundary-less organizational structure which enables knowledge sharing and collaboration both internally, with other divisions and externally with business partners. Agile communities are societies built based on social and organizational agility. Ecosystem agility includes the use of social technologies in business to sense and manage the relations in their business ecosystems to gain competitive advantage.

Agility can be seen as an ability of an organization to sense (know) the business environment (customers, competitors, suppliers etc.) and respond change in time- So, it is more than flexibility – it is responding in a "right" place in a "right" time. Based on discussion sessions' discussions, being agile requires employees' and managers' ability to learn as well as taking care of the learning processes. In practice it means learning from experience/history by breaking up routines and creating new ones, creating possibilities for participation, creating spaces and forums for creating and sharing of knowing, utilizing social interaction and social support and taking time for reflective processes [6, 5, 3].

We suggest that organizational learning and agility might be increasingly enabled by social technologies. However, ironically organizational learning capacity and implementation of social technologies that enable organizational learning depends on organization's present capacity to learn. Therefore, social technologies have a potential to enable and disable organizational learning. One risk in organizing practices heavily on social technologies is that organization and employees might become too dependent on formal systems and they might overlook the potential of less informal usage of organization memory [2]. The added value of social technologies and its' effects on organizations agility are depending on changes in organizational structures, processes, practices and culture [4].

4 Conclusion

Organizational learning, agility and social technologies are intertwined in a complex way. It is essential to note the driver in each case, either technology or agility or organizational learning? What is the main focus in utilizing social technologies and developing organization's ability to learn and be agile? Is it in increasing business and competitive intelligence, in increasing the knowledge sharing and co-creation and/or in collecting information and making it easily available? Learning is enhanced through community-based and explorative learning. Generating and sharing of knowledge were seen essential. The challenge is to create spaces and forums for knowledge co-creation and using organizational memory in a meaningful ways as a source of learning. But in what extent these processes of knowledge construction and sharing should be enhanced through social technologies?

It was suggested that social technologies should enhance organizational learning which then leads to organizations' agility. Social technologies should be "easy to use", flexible and handy when enhancing learning as well as usage and construction of organizational memory. It is noted that there is remarkable potential (organizational memory & customers) as well as challenges in utilizing social technologies. However, it is important to examine the added value of social technologies in work context. In general, the benefits of social technologies include quick exchange of experiences and knowledge, easy access to information, allowing many people to access information simultaneously and making it easier to reach people. In addition to this social technologies offer possibilities, such as, breaking up old routines and building up new ones, linking organization to customers e.g. through customer-driven innovation, generating of new ideas and processing them on the community level, connecting dispersed people, finding answers quickly and allowing openness. These processes were seen to enable sharing and thus learning.

But the impact of social technologies on agility and organizational learning is limited if employees do not have skills and motivation to use social technologies. There is often need for training and creation of collective principles of using social technologies as a part of work processes in the organizations. Collective negotiation processes and discussion forums ensure added value for utilizing new technology as part of work processes as well as creation of collective principles concerning the new work practices. Employees and managers preconceptions, attitudes and reactions are reasonable to make visible and open for discussions. Utilization of social technologies calls for transparency of agreements and practices. Employees also need to have skills enough for utilizing social technologies which can be reached through facilitated peer learning and internal training.

Customers are increasingly becoming powerful in the current business environment. In agreement to Sambamurthy, Bharadwaj and Grover [7] the role of customers could be summarized as "a source of innovation ideas, as a co-creator in the development and design of innovative products and services, and as a user in testing the product or in helping other users learn about the new product or service" (pg. 245). However, the usage of social technology and the level of agility are depending on the contextual factors too like type of organization, field of profession and type of work. Different types of organizations and work have different needs for using social technologies as a driving force of organizational learning and agility. The justifications for utilizing social technologies should be based on missions and visions of an organization. Referring to one discussion session's participant's vision: "Social technologies should be an integrated part of enterprise resource planning (ERP). It leads to integration of business processes and learning which in turn has the potential to positively influence agility."

References

1. Li, Q., Nagel, N.R., Sun, L.: Migrating to Agility 2.0: How Social Computing Creates Strategic Value. Organizational Dynamics 40, 119–126 (2011)
2. Robey, D., Boudreau, M.-C., Rose, G.: Information technology and organizational learning: a review and assessment of research. Accounting Management and Information Technologies 10, 125–155 (2000)
3. Blackler, F.: Knowledge Work and Organisations: An Overview and Interpretation. Organization Studies 16(6), 1021–1046 (1995)
4. Chui, M., Manyika, J., Bughin, J., Dobbs, R., Roxburgh, C., Sarrazin, H., Sands, G., Westergren, M.: The social economy: Unlocking value and productivity through social technologies. McKinsey Global Institute (2012)
5. Wenger, E.: Communities of Practice. Learning, Meaning and Identity. Cambridge University Press, New York (1999)
6. Tikkamäki, K.: Työn ja organisaation muutoksissa oppiminen - etnografinen löytöretki työssä oppimiseen (Learning in Changing Work and Organizational Contexts – Ethnographical Discovery on Workplace Learning.), Doctoral dissertation, University of Tampere, School of Education. University Press, Tampere (2006)
7. Sambamurthy, V., Bharadwaj, A., Grover, V.: Shaping Agility through Digital Options: Reconceptualizing the Role of Information Technology in Contemporary Firms. MIS Quarterly 27(2), 237–263 (2003)

Author Index

MIX
Papier aus verantwortungsvollen Quellen
Paper from responsible sources
FSC® C105338

If you have any concerns about our products,
you can contact us on
ProductSafety@springernature.com

In case Publisher is established outside the EU,
the EU authorized representative is:
Springer Nature Customer Service Center GmbH
Europaplatz 3, 69115 Heidelberg, Germany

Printed by Libri Plureos GmbH
in Hamburg, Germany